Because
I
Love Him

How Girls Become Battered Women
&
Why They Stay

by
Jasper Jameson

100% of author net profits go to victim recovery programs,
adolescent rehabilitation and animal rescue

Published by
The Trust for
The Human & Animal Salvage & Restoration Project

For reproduction permission or information on quantity or individual discounts, contact trust
@
(765)292-2590
or
victimservices@ccrtc.com

For more information on programs, publications and our survey please visit our website
@
www.elysiangardensinc.com

Copyright © 1985 – 2006 Jasper Jameson

ISBN: 978-0-6151-3980-7

All rights reserved under U.S. copyright, including the right of reproduction in whole or in part, in any form

*Dedicated
to the victims, both human & animal,
who patiently teach me
how best to serve them*

Acknowledgements

Thanks to those who took me in, as a teenager, giving me food and shelter, with no ill-intent. Shame on those of you who did it for the opportunity of exploiting a little girl who already had enough problems to leave her shelter and food source. Thanks to Jim Connor. You saved my life and you know how. Thanks to Dr. John Searight. While my father wasn't listening, I heard you and was validated.

Thanks to Phyllis Wyatt who, no matter what, insisted I had value and could succeed at anything. Thank you for loving me unconditionally and for always being there. You're a kind, gentle spirit, that never hesitated to love me and has enhanced the lives of many. Unselfishly, you listened for hours on end.

Thanks to Peggy Burdsall for knowing how to teach violent crime survivors and for the kind, gentle nature at a time when nothing else would do. Thanks to Pat Crawford for introducing me to Buddhism and for the tough, hard, demanding and uncompromising nature at a time when nothing else would do. I will always be grateful for your unending ability to yell, "Get up," nonstop, after the brain injury.

Thank you is not enough to the doctors who treated me at a time when that was not a popular thing to do: Englestein, Foreman, Hingtgen, Stein, Das and Feng. You were proof that your profession could not be defined by the least of you. You stood out as superior, proving to me that while 50% of your profession graduates in the bottom half of your class, another group are the cream of integrity. Thank you to Wong and the unknown nurse for telling the truth and warning my husband and to Gerri Zebrasky for protecting my body, when I couldn't, until it could be moved.

A special thanks to all of the wonderful teachers, of all species, that I have enjoyed (or not) and been blessed to learn from. A special kick in the ass for all of those who could have let me learn differently or had no place to teach me at all.

Thanks to Beth Beams of the Center for Nonviolence for her endless editing to soften my honesty and often abrasive presentation and for taking me to my first training in Baltimore, almost three decades ago. Thank you so much for working to make sure my words stay as politically correct as my heart. Thank you to the Domestic Abuse Intervention Project for the early training materials that focused as much on integrity and victim needs as it did on the dynamics of violence against women.

Special thanks to my family (children and animals) who were neglected as I worked, (or lay) in the trenches, collected research and worked to meet deadlines and goals. Special thanks to my husband for financially supporting our program when it fell short, so that I could operate without financial compensation or having to compromise the best interest of our clients. Truly, without that contribution the other women and I would not have been able to enjoy the blessing of this work, in this way.

I could go on like this endlessly. If I did, I would name people like the unknown truck driver that changed my tire somewhere in Texas, an act that may have kept me from being further traumatized. My point is that we offer acts of kindness and don't know what impact they may have had. I have been offered so much of this kindness and am grateful.

Along the same line, another kick in the ass to those who offered cruelty, whether they realized the full impact or not. For example, shame on the sister-in-laws who felt that I should be hazed as opposed to welcomed, in their family. Along with my daughters, we were so excited to add so many sisters and that we might finally have significant, positive relationships with our new female family. And a bigger shame on you for teaching your children to do the same.

About Victim Services & Elysian Gardens

Victim Services and Elysian Gardens are both divisions of an irrevocable, charitable trust, The Human & Animal Restoration & Salvage Project, whose mission is to "reduce suffering". Victim Services designs and implements programs for both human and animal trauma survivors, for the previous eight years, through Indiana University. Our resources are funneled into victim prevention & recovery programs, adolescent rehabilitation and animal rescue.

We neither seek out, nor receive, grant money or any other type of funding that could leave us beholden to anyone but the beings we serve. This provides us the opportunity to make decisions based only on the best interest of those we serve. Our sources of funding mean that we operate solely at the will of the community and come from a variety of businesses and services owned by the trust. It is operated by those we provide services to, volunteers, interns and highly experienced service providers.

Main Funding Sources

Elysian Gardens is a 6+ acre horticultural park with thousands of varieties of plants. It can be leased for weddings, receptions, family reunions and other events where a peaceful garden setting is desirable. We are also available for classes, retreats and seminars. Elysian Gardens provides life-time sanctuary to traumatized animals and it is extremely beneficial to the human trauma survivors who serve the animals and contribute to the gardens. The pairing of human and animal survivors is a wonderful complement to the welfare and education of both.

Elysian Gardens Outlet is a 20,000 sq. ft. Home & Garden Import Store. We sell hand-made home and garden art from around the globe along with field grown perennials and herbs, dried floral arrangements, exotic plants and trees and other unique gifts and décor items. Your group or organization can host a pottery party in our beautiful store at no cost. Other charities can use this high traffic location for the sales of their product for fund raising, usually at no cost.

Elysian Gardens Outlet is a retail development that sits on 8+ acres, located on a high traffic federal highway. This investment is also owned by the trust. It is being converted to another private park that houses socially responsible, complimentary businesses creating a garden, community concerned retail development. We currently have finished and unfinished space and lots available.

This development includes the Community Safety & Recovery Center where survivors of violent crimes, their loved ones and other concerned members of the community can go for information, support, classes and other services. The Community Safety & Recovery Center is also available to other educational programs for classes.

<u>Some Classes Available</u>
Why Battered Women Stay
How Girls Become Battered Women
What Perpetrators Look For In A Victim
Recovery Tools For Trauma Survivors

<u>Trainings Available</u>
Working With Victims/Survivors of Violent Crimes
Why Battered Women Stay
Producing Victim Impact Panels
Designing & Implementing Victim-Offender Ameliorations
Restorative Justice Programs
Amelioration/Mediation Training

There are a number of other goods and services available. These will be posted and updated on the website and include: *Because I Love Him* in book, documentary and as a training, *Letters From A Batterer* and many other educational goods and services that fund our operation and enhance yours.

Elysiangardensinc.com
Email: Victimservices@ccrtc.com
Phone (765)292-2590

About the Author

Jasper Jameson has researched the human and animal response to trauma for more than twenty years and designs and implements programs to help with the recovery process. She has worked with hundreds of victims/survivors and the offenders. This includes battered women and the men who abuse them, survivors of sex crimes and sex offenders, victims of white coat, white collar crimes and the American Medical Association. She has worked with the secondary survivors of homicide and those who killed their loved ones, combat veterans, racists and hundreds of abused and traumatized animals. Previously both undergraduate and graduate students at Indiana University could study under her for 4 to 6 credit hours of 400 level criminology.

She has trained law enforcement, professors, medical administrators and other service providers on the dynamics of domestic violence, incest and child abuse. Most importantly the author teaches the victims (both human and animal), how to recover and has brought children and batterers together to teach batterers how their actions affect the children who must endure it. Her victim impact panels have included medical mistakes, domestic violence, racism and sex crimes.

The author has made videos on domestic violence, survivors of sex crimes and abused children. Her work with offenders has given her a unique perspective that is extremely beneficial to the females she teaches, providing information on what offenders are thinking and how they pick their victims.

As one professor put it, working with victims, offenders and animals the author is familiar with the whole picture of violence in our society and can readily connect the dots for those who want to learn. She is a consultant for mediators and is able to present the issues to adolescents, survivors and professionals alike.

As a formerly-battered woman the author can deal with subjects that may otherwise be considered too sensitive or politically questionable. For the sake of entertainment, teaching and downright survival, the author brings the levity, optimism and honesty needed to facilitate learning.

Because I Love Him:
How Girls Become Battered Women
&
Why They Stay

By

Jasper Jameson
© copyright Jasper Jameson 1985 – 2006

Published by
The Trust for the Human & Animal Salvage & Restoration Project

This work is protected under U.S. copyright law and cannot be reproduced without written permission.

All names have been changed to protect ourselves from the guilty. Any resemblance to offenders alive or dead is probably due to their unique methods of abuse and our inability to disguise them.

We are collecting research on trauma survivors of all types. Please see our website and respond to our survey @ Elysiangardensinc.com

Contents

Introduction

Chapter 1
Round Rooms & the Reality of Woman Beating

Round Rooms ...1
The History of Violence Against Women & Children ...18

The Perplexing Behaviors of Battered Women & Other Trauma Survivors ... 23

Returning To & Defending the Batterer ...23
Panic & Anxiety ...28
Self-Mutilation ...28
Shame ...30
Hypervigilance ...30
Addictions ...31
Sexualizing ...32
Numbing Out ...33
The Nature of Trauma & Remembering ...34

Chapter 2
How Our Girls Become Battered Women: The Making of a Battered Woman...38

The Nacirema People ...41
Our People ...48
The Appropriate Victim ...49
Savvy Perpetrators ...50
Violence, Abuse & Other Dysfunctions As Generational ...58
Revictimization ...59

Chapter 3
Why Battered Women Stay: The Keeping of a Battered Woman

Popular Explanations ...69

Resources...70
Religion ...70
Social Expectations ...70
Learned Helplessness ...71
Female Masochism ...71

Why Battered Women Stay: Traumatic Bonding & the Development of the Stockholm Syndrome in Battered Women ...73

Victim Responsibility & Examining Our Choices ...76

POW ...82

Implications & Necessity of the Bond...91

Chapter 4
Tool Box for Trauma Survivors &
Those Who Love & Support Them ...98

God ...102
Instincts ...103
Facing the Problem ...107
Getting Over It ...109
Detachment ...117
Post Traumatic Stress Disorder & Vicarious Trauma ...122
Panic Attacks ...123
Feelings ...126
Dissociation ...129
The "F" Word (forgiveness) ...130
Trust ...133
Why Me? ...134
Things Perpetrators Look For ...139
Helping Our Kids & Breaking the Cycle ...141

Some Other Issues ...143

Family & Friends ...143
Children of Victims/Survivors ...144
Why Children May Lie ...145

Chapter 5
Service Providers & The System: The Batterer's Use of the System & Society as A Weapon ...146

Hereinafter Referred to as Mother ...158
Batterers Use of Counselors & Mediators as a Weapon ...175
Victim's Justice Center Position Statement on Forced or Court-Ordered Counseling & Mediations Between Battered or Formerly-Battered Women & Batterers...182

Forced Counseling & Mediations in Domestic Violence...183

Victims Inability to be Honest ...184
Giving Batterer More Ammunition ...185
Message that She is Equally to Blame for her Victimization...185
Covert Intimidation ...185
Using Intervener to Abuse Victim & Support Batterer ...187
Conflict of Interest ...188

Some Things To Look For in Batterer's Groups ...191

Monitors ...191
Giving Victims a False Sense of Security ...193
Keeping Victims Informed ...193
Empathy Considered Guilt ...194
Collusion of Facilitators ...195
Counselor/Facilitator & Offender Bonding ...197

Chapter 6
Common Offender Arguments, Case Problems & Intervener Mistakes ...198

Battered Woman/Victim Looks "Crazy" ...198
If Someone Wants to Kill You, They Can't be Stopped ...200
Victim Behavior Isn't What It "Should Be" ...200
He Says, She Says ...201
I Lost Control ...202
Victim Stance ...202
Provocation ...203
Labeling the Batterer ...204
Labeling the Victim ...205
"There is No Reality..." ...206
The "How Do You Feel About That?" Game ...208
Mutual Combat ...210
Minimizing Damages ...211
Victim Impact to Teach Empathy ...212
Why Battered Women Protect the Batterer ...216
Victim Blaming ...217
Emotional Abuse as Bad as Physical Abuse ...218
Desperate People Do Desperate Things ...219
Depersonalization of the Victim ...222

Law Enforcement ...223
Victim Emotions ...224
Lack of Training ...224
Unwilling to Invest in Case ...225
Victim Discredited ...225
Law Enforcement as Abusers ...226

Service Providers & Organizations for Victims ...230
Political Action Groups ...232
Victim Advocates ...233
Controlling the Victim ...233
Inform Victim of Options ...234
Follow the Lead ...234
Information, Information, Information ...235

Briefly,
Offender Organizations & Programs

Correctional Facilities ...236
Responsibility & Justice ...236
Setting Examples ...237
Refusal of Training ...240
Service Providers For Offenders ...242
The System...Again...245

Quick Reference

After You Have Been Traumatized...248
Some Things Perpetrators Look For...249
Position Statement on Forced Mediation or Counseling...250
Fact Sheet ...251
Definitions...253
Sources Cited/Consulted...262
Index...265

Because I Love Him:

How Girls Become Battered Women
&
Why They Stay

Introduction

In an effort to understand my own predicament, I began doing research on domestic violence in 1985. Because of revictimization (the fact that once we are a victim we are apt to continue being singled out by perpetrators), that research could not be limited to domestic violence, but had to be broadened to include violence against women in general.

By examining my own patterns, I learned that I had no idea how to protect myself. Years earlier I had looked around at the women who shared my support groups and realized I was not alone, which is one of the purposes of a support group. But why were there so many of us? How could our violent realities often be the result of our own choices and yet we were not at fault? This made no sense, and yet, having spent a lifetime submerged in the icky goo of the traumas, I knew it was true. I had to know how it could be. I was unwilling to accept a life of abuse and assaults. I was unwilling to teach that to my daughters.

As the years went on, I wrote a piece here and there, presented my research to battered women and service providers, produced videos and benefits, rode with law enforcement, and did anything else that I thought would teach me about victims and offenders. I had a personal stake in the outcome.

As two decades passed, I put this book aside because my own experience of abuse was graphically presented in a three-inch stack of letters from a batterer and once I came to that section of the book it became much too real. He used notes taped to my car, doors, clothes, and any place else he could think of, to degrade and devalue me. The notes pointed out every flaw, every shortcoming, all of his delusions, and anything else that left me feeling as if I were less. Finishing the book meant I had to work with these letters.

With memory alone, we can filter and review the experiences that don't pose too much of a threat. These letters were too painful to touch, much less read. I would have to hear again the degrading, victim-blaming, denying, and justifying, that had once defined me.

Hearing someone you love apply to you every psychological term they could learn can be crushing to the spirit and self-esteem. How would going through it again effect me? As the letters demonstrate, he never seemed to learn words and terms like victim stance, traumatic stress, and victim-blaming. He clung to the terms he thought exonerated him.

In 2004 I realized that it was only the young who would live forever and somewhere along the line I had become wrinkled. The wrinkles appeared overnight, and my mortality reflected off of every mirror (and, unfortunately, even stainless steel). During this mid-life crisis I decided the one thing I had to finish in this life was my research on domestic violence and other trauma survivors.

To do that, we (the formerly-battered women and service providers consulting on the book) decided to pull the letters and use them in a second book. We all knew this would be necessary for me to finish this book. We were right. Once we removed the letters from the book, it fell together.

I knew that some of my statistics were more than 20 years old, so I asked an intern I was teaching to pull recent statistics. I was discouraged to see that, despite the efforts of an army of advocates involved in the battered women's movement, the statistics had not changed in 20 years. How could this be? Why is there no significant difference after the 20-year efforts of so many?

Obviously, violence in the home is a problem that will never entirely go away, but after 20 years of teaching, lobbying, and public awareness campaigns we should have seen a reduction in the numbers. How could this be? I have seen and been active in other movements of oppressed people, and the battered women's movement IS an army, comparatively. That is partially because violence against women affects so many, creating advocates and political activists. Like other movements, the victims often find healing in political action. Why had the numbers stayed the same?

Over the years, I had presented the topic, *Why Battered Women Stay* to several hundred battered women. Not one ever said, "No that doesn't fit. That's not why I stayed."

Their response was always, with a gaping mouth, "My God. Why haven't we been told this? Why isn't this information available to us?"

When we started providing the information to people other than battered women it become clear why there had been no change in statistics. Law enforcement, judges, and counselors would request the information and then ignore or reject it.

The ideas presented here are not necessarily unique. I knew that other researchers had drawn the same conclusion I had, only to have their research buried or dismissed. Why their work was dismissed would become another question on my list.

I knew that in 20 years the statistics on woman-beating had not declined. I knew we were presently giving battered women the information they wanted. I knew that service providers (outside of this field) were rejecting the information. These were the things I did know, a much shorter list than my questions.

So what was going on? Why on earth was the work controversial? I had set out to teach other women who were trapped in violent relationships why they stay. My only goal was to give them an accurate word because "love" was not it, and every single one of them agreed. So what was the problem? Why were the battered and formerly-battered women the only ones who wanted to hear it?

I needed help pulling these questions and answers together. I didn't have time to sit and simmer in it until I figured it out myself - just like battered women don't have time to wrestle with their questions. Like the women themselves, I needed answers fast. Through my workshops and classes, I spoke with advocates, mediators, attorneys, counselors, and facilitators of batterer's groups. I sought out people who had read my research or participated in one of my workshop and people who hadn't. My area of expertise had never been the politics, and I sought out those who were politically skilled at this system.

To my frustration, I learned that most used the methods they had been trained in and were familiar with, which was often starkly different than the training I had received, giving me no answers.

"Jasper, why do you think this information would be rejected in our patriarchal society?" Douglas asked.

"They don't want to hear it because it's threatening, like the days when we couldn't talk about incest and rape. So why are they threatened?" Doris asked.

"Follow the money," an advocate said during a workshop.

Had the numbers been declining over the last twenty years I would have thrown my work out, believing that it was invalid and what we had been doing was working. But that wasn't the case.

As I drove to the correctional facility to do group with my adolescent sex offenders, the answers all lined up in my head, like Tetris, and seemed to organize themselves. A heavy weight lifted from me. Once I knew where the resistance was coming from, I could address it.

Battered women stay not because they "love" the batterer but because of the trauma they endure and the manipulation and coercion that batterers use to degrade them. The combination of trauma and manipulation cause the women to bond with the perpetrator. This leaves the victims with an intense feeling for which they have no words, so they call it "love". That's the closest and most intense feeling they have for comparison.

This is not a popular concept among service providers because it sounds like I am saying the women are "weak". But that is not the case. This is the exact same type of manipulation and coercion on which we spend a lot of resources teaching diplomats and military personnel to counter. They are certainly not considered weak.

When I teach people why battered women stay, they don't necessarily hear me say bonding. They hear me say that a large population of women are "brainwashed". The thought that we can be "brainwashed" is frightening. People want to believe that is something that can only happen to weak, cult members. Even though I am not saying the women are brainwashed, that is how it's received, and that is not politically correct.

Talking about the manipulation and coercion, is okay. The Domestic Abuse Intervention Project (DAIP) had it charted when my formal training began some 25 years ago in their Power &

Control Wheel. It is the impact of that manipulation and coercion, the bonding, that is supposed to remain unspoken. Like incest and rape 40 years ago, this is a secret we are not supposed to talk about, hence no decline in the incidence reporting of battered women. If we are not teaching them why they stay, that means they have to accidentally bump into something that works for them. And we are not able to forewarn young women who are soon to encounter young men who will try to dominate and control them.

If women stay because of traumatic bonding, as opposed to an unresponsive society and system alone, then that means that our interventions need to change. And that means it isn't only society, the system and the men that must change. It means that the service providers could also do some things differently in order to be of more help to the already battered women and those that are being primed to be battered.

Many of us in the battered women's movement have worked hard to end the victim-blaming inherent in asking rape victims how sexy they were or asking battered women what they did to provoke the beating. If I teach women how to counter and resist the manipulation and coercion used by the batterer, I am also telling women they have some responsibility in their own safety and the quality of their lives. I am telling them there are things they can do, and that they are not helpless. This can be heard as victim-blaming. But it isn't. If they are never told what is happening, then how can they counter or avoid it? Yet we meet nothing but resistance, except from the battered and formerly-battered women (which includes many services providers).

While we must always guard against and protect victims from victim blaming, as the last two decades have shown, we cannot impact the problem with false information and lack of education. We criticize women for trying to change the men they love and yet we, as service providers, are doing the same thing. Instead of teaching young girls and women how to avoid victimization, escape it when they can't avoid it and then recover from it, the current approach of many is to spend our resources trying to change the men, the system and the society, which are as resistant as some of the sturdiest bacteria.

While we throw the word empowerment around, it now seems as if that is only popular if the truth is not ugly, politically incorrect or distasteful. This makes getting the information out truly an uphill battle. We can give women the information and let them decide if it fits - which could lead to an immeasurable change in their and their children's lives. Or we can work ridiculously hard to offend no one, maintain the status quo, and see no changes in the number of battered women as the statistics prove.

It is easier to believe that women stay because of patriarchy, resources, social expectations, etc... because these are things outside of ourselves, mostly out of our control. And these are major contributing factors. But they do not explain her answer to the ever present question, "Why do you stay?" And that answer is a clue we have to acknowledge and explain.

If batterers are using the manipulative and coercive techniques used against enemy combatants and in hostage situations, then that means we need to start dealing with men who beat women in the same way we would deal with a hostage taker. Wow, talk about an unpopular concept for politicians, law enforcement and the system in general! These are their friends and brothers being arrested. To acknowledge this would mean major changes that would seriously aggravate power brokers.

As media, judges, journalists, law enforcement, counselors, etc... we have no right to limit the information that battered women receive. Give the women the information and <u>then</u> ask them why they stay. If we don't give them the information, we can't expect them to change their family traditions and we have no right to berate them for staying, as we bear some responsibility for their trauma.

This book presents one well documented case. My experience has been called extreme by people who have never been beaten. That is just not the case. In one way or another I have worked with hundreds of battered women. Crushed and degraded, they tell of being forced to have sex with animals and other men. Hedda Nessbaum was rendered impotent in saving the life of her daughter, and woman after woman is killed while trying to escape.

I am an accomplished, well educated, woman, with good instincts and high intellect. I am also an old, menopausal, ill-tempered, formerly-battered woman who has worked with, and experienced, a wide range of traumas with hundreds of victims and survivors. I have seen more abuse, by those courts and counselors who choose to be untrained and insensitive, than should ever have been tolerated. Their ability, and willingness, to be used as a battering tool has severely diminished their credibility. I use the word "choose" because any service provider can access proper training at this point. Many simply choose not to.

When I first began training in the amelioration of violence against women there was always discussion on conflict of interest, funding sources, competition for funding, cooperation among agencies, not replicating services, making sure victims weren't paying for services, finding ways for offenders to pay for the services their victims needed etc… These issues were discussed endlessly. We didn't just talk it but we walked it and we weren't popular and that was okay with most organizations. We were changing the system to suit victims.

We had the plans, resolve and conviction to maintain our integrity. We discussed it in unending meetings and the conversations were furthered and enhanced by writings that were copied and passed hand-to-hand from all over the world – we had no internet. The organizations swore to maintain integrity, I believe with all sincerity, because we didn't want to become oppressive, elitist or like the system that was causing such harm.

There were instances of hypocrisy, lip service and misbehavior from the same mouths, but in general, the majority were concerned about integrity in the movement and not morphing into the personalities and organizations that we were helping women to recover from. I know how those advocates, service providers and facilitators were trained 25 years ago, and that was with integrity and a determination to act in the best interest of the victim, yadda, yadda, yadda, rock smashes scissors and, hopefully, paper covers rock.

Things (white clothes, newly painted walls and movements) can become so sullied and filthy over decades. It's so gradual often we don't even notice how yellow our bed sheets, or compromised our movements, have become. Today, organizations work with batterers and refuse services to unpopular groups of victims making sure to keep power brokers happy. They wouldn't consider calling local law enforcement on misbehavior because they are getting referrals from their kin. They wouldn't consider stepping forward and saying, "We saw the video of those officers tazing her for not being quiet when told. Each one of those officers were three times her size and that was not necessary. She was no threat. She was not resisting." They are insisting victims take an MMPI prior to doing any counseling and try to intimidate new organizations out of a fear of limited resources.

Facilitators of batterers groups openly blame victims (see *Letters From A Batterer*) and victim advocates remain silent while talk show hosts run entire shows on how battered women are masochistic and provoke the abuse. Judges are forcing women into mediations and joint counseling, facilitating the forbidden interaction. I know they know better.

We now have organizations blackballing and refusing to work with advocates, service providers and facilitators that do not agree with them as opposed to the long, productive discussions we endured early on. They need to be reminded of their poli-sci 101. We need all facets of a movement – from the radical liberal to the ultra conservative, from the Malcolm X's to the Martin Luther Kings because each position serves a different purpose.

Had these organizations not acquired the power to change the system, they would not be colluding with the system, to keep their power they acquired by challenging the abuses. They currently squander power for media attention and pocket change. We get as many calls now from victims hurt by service providers as we do from victims of "defined" abusers. One of the biggest losses in the movement is humility. The offending organizations have stopped learning from the victims they set out to serve.

At this time, I think it's appropriate for the groups who are fighting to maintain the status quo to simply hush. They are contributing to the lack in statistical change, and have had decades to do so. Now let the experts speak. We are not helpless, drooling idiots who cannot speak for ourselves. Given the chance, formerly-battered women, who have no dog in the fight (because they are not fighting for election, appointment, funding or clients), can teach our women, old and young, battered and not, how to avoid, escape and recover, from these brutal, degrading relationships. There are many organizations that have maintained their humility and integrity and in doing so they have had to give up their popularity with the power and their opportunities for referrals and contracts. These are also going to be the service providers victims/survivors report a high degree of trust in.

We (Victim Services) do not seek or accept money from any source that could leave us beholden. That enables us to talk about the truth rather than worry about offending a sponsor as with television or worrying about our next grant. We are set up to operate on community support. If I am asked to do something with my programs, or participants, that I feel is dangerous or unethical I can say, "No," without worrying about losing my funding. The truth doesn't have to be popular or politically correct for us to work with it. And many offending service providers have lost that ability so gradually they haven't noticed it.

The most popular definition of insanity is, "doing the same thing over and over expecting a different result." That is exactly how we are dealing with victims and exactly how we are training our daughters to become victims.

1

Round Rooms
&
The Reality of Woman Beating

  I sat in the white wicker chair that contrasted sharply with the soft green room and the warm, roaring fire. With my feet propped on a log in front of the fireplace I enjoyed the soft texture and blend of the pinot noir and Bill Withers in a beautiful sanctuary that was my thirteenth restoration. I had worked hard restoring house after house to create beauty and safety in structures that witnessed terrible danger and ugliness. While these structures witnessed horrors that would haunt, they would never be able to bear witness. I would.

  Aaron's friends boisterously staggered down the two flights of stairs. Drunk, they said their good-byes, in the manly way of course, and Aaron disappeared. They had been "jamming" upstairs for the last four hours. Through the archway I saw Aaron reappear in front of the staircase and I smiled. These were times he often felt playful and loving, a wonderful contribution to the sanctuaries I built.

  When the look on his face registered in my mind I remembered that this was also a time where he could be primed for violence. I looked down and saw the duct tape in his hands. My first thought was that he was upset because an amp or a cord or some piece of equipment had broken. As he approached me it didn't register that I was about to be "fixed". By the time he grabbed me, threw me to the floor and I heard the tearing of the tape I realized that making anything better, at least by my definition, was not his goal. Terror set in as I felt the tape bind my wrists and ankles.

While he had hit me, terrorized me and threatened me before I was not prepared for the beating that would ensue with this novel use of duct tape. I was sure he had now tried everything to fix me. If I knew what was wrong with me I would have gladly expedited the process. But I didn't. I had no idea why the husband I had just left beat me and even less of a clue as to why Aaron beat me. Like society, I blamed myself for the brutality in my life and I had no idea what was so wrong with me that even duct tape couldn't do the job.

There was no hysteria or "loss of control" in Aaron and his calm premeditation made the experience all the more terrifying. In my naiveté I still believed that all woman beating came from a loss of control. But this was not my experience as he violently but methodically bound my wrists and ankles and then ripped my clothes from me. The speed of it added to my disorientation.

He turned me over and over before finally, face up, naked and bound he straddled me with all 260 pounds. I remained silent, afraid that my daughters would wake up. They had already seen so much in their little lives. Out of their presence I referred to their father as the fetus beater because his brutality started during pregnancy and pregnancy seemed to make the beatings worse. As Aaron brutalized my body I kept my mind focused on my babies, determined to hold my tongue.

While Aaron's weight perched on my abdomen, as my ex-husband had done during my terms as an incubator, he hit me back and forth, right side, left side over and over until, through my dissociation, I heard screams. After a moment I realized there was more than one person screaming and none of them were me.

Being the oldest child of a violent, alcoholic cop I had learned early how to take a beating. My siblings were always amazed at how I could take a beating from our father and not respond at all, much less shed tears. But at this point in my life there was a new weapon for the men in my life to use, my daughters.

I did not want them to have to learn how to take a beating, as I had. At the time, I thought I would kill before I allowed them to be harmed. But I was ignorantly allowing so much harm to seep into them. Still, they were a nifty tool for controlling me. While they had never tried duct tape, my severely dysfunctional birth family and ex-husband had been using these little girls to hurt me since their arrival.

During an earlier beating Aaron had learned how efficient using those little girls could be at controlling me. During that beating I was refusing to respond when Aaron jumped off of me, headed toward my sleeping daughters and growled, "I'm gonna get those girls."
I immediately obliged him with enough begging, crying and pleading to satisfy. I was learning that part of Aaron's gratification came from my response. That night he learned that threatening the babies would get it.

Hearing the screams, I turned my head to the left, toward the staircase and there stood my two little girls. They screamed, cried and clung to each other in their little, ruffled, floor length strawberry shortcake nightgowns. With their arms wrapped around each other, faces drawn in terror they screamed, "Get off my mommy. You're killing her."

Prior to their arrival I was dissociated, projecting myself into the fireplace where it was safe and warm, the same place I was enjoying prior to this rude interruption. This projection was always a last ditch effort to protect my mind at a time when I couldn't protect my body. Dissociation is when, during a traumatic event, we try to protect our mind by disconnecting it from our body.

When I saw my babies I knew I had to keep all my parts together. This was no longer just dangerous for me but they were now within Aaron's field of vision. Now I begged and cried, which generally pleased him. As he lifted his weight from my 100 pound, naked body he started punching me in the stomach.

I stared at my daughters, fighting back tears and at the same time trying to show him enough pain to satisfy him. I was stuck between his desire to see me suffer and my need to hide it for the girls. I had to measure my response to the trauma. It was harder to show the pain because that just wasn't the way I had always survived it. My best tool was to high-tail it out of that helpless body and give the woman beater no response, at least no response that I could control.

Aaron disappeared from my view. But as I lay motionless on the cold, wood floor in front of them, bound and naked, I watched the deep eyes of my babies follow him. At that moment they were my eyes. Their nonverbal was all I needed to see. Their little faces, no longer innocent, suddenly turned white and I saw the terror heighten right before their screams turned to hysteria. They clung tighter to each other and began sucking air, heaving and muttering unintelligible syllables. I couldn't understand a word they were saying but, just before he rounded the corner in the foyer, I knew that what they were seeing had to be ugly. And, of course, it was.

Aaron appeared carrying a large butcher knife. Now efforts to continue rationing out my reaction were overtaken by the enormity of it all. As he approached I tried to crawl, bound at the wrists and ankles, like a naked worm, out of his reach. I worked my battered and bruised body hard to simply put inches between us. He grabbed me by my ankles and hoisted them into the air, hanging me like a newborn, slicing the duct tape and both ankles in one smooth swoop. Somehow, I think he had done that before.

Dropping my legs to the ground he grabbed for my wrists. Still confused I didn't realize he was trying to free me as I struggled to get my legs under me. The girls were only feet from the front door but I feared that if I yelled for them to run he would turn his focus to them. I felt such shame that they were seeing me this way and such sadness that they now knew true human nature. During their father's beatings their view was usually blocked by the uterus meant to protect them. They now had an unimpeded view to Aaron's violence and I feared any wrong move on my part would turn his attention to them.

Holding my hands into the air he sliced the duct tape that held my wrists. He then let go of my hands and I crumbled to the floor. Aaron turned and walked into the parlor. Through the newly painted pocket doors I watched him stab the eight inch long butcher knife into the wall about seven feet up. He walked past my babies and up the stairs. Sara reached me first and I grabbed her, pulling her on top of me in a crude effort to hide my naked, battered body from her younger sister.

I awoke the next morning in my own bed. My babies slept peacefully beside me and I took a moment to study the differences. Sara was a six-year-old, fair skinned, straight haired, blond. She never hid the first-born traits that could make her a handful. She was the first born of the first born of the first born of the first born of the eldest of the first born. That was as far as I had been able to trace it. Given her personality, I think it went on to the beginning of time.

Spooned in Sara's belly lay Amanda. Sara's light complexion contrasted starkly with her sister's dark complexion and long, brown, curly hair that made people smile with "cute". At one point, Sara had become so jealous of the curls that she used a disposable razor to shave them. Sara was furious when they grew back. Amanda had the quiet, old-soul type personality while Sara was seldom silent and needed to learn every lesson on her own.

Their sleep was not peaceful as they tossed and fussed. Trying to stretch the silence I lay quiet admiring my babies as only a parent could, not yet remembering the night before and totally befuddled as to why the babies were in my bed, as opposed to Aaron.

Up until I left their father, about a year earlier, we had always shared a bed. But since Aaron came into our lives the girls shared a bed and I shared a bed with Aaron. Amanda turned over and I saw a streak of blood on the side of her cheek. I sat upright so quick that I woke them. Panicked I checked them trying to figure out where her injury was. I questioned them as I rolled, poked and prodded.

"Mommy, it's you. Don't you remember? Last night? Mommy you're bleeding," Sara said sadly.

It all flooded back like someone opened up the top of my head and emptied a dump truck full of garbage, confusion, shame and noise into it. It was the same confusion and shame I had felt the mornings after a brutal beating from their father or my own father.

"I'm going to get ice for your face," Sara said, climbing out of the bed. Standing no taller than three feet, she was the one that mothered us all.

"No! Where is he?" I ask.

"It's okay mommy. He left last night," she said.

Sara left to get ice but quickly returned. I could see the fury in her little face.

"He's sitting on the couch, told me to get my ass back up here. Bastard," pausing to frame a thought, "Mommy are we being held hostage?" she asked.

I didn't respond.

I certainly didn't believe we were being held hostage but had no idea what was going on and no idea how to respond to such a straightforward question from such a little girl. If we weren't being held hostage then what in the hell was this? I couldn't explain what was going on to myself, much less to a child.

He yelled up that I just wanted attention and that they were not to cater to me.

"Mommy what is cater?" Sara ask.

"He doesn't want you to be nice to me," I explained.

As the years went by I would sadly realize that was one request that she would incorporate, subconsciously, as she defined our relationship. In a matter of minutes we heard his weight coming up the stairs and I fully remembered the terror of the night before. I pushed the girls down between the wall and the bed and threw all but one of the blankets over them.

"Crawl under the bed. Don't crawl out. Stay," I whispered.

I covered myself with the last blanket as this waking nightmare came through the door. As his eyes met mine the fury simply drained from his face and I saw guilt, shame and compassion. That's when I knew it must be bad. I had never seen those things in his evil, callous face before and I never saw them in Larry's, the father of my children, or the face of Jim, my father.

I sat curled on the couch avoiding eye contact with my sister, Rena. I was wrapped in a blanket so she couldn't see the sliced ankles and wrists. I was so tired and I ached and throbbed with even the slightest movement. Rena didn't mention the purple, swollen face or the fat lip. Just dropped in, didn't stay long. I knew she was just rubbernecking. Where we come from woman beating was the norm. Apparently not even worthy of mention. From where I sat I could see the knife hanging in the wall, a symbol of tranquility, peace and self worth - up high, out of reach and a potentially lethal pursuit.

As children, violence in our home was not only acceptable but expected. I remember at 18 years old when my father-in-law du jour told me that he had never hit a woman. I was surprised. Even though I knew woman beating (child beating, animal beating, racism etc…) was wrong and never hesitated to speak my mind, I truly thought brutality toward weaker souls was considered not only normal but acceptable to anyone with the power to do so.

I was the oldest child in my family of origin and Rena was about eighteen months younger. Our father was only a handful of years out of a Communist Chinese prison camp and he brought the guards home as his model and the techniques as parenting tools. Rena and I were intermittently terrorized and brutalized. Our father had been taken hostage at only seventeen years of age and now he inflicted what had been done to him.

In addition, my father's father was notoriously brutal so even without the input of prison guards, domestic violence was going to be inescapable for us. And as I sat curled on the couch, facing the sister who also suffered a life of brutality, I was unaware of how the Communist Chinese would influence my efforts to understand my history.

Sara, knew Rena's phone number and I suspect she had called her aunt for help. Sara didn't yet know that her aunt was being beaten by her husband, and on occasion, still being hit by our father. I thought that it would take many years before my daughters learned the hard lessons about relationships and as I write this, a decade and a half later, I fear they may never get it.

That day, after seeing my face, Aaron called a crisis line and got us an appointment with a counselor. The notion that beating me was wrong and he needed to go to jail didn't enter my mind. We, as a couple, needed help. He persuaded me that something was wrong with our sex life and that was the reason we would seek professional help, nothing to do with beating your partner half to death.

And aside from the fact that he felt some type of guilt over the incident I was forbidden to remove the knife from the wall. It hung firm and threatening for weeks. The one attempt I made to remove it and the one request Sara had to take it out was met with frightening threats. That knife protruded as a warning despite Aaron's occasional proclamations of responsibility and remorse.

Aaron went from using adhesives to fix me, to recruiting every mental health provider that needed to fill a time slot. And while we waited to get into the first appointment I wasn't allowed to mention the violence because it made him feel guilty. Yet the knife mocked the girls and me as a grim reminder of our recent history and our certain future.

By the time we got into the first counseling appointment the swelling in my face had decreased and turned to a nice shade of green that matched the sweater I wore. During the session Aaron minimized the attack on me and persuaded the counselor that it was "in the past." He was one of the most charming men I had ever met and he made sure any service provider we saw was as charmed as I was during our courtship. He never failed to display his charm and shared it with anyone who might help to manipulate me.

The counselor agreed with him on the definition of "past" and they decided that I either needed to get over it or move out. I was initially appalled that "in the past" could actually occur before bruising healed but, the counselor said I either had to forgive him or get out of the relationship and "they are the experts".

Being a full-time student, single parent, with no income and no place to go I decide that maybe he was right. It was in the past and I should forgive Aaron. Besides he had told me on numerous occasions that he would kill me before he let me go and I believed him. Three weeks later he nearly killed me anyway. It gets to the point that you know he's going to kill you. The question becomes:

do I die in the privacy and small comfort of my home? Or do I die at my place of employment, in front of the kid's school or like a dog in the street being shot by a rabid cop?

We sat in the living room, dressed and ready to go. The girls were with Larry for the weekend and Aaron and I were going out with friends. They weren't our friends. They were Aaron's friends. Once we became a couple, my friends were shut out and I was expected to take his group of misogynists as my support system and allies. Aaron was in a bad mood, angry. He slammed back more wine as we waited for his friends to arrive.

The bruising in my face had finally faded and I was dolled up in a pair of flat sandals, a denim mini skirt and a tank top. As short legged and flat-chested as I was, this was a pretty benign outfit. Our night out drinking hadn't helped his mood and by the time we got home it was a full blown fight over the outfit he loved when we left. He sat down in a chair in the living room and I headed upstairs.

I had chosen this home because of the restoration it needed. You couldn't find window cleaner anywhere but drywall cement and paint cans seemed to chase you. As I went up the stairs, drunk no doubt, a can of paint went thudding down two flights of stairs, losing its lid somewhere along the way.

Standing at the top of the stairs I looked down at that gallon of spilled paint. I didn't yet realize that I would be looking at my hands, hair and feet outlined in this shade of yellow, mixed with my blood, over the entire house. I did not realize this was the last time I would see that paint in such a manageable pool. I felt his every footstep shake the house and before I saw his tense body I knew what was going to happen.

As he stepped right into the pool of paint, with a splat, I put my back to the wall and slid to the floor, limp. I know that it doesn't hurt as bad when you let go of all your muscles, feelings, reasoning, thoughts and most importantly, your "self". I don't own my body, or dare come near it, as Aaron grabs my still sore ankles and pulls me down to a landing between the two flights of steps. As he pulled my ankles my head thudded down each step.

I was a spectator as my body was rolled over and over in the thick, yellow paint. No feeling or thought only a slight resemblance to anything that could be construed as living. No matter which way he turned me, threw me or rolled me I stared straight ahead, blank, projecting my mind outside of my body, the only safe place for it. The girls were not home so I did not have to respond. Time became irrelevant but I knew his anger would not be quickly spent. It never was.

When I felt myself still and knew he was gone, I quietly crawled up the stairs, trailing yellow ooze like a slug, into the bathroom. I slowly removed the gooey clothing that had become heavy with paint. I carefully piled the clothes in the sink, ironically trying to avoid any drips, and started the water in the claw foot tub I had added to the finished bathroom. I felt the floor vibrating and turned to face the six foot frame of the man I was certain I loved, whose anger my strength could never match. Why did he need to go another round? I wondered. I was quiet, submissive and compliant.

His unharnessed rage was more energy than I had ever seen as he grabbed me and dragged my body to the stairs again, this time threatening to throw me outside. Aaron had frequently bragged about stripping his ex-wife naked, throwing her outside, turning on the lights and calling her father to come and get her. He laughed about her cowering naked behind a shrub and felt a sense of pride in his creative methods of terror. With all of his bravado he shared this story as a conversation topic and laughed about it with his friends.

    I knew he meant it. Again, his threat worked. Naked and covered in paint I begged for my last shred of dignity. We owned a large historic home on zero lot line. The houses were so close that the neighbors could hear you cough. They knew I was battered and never called the police. I didn't want them to see it too. I felt my feelings, emotions, thoughts and "self" flood back through my body, initiated by the shame of being a battered woman.

    I begged and pleaded, fighting against his adrenaline pumped body. Reacting worked again. He stopped dragging me toward the door and began beating me with his fists and banging my paint soaked head on the hardwood floors. Each time my head hit the floor my long, brown hair left beautifully artistic splays and outlines that would later haunt me and prompt many questions from my daughters. Guests never asked. They knew because the paint also displayed his footprints along with a print from every part of my body. That night he beat me for hours in every room of that four thousand square foot house. After a while I didn't know who was doing this to me and it didn't much matter. I stayed dissociated, high up in the ceiling until his anger was temporarily spent.

    I saw the sun coming up as I retreated to my bedroom naked and numb. Yellow paint and red blood covered the black and blue bruises donned by my insignificant body. Finding a corner I backed into it and slid down the wall once again. I felt no pain, only a few basic, rhythmic lines repeating themselves over and over in my brain:

> You can bounce off the walls
> You can scream until dawn
> Hide in the corners and tremble alone.
> You can beg, you can plead,
> No refuge you'll find.
> For the rooms are all round
> With no corners to hide

While I'm sure at some point sleep offered my mind, body and spirit some reprieve. I don't know.

Whenever I hear someone say, "Emotional abuse is worse than physical abuse," I think, and usually say, "That's what people who have never been beaten say."

It's as if they think you can actually be physically abused without being emotionally abused. While pain is relative and what one person might be devastated by another might brush off, I know that physical abuse is emotional abuse with a side dish of ass kicking. Someone who has not already been emotionally abused won't take the physical abuse – at least not more than once. Emotional abuse is one of the predictable primers. Emotional abuse has to happen first.

After being rolled in paint, beaten for hours and terrorized with the threats of being thrown outside naked, my next memory was of lying at the foot of the stairs at Aaron's feet begging for his approval. My paint soaked, bloodied and bruised body was covered in sweat pants and shirt. My hair was pulled stiff with dried paint as I begged and pleaded for him to love me.

I reassured him, like a child, that I would be good. He sat still on the bottom step of the stairs. What he thought or felt is still a mystery. He acknowledged nothing, not even my presence.

This was the moment, curled up at the feet of my domestic terrorist that I ask myself, "What in the hell are you doing?"

This was not a rhetorical thought that slipped through my mind, unfiled. This was an epiphany of survival and from that moment on my life would never be the same.

"What in the hell am I doing?" was not the only question.

It was a parade of questions that I couldn't answer. The questions marched from the surface of my brain to the deepest part of my self-definition. A switch flipped in my mind. I would never see Aaron, myself or even the world the same way again. Why am I begging for his approval? I'm the 14-year-old girl who physically fought her drunken father because of his racist remark. What happened to that 14-year-old? Why haven't we declared war on domestic terrorists? Why am I putting my children through this? Why was this a pattern? What was the pattern? Why was I staying, and more importantly why was I begging desperately for him to be happy with me?

The pleading for approval slowly stopped as the questions quietly wove roots deep down into my mind. Contempt moved from my brain through my body, although I knew better than to show it. Something was different and my heart felt hard and firm. I no longer felt malleable. I snuck a peek at the man sitting on the step above me and my skin crawled. I made sure not to get caught and, like a whipped dog, had no intention of eye contact. I just wanted to fully feel this new hardness. I knew he had to go but hadn't a conscious clue how to accomplish it. My brain began entertaining the following fantasy. I didn't yet know that buried in that fantasy lay my answer to partial freedom.

Solemn & Grace

She walks through the door,
Black silence she greets.
She's sent them away,
Out into the streets.

She knows in her mind
The blood that will run,
Icy and cold,
A loss mourned by none.
Pouring a drink
Of solemn and grace,
No surgance of thought,
No detail in haste

Unpinning her hair,
It falls to her waist
He's waited so long
For just one more taste.
Under her pillow
The guns cold, and hard
No more pain will she feel as
She checks the last card.

Breaking her silence
A knock at the door,
He's answered her plea
To love her once more.
Compassion it bounds
From her soul to her mind
The logic escapes her,
To her pain he was blind

Opening the door
She remembers the face.
A day and a time
When he gave her no place.

Easy she feels, till
He speaks out her name
Remembering the terror, but
This ones her game.

Wrapping around her,
She chills to the bone.
Moving seductively
Disabling the phone.

She lies on the bed
Lace falling free
Numb to the presence
Of a man she can't see.

Footsteps she hears
Approaching her bed
She pulls from the night
The weapon of dread.

He cries out her name
As the flesh runs to red.
The bullet it echoes
From the hole in his head.

Pouring a drink of solemn
And grace,
Enabling the phone
She covers her face.

Clinging to the calves of his legs I begged for Aaron's love and approval. I desperately needed to know that everything was okay. If he was happy with me then I had reduced my chances of another beating. If he loved me then maybe he wouldn't kill me. Now, somehow, I was abruptly pulled back out of my body and looked down at the battered and broken woman sitting at the feet of the brutal, heartless terrorist that controlled her. For a moment I was no longer seeing the broken piece of junk I had been taught all of my life that I was. But I was what appeared to be a helpless woman who was broken. I looked upon her with compassion and sadness rather than the contempt that reflected the opinions of my parents and ex-husband.

I saw the sliced ankles peeking out from underneath the sweat pants. I saw the rigid yellow hair pulled back so it wouldn't mess up Aaron's clothes and I heard the pleas for acceptance and safety of a woman-child who feared for her life. The contrast of the large frame of the violent misogynist, totally detached from the pleas of his crumpled, tiny, powerless victim, was striking.

I remembered, after one beating during my first pregnancy, how large Larry seemed, even though he was a relatively small man at five ten. I had crawled from the kitchen, where he had been pounding my head on the floor, to the bathroom. As my body cleared the bathroom door I closed it and locked it. Curled up between the tiny space between the toilet and tub, with my head laying on the toilet, I listened as he removed the door from the hinges. As he finally came through the door his size was striking. Six foot four or five foot eight, there wasn't much difference from my point of view.

No longer detached from my body but viewing the scene from the space I actually filled and shared with Aaron, I could see with clarity the hollow spirit of a man who had no heart, no compassion for the suffering of another and I could no longer ignore what I saw. I could no longer ignore the cold, empty space that his body used or the dark absence of a spirit that cries for, or even notices, the suffering of another.

Still sitting at Aaron's feet, but no longer clinging I knew that this was the beginning of a long road and I knew the road would have to be strewn with a lot of answers, if I was to find my way. As a child and then a teenager I seldom had much more to do than academic pursuits. Until I became an "habitual runaway" I spent my short life, all 12 years of it, watching the world go by from my bedroom window. Which made being an A student and finding answers to questions pretty easy. During my "childhood" my only access to the world was through books and research and I would soon learn how that experience would contribute to saving my life.

I had done this before on other issues and I knew that when the questions hit me this hard, my brain lights up like a bon-fire and I am in for a long, fascinating journey. That was what I knew. But at that moment what was more important was what I didn't know. I didn't know how many generations back this journey would take me. I didn't know I was, at that moment, connected to victims of terror and violence of all types, in every cubby hole on the planet. I didn't know the research would lead to Communist Chinese, POW'S, cult members and abused children. I had expected this moment of clarity to guide me through insights on battered women but I didn't expect to find my answers in correctional facilities and shelters, working with sex offenders, woman beaters and even killers.

I didn't know that I would have to acknowledge and pick apart a painful childhood and adolescence, virtually turning myself inside out, like a sock, for examination and analysis. I didn't know that my parents had left their own yellow footprints deep, in every crease of my brain. I didn't know the road these questions would lead me down would be worthy of a life's work for a lost, unloved little cop's kid they called "Piglet".

As I lay at his feet I was also totally unaware of how much damage the beatings had done to the body I fled from with dissociation. The body that I couldn't protect from Aaron or Larry, the spine that bore the weight of all the men I had loved, including my father, was seriously damaged. And when the chaos and fight for my life waned thus reducing the dissociation, constant adrenaline and other chemicals my brain needed to drown me in for survival, I found that the weight of those men had been more than my abandoned body could bear. I would find the physical damage was serious and permanent and hat was pale compared to the emotional damage.

Never again would I be the same. I no longer saw a God in the man that beat me. In the flash of a moment he went from an all powerful man that I desperately needed to please, to a terribly evil, callous perpetrator who thrived on the power he attained from the suffering he could create. I saw a beast that was fed by the begging and pleas of the tiny women he brutalized and humiliated.

The questions flooded my brain, excited me and gave me reason to continue. I had seen something, in that moment at his feet, that I needed for survival. While I was repulsed by the pig that controlled me, the end of that relationship would have to be his choice and would take a long time to achieve. The revelations were mine, not his. Had I shared my new thoughts I feared he would kill me. He had to be the one to move on. I knew the price of asserting my right to self determination could be my life.

As Aaron dragged me from counselor to counselor, in an effort to find out what was wrong with me, I threw myself into research. He went through the typical gyrations of a batterer and I, sometimes more, sometimes less, retained the characteristics of a battered woman. But from the moment I begged for his acceptance, at his feet, I would never be the same. I was changing. While denying the obvious was something my mother had perfected, I couldn't unsee what was happening and was changing as fast as I was learning.

The History of Violence Against Women & Children

According to FBI statistics a woman is beaten every 18 seconds in the United States (FS) and, according to Susan Forward, in her book *Betrayal of Innocence*, 1 in 4 females will be incested. A 1985 FBI report states that "30% of all female homicide victims are killed by their partners" and the National Coalition Against Domestic Violence has reported that in more than 50% of wife abusing families the children are also battered.

While some of these statistics seem old, recent statistics are no different. The Bureau of Justice Statistics Special Report:

Violence Against Women, August 1995 asserts that one million women a year are beaten by an intimate partner. Other estimates are higher. The 1996 Report of the American Psychological Association Presidential Task Force on Violence and the Family reports that four million women are seriously assaulted every year by an intimate partner and Strauss (1978), *Wife Beating: How Common and Why*, asserts that violence occurs in half of all domestic relationships. These are simply the statistics on violence against women perpetrated by their lovers. These do not include other types of violence like rape, stranger assaults and robbery.

According to the Los Angeles County *Protocol For the Treatment of Rape & Other Sexual Assault*, one out of every 2.8 women will be raped at least once in their lifetime. While this may seem shocking to many people, it is not surprising to those of us working, or wounded, in the trenches. I contend that all females are assaulted, in one way or another, in a lifetime.

Having grown up believing that all men beat women, these numbers were not shocking to me. What was shocking was that this was seen as a problem and that there was an entire movement to stop violence against women and children. The fact that there was a movement gave me the hope I needed. I embraced the notion of a life free of violence and set out to learn everything I could about how I came to be covered in yellow paint, clinging to the ankles of a brutal man.

In all of my research I saw nothing about what happens to the children of battered women after the women leave the batterer. As a young mother, and an even younger victim advocate, I expected leaving the batterer to be the end of the damage to the children. There was no red flag to warn me that the manipulation and coercion used by batterers does not just end when the woman is able to leave. No articles or studies warned me that his need to get even would extend to my children and that Larry would choose any tool he could find to continue manipulating and controlling me. This lack of information would later haunt me. There had, however been a subtle warning that did not register on my broken radar screen.

When Larry found out that I was going to leave him he threw the kids and me out without even a baby bottle. Sheriffs deputies escorted me back to get diapers, clothes and bottles for the one-year-old on my hip and the three-year-old clutching my thigh. I was forbidden to take the dog, which Larry had always hated and beat as if she were also his wife. He told me he would kill her and none of us every saw Tessa, our beloved Great Pyrenees again.

The courts, during the divorce, had the Domestic Relations Counseling Bureau (DRCB) assess both of us in order to make recommendations as to custody and visitation. Larry had always sworn that, one way or another, he would take my children from me and this fetus beater was now seeking sole custody of two little girls. Despite the fact that the courts refuse to consider violence against the mother, after many tests and sessions with psychiatrists, the courts ordered that I have sole custody and that their father have no visitation until he completed counseling.

The social worker for the DRCB called me into her office and said, "You are going to have a long hard road ahead of you." As a young woman with seriously impaired judgment I had no idea just how serious she was. Her warning was just vague enough for me to assure myself that there wasn't much else he could do to me. After all, he wasn't beating me anymore. This social worker would prove to be right in ways a young woman could never imagine but which would exhaust and crush a middle aged mother.

The decision of the court angered Larry and he refused to do any counseling or even speak to his baby girls. An older, wiser woman would have counted her blessings but my daughters were now calling any man they saw, "daddy" and, along with Larry's sister-in-law, I worked hard to explain to him how young girls can be affected by not having a father. He began taking visitation again and a filthy seed had been planted that I would unfortunately live to harvest.

As I subjected myself to one after another intervention, of Aaron's design, I continued trying to learn about myself through research. I went from researching and studying to teaching others. A stark contrast and contradiction in my life was teaching cops, service providers and the public about the violence battered women live with and keeping the secret that I was being beaten, stalked and controlled. For all the world knew my life was violence free, while all I had ever known was a world of violence.

Throughout Christian history women have been viewed as the downfall of man. One of the best ways this is characterized is by the story of Adam and Eve. According to Maria Roy, in her book *Battered Women*, "As a result of this myth much of today's Christian world has rationalized the mistreatment of women."

Christians are not the only religion to paint women in an unfavorable light. Quoting from the Hindu Code of Manu No. 5 (circa 100 A.D.), "In childhood woman must be subject to her father, in youth to her husband, and when her husband is dead, to her sons. A woman must never be free of subjugation." I learned this quote from Aaron who looked for any support for his behavior. He never had to look hard; religion, any denomination, provides an abundance of support for the abuse of any soul weaker than men.

This was the point at which Aaron decided he wanted to be a preacher. He thrust himself into the teachings of a multitude of religions and used God to conceal his cruelty. He cloaked himself in a book called *A Course in Miracles* while I prayed for one. He hid the suffering he caused behind a veil of flowery words and psychological terms. He cuddled up next to a God that would never turn away from suffering, while I shook my fist at the heavens wanting to know "why?"

I found that it wasn't only violence against women that had a long history. Child physical abuse has also been around as long as humans. According to the *Psychiatric Sequelae of Child Abuse* by Jamia Jacobson, Ph.D., "Fossils dug up from the Pithecanthropines to the Mesolithic peoples found a sex ratio of 100 to 148 in favor of males." During the fourteenth century it is estimated that over half of all children died of abuse.

The history of violence against women and children is well documented. I resist citing statistic after statistic because that is not what this book is about. If you are reading this book you already know there's a problem and you're looking for answers for yourself, a loved one or a client.

The Perplexing Behaviors of Battered Women
&
Other Trauma Survivors

While it would seem to make more sense for there to be as many different responses to violence as there are souls to suffer from it, that is not the case. We all (including animals) respond in predictable ways. I had felt such shame over the batterings and even greater shame over the fact that I then found myself begging at his feet for approval. Knowing the facts and intellectualizing my predicament did not alleviate the shame that would take more than statistics, but it did show me that my response to such brutality was predictable and "normal" given the situation. I was not some masochistic freak, as society would have me believe, that deserved the beatings she endured. I was normal within the population and predicament that I shared with so many other women.

Returning to & Defending the Batterer

Putting space between Aaron and myself was not easy. At this point we had separate homes and he spent his time stalking and terrorizing me. He was intent on becoming a preacher and, as demonstrated in our book *Letters From A Batterer*, he was just as determined to make my soul the first one he saved. The duct tape didn't work so he was going to do some type of contemporary exorcism on me. Still, it never crossed his mind to look at his own actions. He was more determined than ever to fix me.

But my life had changed. While trying to survive and escape my batterers with my children and my life, I attended college full-time, mothered my daughters, worked a part-time job and became involved in the battered women's movement. I held a position on the Steering Committee of a local domestic violence network, which in and of itself was demanding, and the girls were now spending every weekend with their father. This gave me the opportunity to work nights, on the weekends, as I tried to give them orange juice instead of cheaper, packaged sugar drinks. There was now an excitement to my life. Realizing I wasn't alone as a battered woman and that there were actually people trying to stop it, I had found a purpose for my suffering.

I rode with law enforcement to teach them about the dynamics of woman beating. I produced and coordinated two large fund raisers for battered women (one being a 21 band benefit at Union Station in Indianapolis). I made videos for service providers and firefighters on how to help the women when they arrived on the scene and I worked hard to safely free my children and myself from the terror that ran through our home, and bones.

It was terribly difficult. I was horribly exhausted and totally overwhelmed. I did the best I could to provide my children with a mother, working nights in clubs, going to school during the day while they were in school and doing research and volunteer work from home while they were home and awake. Childcare was not an option. As young as they were, I left them alone as they slept to work in the clubs. It may have been one of the hardest periods of my life and had it not been for my new mission of answering those questions I probably would have gone back.

Many evenings the girls and I conducted our lives from the big, four poster bed we used as a security blanket. I was in terrible pain and had no idea why. I blamed the problems on stress and exhaustion and did the best I could to meet my responsibilities and parent my babies. They regularly tickled, wrestled and fought over and around my body.

One cool, fall evening an attorney called and I was able to quiet the girls long enough to collect the information. She said that she had a battered woman at her house and the victim needed to be transported to the Salvation Army.

I argued for a moment that to drag me out was silly, "Just take her," I insisted, "I will have to dress the girls and bring them with me."

I quickly realized from the attorney's rantings that she was doing tremendous damage to this woman.
"She has to be stupid to stay," she insisted.

After venting her frustration she told me the story. This woman was a bi-lateral amputee and her husband was taking her prosthetic legs and then beating her. She couldn't escape. After being flooded with the image of a man beating a torso, I immediately left with the girls and we transported this woman to the shelter, all the while talking to her about the reality of leaving. As I returned home I felt a frustration similar to what the attorney had vented. I doubted that this woman would stay away for long. In fact, I would have bet that she would have gone back within days, given her situation. How much did she depend on this man to be her legs, to supplement her income, to provide a buffer to a cruel world?

With all the hurdles that this legless woman faced, she proved me wrong. Years later, as I lay in the same bed, even sicker, she called. She told me that I had changed her life by transporting her and with the things I said on the ride. Now, with 20 years more experience, I realize how rare this is. We intervene and don't see the results. She gave me such a gift. After transporting this woman I was all the more motivated to know why. Why do we stay with men who terrorize us? Why do we go back? While this woman had obvious reasons, a disability, I knew that wasn't the whole picture.

I had been asked by the network I worked for to "monitor" the domestic violence court and for the fourth day I sat in the court room observing one case after another. On this day, a woman appearing exhausted and beaten down, stood before the judge and, with her head lowered, in shame, as if she were the offender, pleaded with the judge to release her attacker, a man who had repeatedly assaulted her. The man, whose freedom she was requesting, was her husband of five years and the father of her three children.

It was 1985 and this batterer had been charged 31 times since 1982, at least five of which were battery charges against his wife. Most of the other charges were alcohol related. The judge asked the victim why she even wanted her husband home and told her that if she didn't get help, her children would be standing before him one day.

She struggled to explain to the judge why she wanted him home. She shifted her small frame around repeatedly but, the judge maintained his eye contact signaling to her that this was not a rhetorical question. Not only could I see the shame but I felt it pierce through me as if he was demanding an answer from me. After what seemed an eternity the answer she offered was tentative and disconnected.

She told the judge that she "loved" her husband and that she could not support her children without him. She said that her church was against divorce, they would turn their back on her if she abandoned this relationship and that her minister had counseled her to make it work. She believed marriage was forever and that her family would respond harshly to her inability to make her marriage work. She explained to the judge that she was certain, given enough time, that she could make this marriage work.

Although compassionate, the judge did not feel the same. Every word he spoke was as if it were meant for me. I saw my own babies standing before the judge pleading with him to release the man who continually beat them. I saw myself proclaiming my "love" to the judge for lack of any other word to explain the strong emotion that caused me to stay. On this day the judge did not oblige her by releasing the batterer.

I returned for the pretrial hearing and listened as the battered woman asked the judge to allow her husband to enter into a plea agreement that would require an anger management class coupled with a substance abuse class. The prosecutor rejected the agreement. The judge turned to the batterer and said, "The state is tired of putting you on probation. You're a bully." And with that, the pleas and proclamations of love from his victim were dismissed.

On another occasion I had been asked to ride with the Sheriffs Department. I would spend an entire weekend in a car doing domestic runs. I had done this with other law enforcement agencies and knew what to expect. The goal was for us to learn about the dangers that law enforcement face on these runs and for me to teach the officer why the women behave as they do. As before, the runs were endless.

We entered homes with screaming and obviously traumatized children and I watched as one woman after another begged law enforcement not to arrest her attacker. This was prior to **mandatory arrest policies** and not one man was arrested that weekend. During one of the runs I watched in horror as an obviously beaten woman attacked the responding officer to protect the batterer. She was arrested that night. The batterer was not.

Law enforcement, justifiably, asserts that these are the most dangerous runs and they are perplexed by the victim's behavior. Are these the most dangerous for law enforcement because they are the most difficult situations to unravel emotionally? If we could teach them what they need to know to untangle these emotionally charged runs wouldn't we lower the risk?

Why would a battered woman plead her attacker's case before the judge? Why would she go so far as to attack a police officer to keep him from being arrested? The answer is logical but for some reason it's hard to see. Her immediate welfare and that of her children are a high priority to her. She knows the batterer will be released after only a few hours in jail. By then he has had plenty of time to stew in his thoughts and the notion that he is actually the victim. He will be even more furious when they release him. Rationalizing attacking a cop may be as simple as remembering that the batterer has threatened, or maybe even come close to killing her and the cop hasn't.

What if he is arrested and they do keep him longer than overnight? What if he is the sole provider? Does she have to give up shelter and food to be safe? If he misses work, loses his job and they can't make the rent, like everything else, it's her fault. Why doesn't she just go to a shelter or the home of a family member? The shelters are often full and are not generally a pleasant place even to visit. He has threatened to kill her and knows exactly where her family members are.

There is a saying, "keep your friends close and your enemies closer." I often felt if I could see Aaron not only did I know what he was up to but I had a better chance of reading him, predicting his mood and then doing whatever I needed to do to make him happy. As I explain later, when a battered woman protects the batterer she truly is working to reduce her own injuries.

Panic and Anxiety

Survivors of trauma often live with terrible, and frequently incapacitating, **anxiety** and **panic attacks** and this includes an overactive startle reflex. The **startle reflex** is something that we are born with and after a trauma this reflex will often become overactive. I don't know how many times I have been startled to tears only to see a look of disgust cross the persons face, who I just scared with my reaction.

Panic and anxiety are often confusing to people who don't experience it. I often hear people refer to it as "paranoia". I explain to them that paranoia is a fear that has no basis – there is no reason for it. On the other hand the person experiencing panic attacks and anxiety has had an experience that tells them something bad is going to happen. They have seen bad things and their fight, freeze or flight instinct keeps telling them that they need to react to be safe. The chemicals in their bodies tell them they must fight, freeze or flee.

In our "polite" society they must repress the urge to flee and fight constantly so they end up living in a miserable state of having those brain chemicals released but having to suppress the effects of the chemicals. Not only does this "high strung" state of being aggravate the people around them but it is a miserable way to live. In Chapter 4 entitled *The Toolbox* I offer some tools for coping with panic and anxiety.

Self-mutilation

Sometimes survivors of trauma will cut on themselves. I call this slice and dice and the urge is as perplexing to victims as it is to those who love them. I have yet to hear any "expert" explain why this behavior is satisfying to the cutter. But ask any self mutilator, if you can identify one, and they will tell you that they feel much better afterward.

Currently my husband and I study the human and animal response to trauma and, at times, house as many as ninety previously traumatized animals, including horses. We were mortified to learn about some of the training techniques used on horses. One of those horrors is called a twitch. This is a stick with a chain on the end.

When vets are working on a horse and they are afraid of the horse they will hold this stick, put the horse's upper lip inside of the chain and then turn the stick. The horses lip is then pinched inside of the twisted chain. Our animals are handled and trained without violence or abuse so we would not allow the use of a twitch.

Not only am I the mom of the place but I am the researcher. I then train the people who care for our animals based on the information I have unearthed from good sources. I came across some studies done by a vet on the use of twitches. She reports that when a twitch is used on a horse endorphins released into the horse's brain is why a small tool like a twitch will immobilize such a large animal. I have heard that it is the same for tattoos and that is why some people become "addicted" to them.

During the beatings at the hands of Aaron, Larry and even my father, pain was not an issue. Of course, it was later but I had theorized that during the assaults I felt no pain because I was dissociated. One day I fell while carrying pottery and cut my hand open. It was so bad that stuffings were coming out. The doctor told me it was fat and refused to transfer it to my breasts. (I have found that, along with **dissociation**, humor works well to relieve stressful situations. Anyway -) After cutting my hand open, I finished what I was doing and hours later went to get stitches. It took about four hours for me to feel any pain from the terrible gash in my hand.

I believe that when **self-mutilators** cut on themselves this is releasing a chemical into their bodies and that is why they feel better after cutting. People have theorized that mutilators do this to prove to themselves that they can still feel pain and that they aren't totally numbed out. People have theorized that cutters do it to get attention yet this is a private, shame provoking act for self-mutilators. There are other theories and there are probably many reasons why mutilators begin cutting but I believe most continue because of the brain chemicals released when they do cut and how those chemicals make them feel.

Shame

There are so many reasons that victims of violent crimes feel shame. We are blamed and shamed by our families, the offenders, ourselves, the service providers we reach out to as well as society in general. We are blamed and shamed when we are ask what we were wearing, what we did, why we were there and why we don't leave. These questions seem benign to the person inquiring but victims/survivors know what the underlying judgment is, "Your behavior is the reason he hurt you".

If the trauma was a nonviolent sexual assault, at a young age, she may feel shame because she was unable to prevent her body from responding to the stimulation/attention. This reality is often seen as victim blaming and therefore omitted from the discussion, leaving females to believe they were the only ones who responded this way, when actually that is how our brains and bodies were designed to respond to sexual stimulation.

Shame manifests itself in as many ways as there are to shame us. It surfaces through self-hated, low productivity, addictions, **sexualizing**, self-mutilation, overeating and so on. The shame causes us to behave in self destructive ways, which causes more criticisms and judgments, causing more shame and, again, on and on. The cycle of shame has to be broken but that is difficult to do in a world that is so willing to protect offenders, justify their actions and blame victims.

Hypervigilance

Victims/survivors of long term abuse, and frequently even one traumatic experience, often live in a heightened state of awareness in an effort to predict and prevent the next trauma. This is especially common to combat veterans, children of alcoholics, battered women, victims/survivors of child abuse and rape.

Sarcastically, people often request that I stop reading their mind and, unfortunately I know all too often what people are thinking and feeling. Experience teaches that if we can watch those in our environment that may do us harm, like any other prey animal, then we can predict their behavior and reduce our injuries. That logic and effort, while exhausting, is accurate. This is one of the residual effects of abuse and can be used as an asset to help others.

Addictions

Unlike slice and dice, seeing the victim's propensity for addictions isn't difficult. Honesty in acknowledging it can be. During Aaron's most brutal years I spent as much time as I could drunk. It turned out to be 3 years of cyclic drinking, followed by hangovers and guilt. I had watched my father spend his life the same way. He had, what appeared to be, one drive in life and that was to sedate the feelings he was overwhelmed with from his childhood and years in a prison camp. It was certainly not an addiction unique to my family.

As I assembled the Formerly-Battered Women's Group for the network, rode with law enforcement and worked with the battered women, I saw how common addictions are. And while I don't understand how anyone could be perplexed by this I saw the intolerance that victims live with. They may have been concealing the violence but the addictions were as apparent as the clothes they wore.

Addiction is a symptom that could help service providers identify the cause, trauma. The addictions show up in so many ways and do not always indicate violence in the home but they are a symptom of something. While my father worked to drown the abuse of his father in alcohol, my sister took every pill she could buy, beg or steal. I watched women shop, eat, steal and sexualize any feeling that might surface –anything to avoid the horror of reality.

Sometimes people create one form of chaos after another to avoid the trauma they are running from. This means of covering up traumatic events is as unique as we are. Some people gamble and some prey on others. People will act in, harming themselves, act out and harm others, or both.

Addictions are certainly effective in helping us cope on a day-to-day basis with the traumas we've survived, but only for a moment. They create much greater problems in our lives and we often forget that a choice we make today can effect us for life. We can pay the price of one choice for the rest of our life.

My sister drugged herself, literally, right into the ground and seriously damaged numerous lives in the process. When my sister died she left a trail of destruction as long as the history that led to it. I believe the thing that will keep her from coming back as a slug, is that my God will consider the mitigating circumstances and will have mercy for the tortured life she tolerated far too long.

Addictions provoke an ugly response from those that victims come in contact with. Judges, law enforcement and the perpetrator use the addiction to discredit her. If they do not probe deeply, counselors may try to treat the addiction, ignoring the source. Friends and family may need to limit contact because of the stress that the addiction puts on everyone around the victim. While sedating trauma with behaviors and substances may provide short term relief, in the long run the victim is only compounding her problems.

My children struggled for years to understand those years that I wasn't available to them. In his final years of life my father has no significant, real relationships. Women shop themselves into bankruptcy and eat themselves into Weight Watchers.

Sexualizing

Sexualizing works the same for battered women as it does for other survivors of trauma and is frequently an addiction. The victim may be behaving in a sexual manner in an effort to keep the batterer or other men happy and therefore reduce her injuries. She may be sexualizing because she believes that if she is more sexual he might have more use for her and therefore be less likely to harm her. She may be sexualizing because that is how she sees love. If her first experience with sex was as a young child and it was not a violent rape but a seduction, that may be what she believes love to be and she may be seeking it from any source that will "have" or validate her. Or she may be using sex as a drug to sedate the onslaught of feelings that keep her overwhelmed and release those often sought after brain chemicals.

Societies response to this addiction is particularly cruel. Females are judged to be whores and sluts. While promiscuity is valued in young men, females can be terribly persecuted for the behavior.

"The language and communication of our society set women up to be victims," states Nancy Henley, in her book *Body Politics*, "There are 220 terms for promiscuous women as opposed to 22 for men; furthermore, the labels for men are stately whereas the labels for women are degrading."

Baggy clothes and weight gain are almost the opposite of sexualizing. We often see women who have sabotaged their appearance in an effort to be less attractive to men. This helps them feel safer when, in reality, they are not. Rape, sexual assault etc… are not about attraction but are about power, opportunity and greed. The woman who thinks she is making herself safer by sabotaging her appearance is terribly mistaken. Sabotaging our appearance is an indication of low self-esteem and human predators pick up on this. During my groups with adolescent offenders we have them list the things they look for when choosing a victim. They always list the same things and unkempt appearance, along with low self esteem, is always there.

Society's response to women who do not tend their appearance in the expected manner is to add to the devaluation and degradation. People, in general, have little **tolerance** for those they see as overweight and judge those who don't dress appropriately. One of the ways we fund our programs for human and animal trauma survivors is a large upscale home décor store. On a particularly challenging day I may run from shoveling horse stalls to the retail store without changing clothes. The response of some of my customers is insulting. Those that don't know me, or our programs, often turn their noses up and one actually looked around at the beautiful store, my boots and coveralls and said, "You don't deserve this."

Numbing Out

Victims often numb out until the danger has passed. They shut down their feelings to protect themselves so that they can do what they need to do. Combat veterans also mention this. It is a way to protect your mind and still do what needs to be done.

Running the rescue facility leaves frequent opportunity to be horrified by the cruelty of life and man's inhumanity toward anything he can catch. If I am caught off guard I could fall apart at the suffering that is often thrust upon us. If I can prepare myself I can numb myself out and operate like an efficient machine – until the crisis has passed. On completion of the task all of the feelings may rush me.

If I am then traumatized, this is called **vicarious trauma** and victims/survivors frequently suffer from it, along with law enforcement, counselors, combat veterans and anyone else subject to seeing the trauma of others. Numbing out serves an important purpose. Trying to function while overwhelmed with panic and trauma doesn't work. Putting aside feelings that could get in the way of our performance could mean the difference between life and death. We may not always be in control of numbing out, and we need to be. This control is a valuable tool for the survivors tool-box.

The Nature of Trauma and Remembering

Our response to trauma can provide a great deal of ammo for those around us when they don't understand, want to do us more harm, justify their own behavior or find an easy answer. We may **dissociate** during the traumatic experience. This happens when the victim pulls "herself" deep inside to protect her mind. Often, victims report projecting themselves, or their mind, outside of their body in an effort to keep it safe. You can not control the actions of another, but you can control your response to them. During a traumatic event victims often choose to protect their minds when they can't protect their bodies, with dissociation.

This can cause problems when, immediately after the trauma, the victim can't remember or describe details that law enforcement, or others, feel she should have seen or remembered. This is often used to discredit victims and their account of the event by perpetrators, defense attorneys and anyone else who might benefit.

The victim will usually have access to the memory at a later date, when it feels safer. The memory can be provoked by seemingly odd things like someone wearing the same shirt, a smell or a sound. This can be terribly confusing to people around the victim because they see no connection. This can contribute to the argument that the victim is **crazy** or unstable when, in fact, this is a pretty efficient way of postponing emotional reactions until the immediate threat or crisis has passed.

These sudden memories or feelings can leave the victim feeling like she is losing her mind. She needs to be told what is happening, be reassured that the event is not happening right then, that it is a memory and even taught that this can be an opportunity to roll with it and how to use it to her advantage. The victim may have fears of seemingly odd things. Given time, safety and information, the answer to why these things feel threatening will become clear.

Trauma is cumulative which means that it adds up. A woman will not respond to the second rape as she did the first. The effects sit on top of each other and build. This means that we can be more easily traumatized or that a new trauma will bring up memories of an old trauma (**retraumatized**). We also can become susceptible to vicarious trauma (when we feel the trauma that we see happening to another being).

Often women will not remember childhood sexual abuse until their late thirties. Whether this is a safer period in life or a prime time to deal with issues, this may be when old traumas surface. People often disbelieve the victim at this point (and, as we know, all other points) wondering why they didn't say something sooner. Often they didn't say something sooner because, whether it was **denial**, dissociation or something else, she didn't have access to the memory.

Our bodies seem to remember whether we do or not. I suffered a traumatic brain injury that left me in terrible shape. I couldn't even tie my shoes or read. One day I lay curled up in the bed crying. I couldn't face the world and felt as if it was all happening again. I didn't know the year much less the date.
I heard my husband's voice from the door, "I didn't know whether to tell you or not. Obviously I need to. Today is the first anniversary of the brain injury."
While I still felt the trauma I knew I wasn't crazy. That bit of information offered a soothing balm for a terribly raw experience. As hard as we might try to suppress and deny the realities of our life, they will always surface. I go into this in more detail in *The Toolbox*, because to keep ourselves safe we have to go in and heal

the hurts or we will remain vulnerable, perpetrators will pick up on this and we may be targeted again (this is called **revictimization**).

This list does not cover all of the responses we have to trauma. The Chapter entitled *The Toolbox* offers much more about the issues that trauma survivors deal with everyday. It also offers the tools that the victims/survivors I have worked with have found the most helpful for learning to handle the problems instead of being handled by them.

Working with other women and the research helped me to understand my own behavior but I needed to know how I had gotten to the point of begging at the feet of my tormentor. How did I end up getting into a relationship with a man that derived pleasure from humiliating, torturing and brutalizing women? Doing the research was the easy part. I could make that about other women, impersonal, not me. But it wasn't enough. I was going to have to examine my own life up to that point and I knew that was going to be difficult.

Socrates said something to the effect that the unexamined life is hardly worth living. While sorting and filing my childhood and adolescence would be a terrible strain, it would also be the most important and life changing thing I ever did.

I expected my family to be as thrilled as I was. I soon found that they were not going to be happy about my new venture. It turned out that they would have been happier with a daily colonoscopy; they offered no support. For me to change I would have to examine and confront the demons that bred in the small ecosystem that spawned me – my family.

They tried to prevent that in every way they could. They sabotaged all of my efforts to understand myself and my origins. When I refused to stop excavating old traumas they became as vicious as the perpetrators that caused the trauma. They discredited me with "crazy" and "liar". They shunned me, gossiped about me and used every tactic they could to stop my exploration just so they could maintain their denial and guard the family secrets. I needed someone I could trust to help me sort through the tragedy referred to as childhood and I found her at a local Salvation Army.

2

How Our Girls Become Battered Women

Paula and I would examine my childhood and adolescence with curiosity, commitment and a lot of pain. As we trudged through various events, the feelings they left and my reactions to those feelings, I continued my research. It was the intellectual yen to the emotional yang. The research and intellectualizing were the stabilizing roots that supported and sustained the sapling of a self I now studied.

I wanted to know how a seven or eight-year-old girl who had the audacity to argue with her drunken father over his racist comments could be reduced to a broken mass at the feet of a batterer. What happened to the little girl who, when told by her father that she was born only because of him, argued that she was meant to be?

"That can't be," I said, "I would have come to the world with or without you. I'm not here because you met mom. I was meant to be here, so you don't own me."

Later he would have (and did) knock us to the ground over a comment like that. I think the only reason he didn't at the time was amusement at the spunk the little girl sported. In hindsight, I'm pretty shocked. Where did she come from and where did she go? I remember my father skinning rabbits on the back porch as he tried to explain that the rabbit had no feelings, so it was okay. Even though I was so young that I thought it was Bugs Bunny, I still knew he had feelings and argued my case with the conviction I felt. What on earth could have happened to change such a strong little girl into a cowering woman, defined externally by any cold heart with an opinion and a fist to make it so?

Different cultures see females differently. While the cultures may be different and their opinions of females may be at different points on the spectrum, from birth, females from all cultures are treated differently than males and, in my opinion, this is generally a good thing because females are different than males. We are not the same. We are equal, but not the same.

In all cultures the differences in treatment begins immediately, at birth. Parents play and communicate differently with their daughters. The toys they are given are different. The way they dress them is different and the attitude around their birth can be starkly different. Regardless of what country they are born into, all of our lives females are generally taught to be mothers and wives. Years ago, Lenore Walker presented the theory of learned helplessness as an explanation of why battered women stay. While this theory was offensive to many there is some truth to it. As politically incorrect as it may be to say, we are taught to be helpless in most every area but the kitchen.

We give our daughters dolls to teach nurturing as opposed to tools so they can fix their own cars. Communication studies have found serious differences in the way we communicate with baby girls and boys. And while boys are rewarded for resourcefulness little girls are warned to be "careful", told how pretty they are and encouraged to "smile". Early on the focus for little girls is appearance, bows, ruffles, sugar and spice.

I was always an A student and yet my parents spent a great deal of money sending me to modeling and finishing schools. These schools were terribly damaging to me. I remember the day I stood next to my father, popping with pride as the school told him I had won a scholarship. The director just had to add that I won the scholarship because I needed the instruction the most. While I was labeled as "gifted", I was told I would never go to college, "That was for men" and, as my father explained, that money needed to be used on my brother.

All cultures treat male and female children differently but in some cultures it goes further than a difference in upbringing. Many families in other cultures are terribly upset at the birth of a daughter because they are seen as a burden whereas a son is seen as an asset. In these cultures the female infants may be abandoned or even killed, especially if there are laws in that country limiting the number of children the families can have. Daughters are seen as a liability that they will be responsible for and sons are seen as being able to work and care for their parents in their old age.

If they are allowed only one child by the government, they don't want to "waste" that on a female. Often these infant females, such as in China, meet a horrible end. In some areas of Africa, young girls are subjected to a ritual of mutilating their genitalia. Virginity is so valued that their vaginas may be sewn shut. On the wedding night the husband forces his way through the stitching.

The Nacirema People

There is another culture where the young girls are treated terribly. From birth these babies are painted up like sexy, grown women and then paraded around to be judged on how sexy they look. Often these girls are so young that they are not yet walking and have to be carried by their mothers. At these events, which are legal, you can regularly see infants, three-year-olds, ten-year-olds as well as teenage girls dressed up like hookers, strutting in front of a roaring crowd.

Children in this tribe see the women wait on and serve the men and frequently see their fathers and grandfathers beat the women in the home. For entertainment they watch hour upon hour of violent "skits". Often this violence is directed toward women. Even when the skits they watch are not physically violent, they watch aggressive males control females and the females in the skits respond positively to this strong, "take control" bad boy image.

It is sad, really, because at around 7 – 8 years girls in this culture are resisting the notion that they are for the sexual gratification of men. At this age, despite almost a decade of brainwashing, most of them are tough, resilient and confident. They are ready to change the world and are what we, in this country, would typically think of as tomboys. They still value their intelligence, making good grades in school and they are not focused on their bodies.

At this age, girls in this tribe are more interested in what's fair and the concept of justice than they are in make-up or their appearance. The most uttered term by this age group of girls from the Nacirema Tribe is, "That's not fair" and they see plenty to protest.

At this age these young girls are being taught that they are responsible for the happiness of everyone around them and they are encouraged to be peacemakers at all costs. They are taught that they should not be rude and that they should even be polite to strangers that may be causing every safety alarm they have to go off. Even if their gut is telling them something is wrong they are encouraged to ignore that and be polite.

They are not encouraged to have boundaries. They are taught not to challenge authority even if that authority is their uncle or father wanting sex. Challenging authority is seriously frowned upon. They are told not to be disagreeable or difficult. They are taught that disagreeable is not pretty. Even though they are resisting many of these messages, they are still hearing them.

The religion of this culture preaches that they should be dominated by men and that they should have a man in the family at all costs. The religion tells men that they should completely control all of the members of their family and if the male doesn't stay in the family the religion may "disown" them. Their religions often frown upon women as heads of household, sex, birth control and women working outside the home. Women are expected to "make it work" no matter how brutal the man may be.

In many of the families of this tribe the father leaves them anyway. The children are often raised by only their mother who may allow a series of different men to come in and out of the family as she searches for a male to help her financially and to provide safety from other men. She feels she needs this and often rightfully so. This lack of a male figure leaves the young girls searching for a male role model and they are subject to being preyed upon by men who see this absence of a male in the home as an opportunity.

These "tween" girls live in homes and communities where male dominance is seen as a strength and an asset to the family. If a man is soft and gentle, and many of them are, he may be seen as a less desirable mate and is often made fun of by other men who see him as girlish and feminine.

And if the father stays he may be quite brutal. These girls watch as their fathers brutally beat their mothers and grandmothers and then they see the women accept this and stay. They are old enough to make enough sense of the perplexing contradictions in their tribe to know that making waves could cause them even further injury.

As powerful and autonomous as these girls feel at this age they are still being discouraged and degraded. Some of these girls have a lifeline. There are people in this culture who know that what goes on is wrong and they try to help as many of the young girls as they can. If the girls have support they may hold on to who they are for a short time and keep plugging along, but all too often the support is too little or nonexistent.

It is not unusual for family members to use these girls for sexual gratification. These girls are raped, sometimes violently, sometimes gently, from a young age and these girls often begin confusing sex with love. They may come to believe that their only value is in their sexuality and that no one would love them unless they have sex with them.

While verbally the Nacirema culture says that this is wrong, the culture behaves in ways that conflict with this statement and the young girls become very confused. The sexual assaults may feel good and their young bodies respond to the stimulation. This causes terrible guilt and shame for the young child. The culture says this is wrong but the girl is being given attention, and love and sex may become terribly intertwined in her mind.

By the time these girls reach the age of about 13 it has all started adding up and they struggle to resist the pressure that this tribe is putting on them. They are prepared at an early age to be sex partners. After, and sometimes even during, puberty their chests are stuffed full of toxic material so that their breasts are grossly exaggerated. This is done to please the men of the culture and to make her more appealing to a larger number of men. This substance is considered a "biohazard" in the United States.

The Nacirema girls often begin dressing and behaving in blatantly sexual ways and other people call them sluts and whores even though they may have been dressed that way and paraded around prior to puberty. These girls often continue trying to get attention by sexualizing and the community judges them harshly even though that may have been how they were brought up to acquire attention and love.

And while the men of the culture judge them and call them sluts they are happy to force upon these young girls sexual attention.

Many of them do try to seduce men. If the men that assaulted or raped them early on were particularly brutal the young girls may believe that if men like them, they will have more value and therefore the men may not harm them as badly. Or, as I mentioned, if the assaults were not brutal the girls may confuse love and sex. This causes them to seek out sex as opposed to love.

After the society has prepared them both mentally, emotionally and physically to sexually gratify males, the females are often raped and assaulted by men and then blamed for the men's behavior. They are told that they were too sexy and that it is their fault. And sexual assault for them is not unusual. It is estimated that 3 out of 4 of them are sexually assaulted prior to reaching the age of consent, 18.

As teenagers they often enter into relationships with young men who beat them and see them as property. As terrible as it sounds, it is important that they are seen as property because they will be safer. Women and children in this society that do not belong to other men, are seen as fair game and are targeted by men who would do them even greater harm. When they are beaten by their boyfriends or husbands they are blamed for that too. Their communities believe that they must have done something to deserve it or provoke it.

Education for them is often not valued and when they do reach the workforce they are not paid as much as the men. Some of these young girls are so injured by what this society does that they actually stop eating and die because they are afraid of food and getting fat. Often these young girls will eat, against their better judgment, and then feel compelled to vomit the nourishment up so that they don't get fat. The contradicting pressures on the young girls can be so great that many of them will take sharp objects and cut on themselves.

These people force their young girls to view pictures of extremely exotic, perfect women for as many as 12 – 14 hours a day. The girls don't know it but the pictures that they see all day long are pictures of composite women. A composite picture is one that uses one woman's head, pasted onto another woman's torso and still a different woman's legs. The girls aren't told that these are composite pictures. They are told that women look like that, and they should too, and encouraged to imitate the pictures.

They are in a catch 22. They are told their value is in their appearance, but the role models they are given are unattainable. They are told that their value is in their sexual attractiveness but if they want to have sex they are bad. They are shown that sex will get them attention and then they are treated as dirty for engaging in sex. The girls see that women are minimized and discredited if they have large breasts and made fun of if they don't. Their bodies are often grabbed, touched without permission and treated like public property in their places of education and subjected to lewd remarks from their peers as well as their elders.

Because of these contradictions and the catch 22 that these girls find themselves in, they learn to play coy. They may say "no" to sex when they actually mean "yes". They see this in the skits they watch day in and day out and they know that to admit they want sex may set them up to be judged by their community. The message is that bad girls want sex and good girls don't. So instead, they pretend that they don't want it. This is very confusing for the young men in the community because some people are trying to teach the young males not to exploit the young women and the mixed messages are terribly confusing for all.

For entertainment it is customary and accepted to publicly ridicule these girls by making fun of the color of their hair. The lighter the hair color, the less intelligent they are seen to be. They are ridiculed at social affairs and never grow up without hearing jokes about how bad they stink and how their vaginas are filthy. They are encouraged to disinfect themselves after having their hand near their vaginas. If their breasts are not yet stuffed with toxic material and they are small, they are made fun of. If their breasts are large or the toxic material has already been inserted they are dismissed as sex toys and not taken seriously in other pursuits.

While the young women are able to resist the social pressures in their preteens, by the time they are into adolescence they become less and less likely to resist the thinking they are force fed. Eventually most will internalize the degradation and devaluation. By their teenage years these girls believe that they are seriously flawed and that their only value is in appearance and their ability to sexually stimulate the men in their community.

By high school the girls of this culture pretend they are stupid and their math, science and I.Q. actually begin to drop. The resiliency and optimism they had in their preteens disappears and they become more quiet and sullen. As children they were constantly told they were pretty but as teenage girls they are told that they are never good enough. The message changes after puberty as they try to look like that composite woman and please everyone around them.

They begin smearing chemicals all over their face in an old fashioned ritual that they have been told will make them more desirable to the opposite sex. The young women are pressured into ripping holes in their bodies sometimes in their nipples, vulva and labia. They are taught to flood their vaginas with chemicals on a regular basis so that the "odors" don't bother other people.

When young women in this culture are assaulted either physically or sexually they don't often tell anyone because they have all known at least one other young woman who told the secrets. They saw what the tribe did to the other girls for talking and they've decided that it's not worth telling. They know that if they tell, the family member that raped them is allowed to stay in the home and they are taken someplace far away from their homes, friends and family. They know that if they tell, other men in the community will shun them, call them liars and see them as "fair game".

Many of the women also join in this practice. The girls in this culture know that if they tell family secrets all of their aunts, grandmothers and siblings may turn on them. To these young girls it is just easier to tolerate the violations and rapes than it is to be rejected and mistreated by their families and the community. Often, when one family member starts having sex with the young girl the other male family members have unspoken permission.

As women they are sometimes ejaculated on in the crowded marketplaces or while they are en-route. They are frequently grabbed and touched in the work place and they may have no recourse because they need to feed their children.

They may have surgery after surgery to make themselves more appealing to men and the toxic substances stuffed in their chests more often than not cause them terrible problems. As they get older many of them suffer terribly from crippling diseases because their bodies try to attack the material. They almost always have to have multiple surgeries to maintain this toxic substance and often feel like it would just be easier if they had a zipper under their breasts that gave the medicine men access to their chest cavities. Sometimes the women die from the toxic substance but the society feels it is more important that she be a sex toy rather than healthy.

This is how the women of the Nacirema Tribe are raised and taught, and when they find themselves being beaten and raped they are blamed and then ask how they could let it happen.

The American People

While we can grasp our chests and shed tears for the young women in China and Africa it is important that we look at our own hypocrisy. As those of you who were in Mr. Priller's eighth grade Social Studies class already know, the above described country is the United States and these people are American spelled backward. The previous description is done with accurate words as opposed to the gentle terms that we use to persuade ourselves that these things are okay.

When we call these things breast "enhancement," "beauty pageants" and "molestation" it becomes easier to tolerate because the words are softer. When we call it what it is, making babies look like hookers, stuffing teenagers with toxic substances and assault, these things become less tolerable and makes us more uncomfortable talking about it.

Like most children, little girls spend a great deal of time in front of the television, see the billboards on the interstates and notice the magazines that are a staple at check-out counters. Whether directly or indirectly little girls are told that their looks are more important than their brains and they believe that intelligence in women is unattractive and undesirable.

They eventually begin trying to hide their intelligence. Mary Pipher, in her book *Reviving Ophelia*, talks about how females begin disguising their intelligence by high school. She notes that at that point the Math, Science and I.Q. scores for girls begin to drop.

Regardless of our parenting, our young girls are still exposed to media images that are unrealistic and show female value in beauty. Our young girls are bombarded with the images of composite women. I am always shocked at how few people are aware of the fact that the images they see are airbrushed. They are not aware of the fact that the model on the cover may be one woman's face with another woman's abs and yet another's legs.

Young girls hear people laugh at jokes about their vaginas and girls actually believe they smell like tuna. Blond jokes are not considered terribly inappropriate and the "itty bitty titty committee" is familiar to all small-chested females.

The Justice Department asserts that 3 out of 4 of our young girls are sexually assaulted prior to age 18 and this figure does not include those girls that have witnessed domestic violence, been physically assaulted or experienced other non-sexual abuse. After having contact with thousands of victims and working with hundreds, I contend that all of our females are sexually assaulted prior to age 18.

Females are often raped and then blamed for the perpetrators violent, greedy behavior. As little girls we are encouraged to be cute and smile, as women we are encouraged to be sexy yet when we become the victim of a sexual assault the question becomes, "How sexy were you?"

As women we are ejaculated on in buses and subways and degraded as a matter of entertainment through "jokes" and images. Our young girls see women stuffed full of silicone to better please and attract males. This devaluation and degradation of young women takes a heavy toll. Young females manifest our societal dysfunction and abuse through lowered expectations, eating disorders, self-mutilation, addictions, sexualizing and worse. We subject our young girls to all of this and then shake our heads and wonder how they could end up in a violent relationship.

The Appropriate Victim

Another way that girls become battered women is through the notion of an appropriate victim. Once a female has been "sullied" males can more easily justify using her for their own gratification. I include more on this in this chapter under the section called revictimization. Not only are previously traumatized females a more appropriate victim, but single women are seen as easier and more appropriate targets.

Women who are in a relationship are generally safer. There are real safety issues involved for females who are not part of a couple. Having worked with many batterers and sex offenders, I know that perpetrators are more likely to see women in a relationship as someone else's property and more likely to regard her as off limits.

Children from a single parent home are more likely to be targets. Offenders may fear retribution from the male or just have more respect for a woman or child who is the property of another man. Also, the members of a fatherless family may be more vulnerable because they are seeking that relationship. And while perpetrators know this and try to appeal to that need in their victims, consciously or not, women know this too and may make poor choices in an effort to add this male figure to theirs or their children's lives.

Savvy Perpetrators

By the time our young girls reach adulthood and the age of consent they have been well prepared to not only be battered women but victims in general. And when they do meet a man that will use violence to achieve his goals, it's not like he's wearing a sign proclaiming his intention. We wonder how a woman gets herself in this situation. We blame victims of violent crimes in so many different ways and in domestic violence situations we start out by wondering how she got involved in the first place. Victims of rape and domestic violence are blamed when we question their choices and accuse them of provocation. Even in my homicide ameliorations the victims were blamed in one way or another for their death.

Like child molesters and "strangers" you can not walk down the street and pick out the batterers. He has no sign posted on his forehead warning women. Often men will give verbal and nonverbal clues early on in the relationship, but we have historically been taught to dismiss our gut instincts and what we know. For example, jealousy and possessiveness are red flags yet may be seen as protection, caring and love. Because of our failure to teach young women, and the dysfunction they grew up in, they may not even recognize the red flags as warning signs.

Young kids and small animals know an ugly person when they see them and yet, out of politeness, parents still force little kids to let strangers hold them, Grandma kiss them and to sit on uncle Herbie's lap. Whether the child's instincts are right or wrong at that time, about that person, when we force them to violate their instincts and to be polite or to submit to authority, we are setting them up to do it later in life. And then it could be fatal. By forcing them to always submit to authority they are not learning to challenge it when they need to. We want our children to fight against authority figures when an authority figure tries to drag them into a car.

When we, as a society, accept woman-bashing jokes and sexualizing women, why would a young woman see these behaviors as a red flag? And if the young woman grew up in a violent home, a man's controlling actions could be an indication to her that this is a normal man.

Victims may feel stupid or ashamed that the perpetrator was able to harm them. The fact is that when a person becomes the victim of a violent crime they are blindsided. The perpetrator knew his intentions all along, but the victim doesn't find out until the first blow or weapon appears.

One time my daughter, who had just gotten her learner's permit, said, "I don't need to put my seatbelt on. If I see I'm going to be in an accident I'll put it on real fast."

I looked at her in disbelief and then reminded myself that this was why she was still considered a child.

"Why do you think it is called an accident? If you had time to get your seatbelt on then you would have time to prevent it," I said.

It is the same with being victimized. If the victim saw it coming it wasn't consciously. While victims feel embarrassed, ashamed or stupid that they "let it happen" the perpetrator had time to plot and plan. Having been taught to be a pretty, polite, peacemaker, she is at a serious disadvantage when being picked and groomed for a violent crime.

At the age of 14, I had been an "habitual runaway" for two years. I lived on the streets when home seemed too dangerous, and back home when the streets were overly hungry for a tiny, 14-year-old girl. When the streets seemed as if they would consume me I would return to my parents knowing that "eaten alive" was just as possible there. I was at high risk of being wasted in either place and constantly had to decide which was safer.

From a young age fending off sexual assaults from the friends of my parents and male relatives was a part of life to be maneuvered, like the streets I often lived on. Home was a place where the physical assaults from a violent cop and the vicious, unpredictable attacks of a mother were as normal as family dinner. And because we were required to engage in family dinners, the assaults and the meals often occurred together.

Both parents struggled with issues that usually kept them occupied in one way or another. The fact that I was my mother's favorite target made life all the more difficult. If I would have only had to worry about being a "handy" target it would have been easier. I could have stayed out of her way. But that wasn't it. I was the target. Sleeping in abandoned cars, in the dead of an Indiana winter, was often a reprieve from the constant threat posed by family and their friends. As a 14-year-old virgin I had a 25-year-old engineer in my sights, as a way out. Virginia, the woman who gave birth to me, said I was never a virgin but I wanted to believe she was just being mean. Deep down I always wondered if she knew something I didn't.

Denial is a fascinating and frustrating human coping tool, but it is extremely dangerous. Animals don't practice denial. If they ever did, natural selection ended the practice real quick. You do not see prey animals that will remain in the presence of a predator refusing to believe they are in danger. A zebra will not deny that they watched their mother brought down by a lion and therefore believe lions are safe, just because that memory is uncomfortable. But humans will deny the obvious regardless of the potential for harm, repeating the same dangerous behavior over and over.

By this time my spirit and desire to survive had become enough of a bother to my family that they were beginning to just let me be most of the time. They had gone on a family vacation and I had persuaded them to leave me with a friend's family, but we didn't tell my friend's parents about the arrangement. This left me free to party and hang with the man I was determined would be my husband, my escape hatch from the violence.

The apartment Stan lived in was a flop house for college students and the party never ended. At 14, I was surrounded by men from all over the world who were enjoying their 20's. When Stan left the apartment, so did I. I didn't fit and had no idea how to interact with his roommates.

This particular evening he had to go back to his hometown for the night. I was supposed to be staying with my friend, my parents were out of town and my dad's brother, who I had been around all of my life, was staying at the house. I left Stan's apartment in the middle of the night to walk through the dark back alleys of the neighborhoods and shopping centers.

I had a rich history with these areas and learned them at an early age. I would never forget which areas where I had been assaulted, which spots the local pervs proudly displayed their organs to little girls and the one spot where I had been robbed at age 7. As I walked quickly through the streets, the fear of the loose dogs left me in a sweat. At that time of night people left their dogs loose and they took offense at passing teenagers. I knew from past experience which dogs meant it and which were all show. I knew from past experience there were men in the bushes, hiding behind the dumpsters and standing behind the screen doors of their castles.

I am surprised at how many people say they have never experienced fear that made them literally shake. They act as if that's just a figure of speech or movie dramatization. I assure them, peoples' knees will actually knock together and their jaws will chatter from fear of the agitated collie laying in wait or the teenage thug that wants whatever you may have squirreled away for a pack of smokes. I came to learn that often the actual assault, or proud performance by a man masturbating in the window of his home, wasn't as bad, at least for me, as the fear of waiting for it.

My arrival in the middle of the night would have raised some questions at my friend Joan's house so I went a little further down the block to my parent's house. Walking in that door felt like a relief and an accomplishment. But it was at this point in my life that details and descriptors would begin going beyond the common use words of a 14-year-old. On that night it felt safe because there was no father there to assault me or a mother to belittle me. But I was wrong.

Walking through that door, on that night, would forever change my life and I would need to develop a whole new vocabulary to express my world. I did not know that this would be my first lesson in victimology, the unofficial beginning of my career. I did not know that this would be my first lesson in sex offenders and the female response to sexual assault through the power imbalance of age, sex and blood relation. I did not know this would be the night when the term "blood relation" would take on dual meaning. I soon saw what coercion, manipulation and threats looked like. It would take another two decades for me to analyze and understand the grooming that had led up to that ambush on that hot August night.

That night, my father's brother, the uncle we all looked up to as cool, straddled my chest, with his full adult weight, and ejaculated on my face and neck. This is an abbreviated description of the hours he spent using a trusting little girl to satisfy his sexual greed. As brief as the description is, it conveys more than I understood at the time. While I had a much older boyfriend we had never done things like this. Our interactions had not yet gone beyond "second" base and I was confused to be overpowered and shown what a penis actually did.

As silly as it sounds, I was so worried that the neighbors could see through the window. I was so embarrassed and, for years, I was certain that the whole world knew what I had caused by going home. When my uncle pulled his weight from me I locked myself in the only room that had a lock. Ironically it was my parent's. I cried all night as he pounded on the door pleading with me to come out and offering to make me a steak dinner. At daylight I ran to my friends to wash…and wash, and wash.

As I fled, my uncle yelled behind me the same words as the night before, "If you tell anyone your dad will kill me. He'll go to prison for life and it will always be your fault."

But what he didn't know was that it was already my fault. In my mind, I had brought this on myself.

I later found out that the reason my uncle didn't use one of the standard threats for child molesters, "No one will believe you," was because he knew they would. Turned out the whole family knew that he sought refuge in my father's home because he was being pursued by German authorities for child molesting. Apparently the only people who didn't know were his potential victims, the kids.

For months I didn't tell. His girlfriend and her small son had arrived from Germany to join Steve, and she and I were forced to share a bed. She began touching me and, although my uncle never touched me again, he was around every corner laughing at me, making faces and taunting me. And one day I told. I was wrong when I thought my life was changed the night he assaulted me. He was right when he said, "It will always be your fault."
In hindsight my uncle offered me sound advice and if I could do it again I wouldn't tell a single blood relative because even decades later, they have not finished extracting the blood they seek from that confused little girl.

To avoid staying in battering relationships and for the sake of my daughters I knew, as I examined my life, that I had to come to terms with what the adults in my life had done during my childhood. I had to accept that even though I had made some bad choices that night, I was not responsible for what my uncle did to me. I was responsible for doing what teenagers often do best, making bad choices. It is the parent's job, as best they can, to provide a safety net so that the choices don't terribly change, or even end, the kid's life. And for parents knowingly to harbor a relative that is being sought for child molesting should be, if it is not, criminal.

I don't remember seeing my mother for a long time after I told her. The last time I saw her she was screaming and swinging at me and my father was trying to push her to the end of the hall and into her bedroom. She later told me that she was given "a lot of Thorazine and flown to a hospital in New York". At the time I only knew that my grandmother, my uncle's mother, was the only adult around for a long time and her feelings toward me had obviously changed.

The warm, nurturing grandmother, the one who had tried to protect me from my father and mother, now treated me like a stranger. She wasn't mean to me like my aunts would be. She just turned cold. At that young age I had a strong feeling that the reaction of family wasn't just to protect their brother and son. I was often treated as if I had violated my uncle, as if I had somehow seduced him. I felt to my bones that I had violated some unspoken law, but I had no idea what it was. It was as if I had unknowingly uttered words that were foul. It was as if I had betrayed some type of secret. I later heard another author call her family "batterers, drunks and secret keepers". That's when I understood what I had done. I had dared to speak the truth. I had dared to tell the secrets.

My aunts became vicious defenders of their brother. They repeated the stories he told about how I had seduced him that night. They sheltered him in their homes with their children, telling me I should stay away. No longer was I invited when my aunts and more than 20 cousins went to the lake or to our large family reunions. These were not distant relatives and they had been an important part of my life, until then.

As a kid that just found out what a penis did, I had no way of knowing that it was only going to get worse over the years. I thought what they were doing to me at 15 was hell. I had underestimated the power of denial and meanness of humans. In what was left of my 15- year-old innocence I didn't realize how adult women could harbor a hostility toward other young women, even young ones that need them.

These were the adult women that I had been close to all of my short life, the women who had changed my diapers, comforted and even defined me. I later realized that I was not the only young woman that these older, more experienced women unleashed their ability and experience on. One aunt, like a female dog that steals puppies from another mother, attempted or succeeded at taking the children from at least five of my female cousins. She used the courts to devastate them with the loss of their children or they had to suffer the financial loss of fending off the attack .

It didn't matter whether it was second cousins, uncles, great uncles, family friends or drunk cops: protecting their daughter from men, or other adults, was not on my parents' agenda. Sadly, some 30 years later they still don't believe me. A counselor set up a session for me to tell my mother about my experiences. It was Virginia's counselor and I knew the outcome would probably not be what I needed.

While my expectations were low, I had expected more. After pouring my heart and mind out about the traumas men had caused me as a child, Virginia looked at the counselor and calmly said, "She's a liar."
The counselor and I looked at each other, one assessing the other, and accepted that there really could have been no other response.

Like many families, keeping the secrets was the most important thing in our family. But it wasn't just my birth family. On both sides of the family tree I could count the generations of secrets. It isn't shocking that I ended up with a series of batterers. What would have been shocking is if I hadn't.

At 16 years, 2 weeks and 1 day old, I married Stan. The father of a friend of mine met with a judge and told him I was pregnant. He was an attorney who had tried to speak to my parents on numerous occasions about how they were hurting me. You can imagine how that was received. But what that man did might have saved my life.

Getting married at that age may have been the difference between my sister and me that kept me alive. Stan did relatively little damage to me and I graduated high school in the top 10%. I left him on my 18th birthday. To this day Virginia says that allowing me to marry him is the only regret she has about raising me. Interesting and quite telling, the one thing that may have kept me from sharing my little sister's fate at six feet under is my mother's one regret.

Some people will argue that my experiences were extreme or different and that their childhood had nothing to do with their victimization. And in a lot of cases that could be true. I know that there are people who would have found my childhood a nurturing environment. But trauma is relative and we are all survivors of something. If you, or a loved one, find yourself being hurt over and over, then examining your "family traditions" would be wise. And if you are so certain it isn't the problem then why not examine it? No harm done.

Violence, Abuse & Other Dysfunctions As Generational

I know, from working with adolescent sex offenders, that my uncle was a victim of something, probably sex abuse. I am not excusing what he did to me, other cousins and other children around the globe, I simply know where that propensity came from. The bible says the sins of the father are visited on seven generations (or something like that) and this certainly includes domestic violence. I am the first born of the first born of the first born of the first born of the eldest of the firstborn and I come from a long line of battering fathers and battered mothers.

I remember seeing my mother with a busted lip and feeling fury when hearing the tales of the beatings that my beloved grandmother endured. I remember, as a teenager, asking my father, what he would do, as a cop, if he saw a man beating his wife. With arrogance, indignation and certainty he replied, "Well that's his wife. I wouldn't interfere."
Up until my sister's death, upon hearing she had been beaten by her husband, our father would immediately ask, "What did she do?" Who cares what she did! It didn't warrant a beating.

Our mother sent the same messages. The father of my children was also a batterer and everyone knew it because he would knock knots on my head the size of baseballs. He was out of town five days a week so I only had to tolerate it two, at least that's how my mother saw it. It was as if she was disgusted with my weakness and I quickly learned to "endure" as the women before me had done.

The father of my children started beating me within days of saying, "I do". I stayed for five years until one night when I almost killed him. Sara, my first born, and I had returned from a local festival to find him home. When I got through the door, with the stroller, diaper bag and other baby paraphernalia, I realized I was in trouble. He accused me of cheating and anything else he could think of, which was nothing new. I was determined that on that night I was not going to be beaten. I don't know why this night was different, but it was.

I took my baby into the bedroom, locked and barricaded the door, put the baby behind me and laid the rifle on the bed in front of me. This night I was not afraid like I had been at other times. I knew my baby and I would be safe. Fueled by fury and whisky he had no problem breaking through the door and pushing aside the furniture I had against it. As he came through the door I fired the first shot just inches from his head. He continued toward me and I fired the next shot into the wall only inches from his crotch. He stopped, turned and closed the door behind him. That was when I knew I couldn't honor my mother's request to stay in a violent relationship. I also concluded that, based on his reaction, he did think with his crotch.

And that is how it goes. Boys who grow up witnessing woman beating are more likely to be woman beaters. They are more likely to be disrespectful and violent toward women. Girls who witness this are more vulnerable to victimization and more likely to accept a partner's control and violence.

Revictimization

Often women find themselves being traumatized multiple times. This is called revictimization and is another way that young women find themselves in violent relationships. **Revictimization** throws fuel on the argument that the victim must be the problem, that it is the victim's fault. After all, if she is the one common element in the traumas and the offenders are different, it must be that she is responsible.

If it keeps happening to her then she, and every one around her, assume it is something about her. But this is not the case. This is called revictimization and has a number of causes. And only one cure: self-examination. She has to ask herself what type of choices she is making that put her at risk? How does her family history make her vulnerable? What are perpetrators picking up on that make her an easier target?

The answers to these questions, along with the necessary changes in her choices, will lead to lessening her chances of being picked. That an opportunistic predator chooses to take advantage of our perceived "weaknesses" is never our fault. These weaknesses may be as well intended as kindness but are still seen as a weakness by perpetrators. And again, while the choice of a perpetrator or predator is never our fault, we have to look at the behaviors we exhibit that make us look like easy targets.

After spending the first couple of decades of my life being a victim, then studying victims, working with victims and then teaching about victims I started working with adolescent offenders. I was initially unwilling. My training as a victim advocate had left me with the "old school" mentality that the only true victims are those who have never committed crimes against other people. This is not true.

In fact, I had been one of the women that had stormed the legislature (figuratively, of course) and demanded that offender programs be denied funding. We did this with the justification that victims should not compete with offenders for funding (and, in our minds, there could be no overlap between victim and offender). While we were wrong about our definitions of victim and offender and who should receive services, I would later hook up with an offender organization that would prove every point we had argued. But more on that tough lesson under *Service Providers*.

While not all victims become offenders, all offenders were victims. As I said, if you're alive, you've survived. We have all survived something. Working with adolescent offenders illuminated a piece of the puzzle that should be mandatory for anyone providing services to victims. There is a lot to be learned from viewing the whole picture of victim and offender relations and realities. The boys quickly and definitively taught me how they pick their victims and why some females are victimized over and over again. Among other things, the boys, in their own way, told me how much easier it was to rationalize violating someone who had already been harmed.

But how did they know? How were they picking their victims? In my years with them I heard about how they knew the fatherless child would respond to their fatherly behavior. I heard about the girl's low self-esteem and how they tried to hide their bodies under baggy clothes and unkempt hair, the girls that dressed sexy and the girls that "wanted it". The boys identified girls who were weak in their identity and those who were "nice".

Their contribution was from their perspective, the perspective of an offender, and it was important. But, I knew there was still something missing that would help me understand this fascinating area of victimology, revictimization. I would not be able to pull it all together until another major area of abuse, violence and exploitation opened up, engulfed me and refused to spit me back out until I soaked and synthesized as much information on the subject as I could tolerate. And I would find this area of trauma hard to tolerate and potentially career ending.

As a young girl I had been emotionally overpowered by the contempt that my mother couldn't seem to hide from me, and I started praying for God to show me what was wrong with me. I may have been the first six-year-old to work the 12 steps and not even know what it was. Not only did I ask God to show me my flaws but I quickly learned that I needed to be shown a purpose.
"What am I supposed to do with this information?" was a standard, sarcastic response to the pain and suffering I saw in the world. While the question may have started out as sarcasm, I think God took me seriously and set about answering it.

As a child I began praying some version of, "Please show me what you want me to do. Please put in front of me those things I should focus on and keep distractions at bay."

At this point, the world always felt so big that I felt overwhelmed at the notion of going in search of the answers. I needed to trip over them. It took a long time for me to realize that the obstacle course of a life that I maneuvered in frustration, day-after-day was actually cluttered with answers. I just needed to match them up with the questions.

For many years, it was human suffering that I found in my path. It started out as my own and turned into bi-lateral amputees that couldn't flee. Then it was the victimization that my offenders covered by victimizing. Now I was finding traumatized, tortured and beaten animals strewn about my life.

This part of the lesson was more heartbreaking and mind-bending for me than the others, but I quickly realized that traumatized animals were a missing piece of the puzzle. They were a missing piece because they would show me the cues and behaviors that the predator humans were picking up on to single out a victim. They would demonstrate the behaviors, exhibited by victims, that my boys had explained to me.

My prayers quickly changed to objections and pleas, "God, please. I have no experience with animals. Maybe you have me confused with someone else. I have no defense against this. I can't take this. I can't deal with their suffering."
More often than not I just ended my prayer with a disgusted, "Are you flippin' sure?"
And while I never heard a booming voice say, "Jasper, I'm flippin' sure," a parade of suffering animals continued.

I managed a U.S. Humane Society Shelter during a year of college and I often pray for forgiveness for that. They were killing animals in a terribly inhumane way. I participated once before I authored a twenty page paper on why our actions were in violation of U.S. Humane Society policy and set out to change the horrid policy of my shelter. I was unsuccessful and resigned out of fear for my soul, but I was left with the feeling that I should have fought to the death to end that practice.

It was no time before I saw a pattern and started making connections. The animals acted like people. The offenders resembled predators and my victims behaved like prey animals.

And while society has made the connection between human offenders and predators we hadn't taken it to the next step and applied the behaviors of prey animals to victims. I wondered if that was an oversight, just too politically offensive or because we are so different that people thought there was just no comparison to be made.

Some 15 years after leaving Aaron I am running a seven acre horticultural park that houses some 90 rescue animals while carrying a caseload of human survivors that ranges from five to one hundred. To support the effort we also run a large home and garden import store that uses 100% of the net profits to pay for our trauma survivor programs.

This provides me the observation opportunities of animal behavior I need to make the comparisons and to learn exactly what it is that the women I work with are doing, that let the offenders I work with know they are vulnerable. I had started seeing a resemblance in the behavior of the humans and animals, but this immersion was the best way for me to understand how my boys were picking their victims and just what females were doing that caused them to stand out from the "herd".

The first horse that came to us had, according to the trainer, open bloody whip marks on his back. His back is more than six feet off the ground so I couldn't see and was smart enough not to climb up over him. He is a big boy, about 2,500 pounds, named Benjamin Thomas Horse. He caused quite an uproar in the community. Anyone who had an opinion felt free to voice it when it came to the disposition of Benny.

"That horse is dangerous. He has to be destroyed. You can't help him. He's going to kill someone…"

Now for any other novice that advice would be well-heeded. A traumatized animal that big IS quite dangerous. Any animal that big is dangerous, period, and the old farmers knew that adding trauma to that size was a recipe for disaster. As I watched Benny, my heart ached. He was so deeply hurt that destroying him was not an option for me. Not only were his feelings real, but it was apparent he meant no harm. He just wanted to live and to minimize his injuries at the hands of predators (which, in his experience, were human).

The eyes of a prey animal are set on the side of their head so that they can see all around them, better to see predators. They are highly tuned in to their environment and can watch everything around them even when they appear to be paying no attention, like grazing. The slightest rustle or movement can cause them to react much like someone who has an overactive startle reflex. There are humans that startle (or spook) real easy and that is how a healthy prey animal naturally behaves.

They will kick, just in case. They will run and rear and they believe their life depends on it and in the wild, it does. As with humans, these reactions are heightened after abuse. The fact that Benny had been traumatized to his bones, was pitifully afraid of humans, and was so large, made him incredibly dangerous. "Experts" claim that there are two responses to a threat: fight or flight. There are three. It is fight, flight or freeze. Benny would startle if you wore a different shirt and bolt over seeming hallucinations.

Benny's fear made us all the more determined. We took our time and applied the recovery tools that worked with humans to Benny. We worked hard to help this gorgeous, yet pitifully hurt animal recover so that he might live. As challenging as it was, we had a rider on Benny within two years. Other prey animals are goats, rabbits, mice and birds.

Crosby Joe Jameson, on the other hand, came here because he didn't meet American Kennel Club (AKC) standards and we believed that his appearance was so far off the mark for a German Shepherd that the breeder might destroy him. I am using Crosby as the predator example because he is the most primitive dog that we have.

Like people, there are highly evolved dogs and then there are dogs that, if they had knuckles, would still be dragging them. For example, Scruffalopicus Jane would never kill anything and repeatedly tried to nurse my infant granddaughter. She came off of an eight lane interstate and is extremely sensitive. Crosby on the other hand, is not highly evolved and is never unsupervised around any living thing he can fit in his mouth. He has retained the primitive thinking of canines.

The brain is divided into different parts and animals have the same parts we do. Like humans, animals vary on how much they are using the different parts. Scruffalopicus is using her frontal lobes (higher thinking) much more than Crosby. He is still dominated by his more primitive, but necessary, mammalian brain.

The dog's (and any other predator's) eyes are set in the front of their head so that they can focus on prey because, unfortunately, they eat prey animals. Crosby adored me from the beginning and would shower me with the most horrifying gifts. One day, as I dressed for a presentation, he walked into the bathroom and dropped a rabbit head at my feet. He was bewildered as I screamed and abandoned me and the rabbit head which, by the way, was looking right at me.

Crosby, like the cats, would crouch, stalk and hunt anything he thought he could take, and often attempted things he couldn't. This is what predators do. The majority of people are more familiar with predators because more of us live with cats and dogs than horses and goats. I am certain that if more of us lived with prey animals we would have more insight into our own behaviors that can make us targets.

Human behavior is very similar to that of animals. Many victims, survivors and veterans have been diagnosed with Post Traumatic Stress Disorder (PTSD). People who suffer from PTSD often have an overactive startle reflex. They may be hypervigilant, which means always watching (hyper – over and vigilant – watchful). They may have nightmares and night sweats among other symptoms. PTSD is a response to trauma and we see it not only in humans but animals. PTSD occurs as normal behavior in a prey animal. The prey animal who hasn't learned these behaviors is called dinner. But when the animal has been traumatized these behaviors are more recognized.

Dog lovers often watch amused as their dogs bark, cry and run in their sleep. We have dogs that are obviously having nightmares and their experiences are the source. We have all seen dogs that are "hand shy" or urinate on themselves when spoken to harshly.

Maggie May Mulvaney is a bloodhound that was rescued from a puppy mill. She is crippled from being hit by a car and the mill owners did not seek treatment for her. When you are a bitch in a puppy mill the only part of you that has value is your uterus and Maggie's still functioned.

Maggie is an ambassador that we take into public to teach people about mills. She has a permanent scar around her neck where she was tied with a rope. In what should be a peaceful sleep Maggie whimpers, cries and her feet move as if she were running. In the next room I regularly soak my bedding and scream in terror at the night. I wake with nightmares most nights and during the daylight hours my startle reflex can leave me, and the person that happened up behind me, in tears. I am so good at reading peoples nonverbal (from hypervigilance) that people are often certain I can read their mind.

I am in no way unusual. Survivors of domestic violence, rape and combat may startle easy. They become highly tuned into their environment. They may do the human equivalent of "cowering" when they are afraid or they may cover their fear with a lot of bravado. Traumatized humans behave like traumatized animals.

How does this all fit together? Why am I talking about animals and perpetrators in a book about domestic violence? Working with the victims I saw the impact violence had on them. Working with the offenders taught me how victims respond to trauma and taught me why a perpetrator picks one person over another. Society's role was easy to unravel because of extensive research already available, done by the domestic violence and victimology researchers who preceded me. But something was always missing. What is the victim's role in her own trauma? This is an especially pressing and serious question. Can these women, who are being chosen as victims over and over, truly just be the victims of the universe and if so, why?

A predator in the wild will watch a herd of animals and pick out the weakest. This may be the oldest, youngest or sickest animal and this is the animal that the predator(s) will target. They will watch and focus on this animal prior to pursuing it. The young men that I work with do the same thing. They pick out the weakest among us. After a trauma, or multiple traumas, victims exhibit certain behaviors that attract predators. Again, this is not to say, in any way, that it is the victims fault. It is to say that the victim exhibits certain characteristics that she must deal with ASAP to avoid being traumatized again. You can watch our website for a more detailed book on human and animal prey and predator.

Some things perpetrators consider weaknesses:

- "Nice" is often considered a weakness.
- Perpetrators can quickly pick out previously traumatized people.
- Children from single parent families
- Women who are not involved in a "love" relationship
- Bad choices

These are just a few examples of things that might make us stand out from the herd. Perpetrators are able to pick out people who have been previously traumatized and can readily justify victimizing them. I don't know how many times I have heard sex offenders say, "Well her father was already raping her." Or an indignant, "She wasn't even a virgin."

People, and animals, are frequently the victims of violence because they stand out and are therefore picked out by predators. This is one way that revictimization occurs. You may be targeted because you have not dealt with issues that cause you to stand out. For example, if you were sexually abused as a child you might subconsciously show that with low self-esteem. Maybe a woman is using alcohol to help her cope? How long do you think a drunk Zebra on the plains would last? This is as telling to a predator as a gazelle with a broken leg. I go into more detail in the Chapter called The Toolbox about keeping ourselves safe after a traumatic experience, how we show the trauma and what predators look for.

I now had a better handle on what things had set me up to be a battered woman, how I had been prepared to get into the role. But why did I stay for more than one beating? Why did the bi-lateral amputee accept that horrid life for more than 20 years? Why do battered women consistently answer the question, "Why do you stay?" with "Because I love him"?

3

Why Battered Women Stay

Battered women stay for a number of reasons. The reasons are basically the same, but the amount of contribution from each reason varies. Battered women stay because of social expectations, religion, resources and traumatic bonding, to name a few reasons. These are contributing factors and the role that each contributes in each woman's decision is different.

For example, domestic violence crosses all socioeconomic lines, meaning that women with money are as likely to be battered as poor women. So the issue of resources would play less of a role with a victim who is able to support herself. But this victim may be more concerned about what people think, her wedding vows and church, making social expectations more of a contributing factor for her.

The contributing factors influence the victim to different degrees but in situations where certain conditions are present traumatic bonding will occur and be the most important, and most controllable factor for the women.

Popular Explanations

The following are some of the most common explanations for why battered women stay. These are contributing factors that have received a lot of attention over the years. They are worthy of mention, but they are not the primary reason that battered women stay with the men that abuse them. If we look only at these explanations, then women are powerless to end their victimization because these contributing factors are primarily controlled by someone else. These are the most easily described, and convenient reasons because they are outside of ourselves, outside of our control. The following list is not complete. There are many contributing factors but these are some of the most often cited.

Resources

One of the contributing factors that keep battered women from leaving the men that beat them is resources. There is still a significant pay gap between men and women. Statistically, women still earn only 70 cents on a man's dollar. Families more often than not need two incomes and, understandably, women are hesitant to thrust their children into poverty. The faces of poverty in this country <u>are</u> the faces of women and children. Part of this is due to the fact that after a divorce, the man's standard of living is increased while a woman's decreases. Providing orange juice for your child as opposed to a cheap package drink can be a serious motivation for women to stay. Keeping your children in your home as opposed to a homeless shelter will help a mother tolerate quite a bit.

Religion

Most, if not all, of the formal religions look down on divorce, and religion has historically encouraged men to "control their wives." The Catholic Church doesn't readily recognize a second marriage and the divorcee may be denied certain privileges. Religious beliefs can be a strong motivation to accepting violence in your life.

Social Expectations

There has historically been a social expectation that we stay in a marriage, no matter what. In fact, it is only relatively recently that woman beating has been illegal and it can still be difficult to get law enforcement to arrest a batterer. There is a lot of pressure on women to get married and be wives.

We are very clear about their roles as keeper of the home and the emotional well being of the family. Good wives forgive, don't abandon vows in a crisis; any type of deep faith means we take our vows seriously. And single women are often seen as defective and considered to be a more appropriate victim by predators and other types of offenders.

Many of us are taught our entire lives that we want to grow up and marry doctors rather than to be doctors. My sisters and I grew up being told that we would not be allowed to go to college, we would marry. While we have come a long way to explode these archaic ideas they do die hard and it will take the work of many more generations.

Learned Helplessness

While bitter, this theory has some merit as a contributing factor for explaining why battered women may freeze as opposed to fighting or fleeing. We are taught, as females, to rely on others to fix our cars, our plumbing and our lives. We grow up believing that there is a knight in shining armor who will ride up and rescue us from our lives.

Female Masochism

At one point I actually found out that I was working with a Ph.D level counselor who believed the only way to help battered women was to teach them not to like the physical pain. While this sounds so far fetched that it couldn't be so, people never cease to surprise me with the ignorance and thinking errors they carry around. If you are working with a counselor and it just doesn't feel right, move on. Be warned, there are professionals out there who believe that battered women are masochistic and stay because they enjoy the pain & you won't have any warning until you feel the crush in your chest of hearing her say it.

These are also the factors that service providers have been acting on in the last twenty years which, in my opinion, is why there has been absolutely no statistical change in incidence reporting in the numbers of battered women. Without looking at traumatic bonding, a contributing factor that women can control, we will not change the numbers. Without educating women on the cues they send offenders, how they get that "V" on their forehead, they will continue to get into and stay in violent relationships.

While all of the above mentioned issues contribute to a woman's decision to stay in a violent relationship, they do not explain her constant defense of, "Because I love him." There is

more going on here than resources, religion and social expectations. If these were the only reasons that battered women stay then they would answer the question, "Why do you stay?" with "I can't afford to leave" or "My religion prohibits leaving." But that is not what they say. Consistently battered women respond to the question, "Why do you stay?" with "Because I love him." Something else is going on.

The idea that they stay because they are expected to and don't want to deal with social or religious approval is simplistic and disrespectful. The fact is they live with openly expressed disapproval everywhere they turn. Outside the home they are constantly berated for staying and inside their homes they are berated for everything.

Battered women stay because of the coercive and manipulative techniques that the batterer uses. These techniques cause the women to bond with the perpetrator and this bond is so strong that the only word women have for it is "love". They have not experienced any other feeling as intense, to compare it to. The closest word they have to describe this bond is "love".

Why Battered Women Stay: Traumatic Bonding & The Development of the Stockholm Syndrome in Battered Women

We hear the question "Why do you stay?" asked of battered women time and again.
Most of society tired long ago of the answer, "Because I love him." What the battered woman is really saying is, "I am bonded to him because of trauma and the only way I know to describe this bond is the word "love". This feeling is strong and I don't know what it's called."

These victims do not have the information they need to describe accurately the intense feelings or what has happened to them. They are not taught in health class that if a person is exposed to certain conditions, they will respond in certain ways. They are not taught that if they live with intermittent violence, occasional indulgences, isolation etc... that this abuse and trauma will cause them to have strong feelings that feel like love.

No wonder they attribute these intense feelings to love; both feelings are intense and complicated, not easy to explain. When we ask a battered woman why she stays we may as well be asking her how to split an atom, because they have no frame of reference, no words for what is happening. They therefore search their minds for a feeling that does fit and that is love. While love may be illogical, a traumatic bond is not. It makes an incredible amount of sense.

If battered women, their friends, families and service providers had accurate information and a name for why battered women stay, many women would find it easier to take control of their lives, and the people who support them could do a better job helping them to break the bond and escape.

I have watched the concern of law enforcement as they fend off an attack by a battered woman who doesn't want the offender arrested. I have seen the frustration of prosecutors who have taken precious time to build a case only to have the battered woman refuse to cooperate. I know the disgust and fear family and friends feel watching their loved one return over and over to a "lover" who may eventually kill them and who keeps them and their children in a chaotic grip. Until we fully answer the question, "What makes it so hard for her to leave?" we can not have any real impact on the generational cycle of woman beating.

For years we have talked about financial, cultural and religious reasons and these are valid, contributing factors. But the reason that battered women stay is traumatic bonding and the development of the Stockholm Syndrome. This is also referred to as Hostage Identification Syndrome, the Stockholm Syndrome and Traumatic Bonding. I use them interchangeably.

Traumatic bonding was first formally recognized and acknowledged during a bank robbery and hostage incident in Stockholm, Sweden. Authorities were amazed that the hostages being held during the robbery refused to cooperate with them and actually saw law enforcement officials as the villains. This is what we see in battered women when they refuse to cooperate with authorities or are willing to fight law enforcement to protect the man who batters them.

What the authorities in Sweden were witnessing was the hostage's identification with the hostage takers, or a traumatic bond. The hostages had bonded with the hostage takers and authorities were even more shocked when the hostages refused to testify against the robbers. One of the women later married one of her captors.

The Stockholm Syndrome, or victims bonding to captors, has been seen in POW's, abused children, cult members and battered women. The Communist Chinese researched and wrote extensively about the conditions necessary to achieve this bond, in order to get compliance and cooperation. Albert Biderman wrote about these conditions for Amnesty International (*Biderman's Chart of Coercion*). Even though this was done with prisoners of war in mind, this chart describes with amazing detail the conditions of a violent domestic relationship. I don't mean there is a resemblance. I mean there isn't a hair's difference between violent domestic relationships and other hostage relationships where the Stockholm Syndrome develops except in the way we, as a society, respond to the victims.

In her book *Rape in Marriage*, Diana Russell notes, "The techniques used by prison guards also apply to the brainwashing of other victims," and Ginny NiCarty, in her book *Getting Free* says, "Most people who brainwash their intimate partners use methods similar to those of prison guards who recognize that physical control is never easily accomplished without the cooperation of the prisoner. The most effective way to gain control is through the subversive manipulation of the mind & feelings of the victim who then becomes a psychological as well as a physical prisoner." When these authors refer to prison guards they are talking about POW's because the first studies were conducted on the POW – guard bond.

We see the results of this manipulation every time we are perplexed by the behaviors and priorities of a battered woman. We see the results of this "subversive manipulation" when a 100 pound woman jumps on the back of a cop because she doesn't want the batterer arrested. We see how effective this set of manipulations are when battered women protect and plead the cases of the men who beat them.

The bond that battered women feel is the reason that they stay and, as you will see, it actually works in their favor to reduce their injuries. Dee Graham et al in *Survivors of Terror: Battered Women, Hostages and the Stockholm Syndrome* published in *Rethinking Clinical Approaches* says, "The psychological reactions of battered women can best be explained as a result of their experiences of being trapped in a situation that is very similar to that of hostages. Traditional psychological theories have suggested that battered women love and remain with the men who beat them out of female masochism. We suggest that their experiences can best be understood through the model of the Stockholm Syndrome…"

While the research has been available since the 1950's it has never been widely distributed because, like incest, this bond is still not politically correct to discuss. There are many reasons that there has not been a sincere public awareness campaign combined with actively teaching young girls and women the warning signs and dynamics. I don't mean to say that we can end woman beating with a public awareness campaign. We can't. But we can give women the tools they need to combat the manipulation that keeps them in violent relationships and by doing so we can cause a decrease in the number of women that become battered and the number of women that stay.

As long as we do not educate the public, especially the battered women, we can't deal with this tragic truth that leaves a trail of battered, bruised and scarred women and children. Without accurate information on why battered women stay, we can not support them, help their children or help them to understand the situation so that they can get out of their present relationship and avoid it in their next relationship.

As long as we continue to portray battered women as helpless and needing to be plucked out of their situation we will fail to break the generational cycle of violence against women. As long as we place more value on the political correctness of portraying battered women as passive amoebas, with no control over their environment, as opposed to placing the emphasis on teaching them about how perpetrators pick them, why they stay and how to recover, then we will have self blaming mothers whose sons and daughters learn the pattern of family violence.

Victim Responsibility and Examining Our Choices

While it is true that even if you choose to walk down a back alley totally naked you do not deserve to be raped, it is also true that you are much more likely to be raped if you do. We have to look at the choices we make and whether they contribute to our safety or put us at risk. There are many behaviors and cues that offenders look for in a potential victim; those women that are chosen are often seen as **"appropriate victims"**. An "appropriate victim" is someone that offenders can justify or rationalize hurting and feel reasonably sure that they will either remain silent or can be easily discredited. They are the females that offenders say, "were asking for it," or "deserved it." They are often the females that had been traumatized by someone else previously, so the offender may look at them as "fair game".

But we can't even talk about victim responsibility and "empowerment" until we educate women on their own behavior. While the term "empowerment" is thrown around you can not empower someone who has not been educated on safety, choices and even how to think critically about her experiences. To empower our females means that we need to teach them about the world they live in and the choices they make.

If we give women the information that they need, they can identify subversive manipulation when they see it and then can counter or resist it. Without accurate information they have little chance of accidentally hitting on the cause of the problem and this sets women up to blame themselves, be victimized and revictimized.

To demonstrate traumatic bonding and the development of the Stockholm Syndrome in battered women I will use an imaginary woman. We will call her Anne and give her a typical background, whatever that is. As I discussed in Chapter 2, *How Girls Become Battered Women*, Anne has grown up hearing the tuna jokes and seeing all of the unattainable images of what she should look like. She is made to feel stupid with blond jokes and paid less than the men in her office. She frequently watches the men she has trained get the promotions she wants and she lives with messages about the ticking of her "biological clock," all of which may leave her feeling tremendous pressure to find a mate and start her family.

Anne meets a man and she doesn't see any sign that says "I am a batterer". And she did look because during high school one of her friends was in a violent relationship and, while she never understood how it happened, Anne swore it would never happen to her. As if on a job interview, he was on his best behavior. If he had hauled off and backhanded her on the first date that would have been the end of it. But that isn't how it goes.
Batterers do not walk up to women and say, "I am a woman beater and I want you to be in a violent relationship with me."

He's not stupid. He knows that he has to win her and, like all of us, he shows her his best side. She's not stupid either. She is checking him out to see if he would be a good mate. The problem is that he is experienced at this and she is not. He is savvy and knows which women to pick and how to get them invested before he shows too much of his real self. But she has never been taught what to look for in an abusive man and we still blame her for the relationship. Batterers are notoriously charming and, by the third date, Anne was charmed right out of her britches.

She is beginning to have some investment and starts thinking about his potential and expanding her family. She also knows that it's too soon to know the answers to those questions. And **time** goes on…and maybe it's a little time and maybe it's a lot, but it really doesn't matter because time, like trauma, truly is relative.

At this point she has seen nothing but his best side, well, except for the occasional name calling, and she is spending less time with her family and friends. And sometimes he says insensitive things and occasionally she catches him looking at other women, but no one's perfect, she reasons. Every time he's insensitive she feels a little **degraded**, but it is so subtle that it doesn't seem like a big deal. He can be fixed.

She isn't aware of the fact that we get into abusive relationships through a slow and subtle process. It wasn't a part of health class or home economics and she has been **degraded** in one way or another all of her life. He has manipulated her from the beginning starting with the fact that he refused to wear his sign (I'm a batterer) and the manipulation and **degradation** is escalating. He dislikes her friends and family more and more and the name calling is more frequent. And time goes on…

He shows himself in small doses over a long period of **time** and everything is so gradual that the change is barely noticeable. He has thrown a fit or two and she has begun watching his every move in an effort to predict his mood, please him and maintain the peace. She remembers how great he was in the beginning and reminds herself of his potential and besides, every time he gets angry he does regret it.

Anne is really **exhausted** all of the time. She has a child from a previous relationship, a full time job and she's a part time student. One day, during one of his fits he hits her. She is shocked. But it has been such a gradual build up to this point. Maybe her gut instincts have been screaming at her and she has worked hard to silence that voice. And maybe her gut didn't recognize anything unusual because she grew up in a verbally abusive home or simply because of society's **degradation** of women. Maybe with the pressure on women to marry and be part of a couple, she didn't want to hear that little voice inside her.

He is so sorry for what he has done. He can't quit apologizing and he is bringing her flowers. He promises this will never happen again. He's just under so much pressure, she reasons, and he really needs her. He is kind, loving and all of his attention is focused on keeping her and the **indulgence** feels really good to her.

And **time** has gone on…And she is really financially strapped and her child does need a father and he has so much potential and he is truly sorry and her religion says she should make it work and she doesn't want to go back to the single life and how would she admit this failure to her family and friends and there really isn't anyone anymore because she has focused so much on him. She is already terribly **isolated** and…

And he turns up the charm. He swears he will never do it again, brings her more flowers, jewelry and even lightens her load. He works really hard to make it up to her and swears it was a one-time thing. He **indulges** her in an effort to make things right and prove his love. She loves the charm and feels that maybe it was her fault. Deep down he is a nice man.

She has been focused a lot on her work and child. He is working a lot of hours. She decides she should spend more time with him and she shouldn't push him so far. She decides she can watch him more closely and when the stress is too much for him she can help relieve it. And really, she thinks how big of a deal is it to have dinner done and the toilet paper put on the way he likes. They are such **trivial demands**. And **time** goes on…

Even though Anne is **exhausted** she watches him more closely, as if he has totally **monopolized her perception**. She makes sure his dinner is on time. She spends even less time with friends and family because he doesn't like them and she believes she needs to focus more on her relationship. She really appreciates the **occasional indulgences** he offers her and is certain she can help him recognize his potential. And the tension is building…And the tension is building… And **time** goes on..

As **time** goes, on he occasionally uses **threats** which really isn't necessary because once you hit someone the **threat** is always there. He occasionally **indulges** her and keeps her family and friends at bay because they take her time and energy away from him and he's sure that they just don't understand him and they're trying to come between them. He keeps her focused on him and insists she do this and that.

Anne becomes more and more **isolated** and the tension is building and it escalates. She may or may not have something to do with the escalation. It doesn't matter, the next phase was inevitable. She may have "provoked" him to move from the tension-building phase to violence so they can get to the honeymoon phase. This time he has to use even greater force than the last time because that's the nature of violence. He busts her mouth and blackens her eye.

While batterers scream and cry that they are provoked by the women, they fail to look at basic physical power differences and the potential for damage. She could slug him and not even knock him off balance (and this is still domestic violence and unacceptable) but if he hits her he could kill her with one blow. And while the batterer is screaming and crying that he was provoked, he appears unaware of the inherent statement in the argument of provocation. He is saying he doesn't have the maturity to control his feelings, because you can not provoke an action, only feelings.

And who could blame Anne for trying to move the relationship from the tension building phase and just get the beating over with. Waiting for a beating can be as hard as enduring it. Again he is sorry and she watches his every move and mood. She tries not to provoke him and keep the peace because harmony in the home is her responsibility. She tries to please him even with the seemingly **trivial demands**. He controls the money and tells her things like, "no one else will ever have you," and he would kill her first.

She knows that it's in her best interest to keep him happy and she must constantly dismiss the nagging advice of loved ones that she leave him. She is ashamed and embarrassed that she is in this situation and so she really doesn't talk about it. She avoids friends and family because of the shame and persistent nagging and becomes even more **isolated**. Anne knows that leaving him would be futile because he would never let her go and might actually follow through with his threat to kill her.

She remembers hearing that when battered women are killed it is most often when they are trying to leave. Anne grows more **tired** as the days wear on. The tension building continues until eventually he blows up and this time the neighbors call the police. The police stop the initial assault but now she worries what he will do to her when he is released from jail. Now she wonders how she'll pay the bills and where she will go because, hard as she tried, she could not keep the police from arresting him and he is going to blame her.

The police tell her that he will be released in about 6 hours and they drill her about why she stays. Totally humiliated she minimizes her injuries and watches, with the children, as they take him away. He is going to blame her and she will never forget his threats to kill her, as he reminded her that he was all powerful (**or demonstrated his omnipotence**). Every muscle in her body aches, from the assault, as she packs a few clothes for herself and the children. She feels the pain in every movement she makes as the children cling to her legs, screaming, in search of anything that resembles safety. When their crying slows they begin asking one question after another.

Overwhelmed by the smell, Anne sits in the small room provided for her and her children in the battered women's shelter. She knows her tormentor is resting comfortably in his recliner in the home she has created. He knows there is a limit to how long she can stay at the shelter and that once she is out she has no place to go. He knows all of her friends and family…and so he waits.

Anne has been subjected to the subversive manipulation author Ginny NiCarty, Diana Russell and a handful of other researchers acknowledged, unheard, years ago. She doesn't know what's happened because she is busy trying to reduce her injuries at least, and to save her life, at most.

POW

50 years ago a 17-year-old boy is captured by the Communist Chinese during the Korean War. He is captured after four months in Korea and he is **exhausted** by the time he is captured. He believes that being captured saved his life and said he was so tired and hungry that it was almost a relief. He is devastated and **debilitated** from hunger, **exhaustion** and the stress of his situation and what he has seen. He is traumatized by the death and destruction that should not have been seen by anyone, much less a child of 17. He is made to walk for weeks through mountainous, rugged terrain to the prison camp.

When he arrives he is interrogated and **isolated** from the general population. But the **isolation** was already overwhelming. He misses his friends and family back home. He is abused frequently and is occasionally **indulged** with a dead cat to supplement the regular diet. He carries out the bodies of his starved and dead buddies on a daily basis and he stays focused on the moods of the guards because he knows his life depends on his ability to keep them happy.

The guards are **all powerful** and he knows they would kill him before they let him go. He is constantly **degraded** by his own nudity and name calling. He is abused for not carrying out the diseased bodies fast enough and the abuse itself is constantly overshadowed by the **threat** of abuse because, once it happens the **threat** is ever present.

When the prisoners are abused they can frequently find justification. After all they did try to escape, it is important to get the diseased bodies out quickly and the guards must keep order, the men reason. And like our battered woman the **violence is intermittent** and hard to predict despite the victim's efforts.

Sometimes the men are **indulged** with a game of basketball or a substantial meal (relatively) and they are frequently asked to do silly things that just don't make sense, like busywork or "**trivial demands**", says the former POW.

After 47 years of freedom this POW still speaks fondly of one of his captors. He readily credits his captors with saving his life and says if they hadn't taken him to China he would have died. He speaks of how well educated the guards were and how he would talk for long periods with them.

He was young when captured and a couple of the guards spent hours listening to stories of his family. The POW feels a great deal of shame for any of his positive feelings and blames himself for being captured and his fond feelings for one of the guards. Like the battered women, no amount of reassurance can ease his guilt and feelings of responsibility for the situation. He warns me not to speak of this because society doesn't understand. Many of the men were highly criticized for having positive feelings toward their captors and these positive feelings were misconstrued as cooperation.

He tells of the constant voice that broadcasts through the camp reminding them of how their predicament is their own fault and they should repent. He tells of how the men who developed a bond with their captors were blamed and shamed upon their return. He believes some were even prosecuted.

Fifty years later he washes down his shame with alcohol. He bonded to his captors to reduce his injuries and to save his life. This doesn't mean he cooperated with the enemy. It means that he behaved with good and common sense in an unusual situation. How smart would he have been to constantly aggravate his captors?

Hostages, cult members, abused children and battered women frequently bond with the perpetrator. This bond is in their best interest and can reduce their injuries. Yet they are shamed, blamed and even tried by juries for "allowing" this bond to occur. This has also been called Traumatic Bonding, Common Sense

Syndrome, Stockholm Syndrome and Hostage Identification Syndrome.

In *The Stockholm Syndrome: Toward an Understanding*, Irka Kuleshnyk of the New School For Social Research defines the Stockholm Syndrome, "The group of behaviors usually made in reference to the Stockholm Syndrome emerges when hostages and their captors are **isolated** by authorities and when hostages experience positive feelings to their captors, which the captors reciprocate. In addition the hostage often feels negative feelings toward authorities." Kuleshnyk also asserts that the bond tends to develop exclusively in lengthier situations.

The fact that the captor (batterer, hostage taker, perpetrator) reciprocates these positive feelings is how the victim is able to reduce her injuries. The fact that time is an important element is why we don't commonly see this bond in stranger rapes, property crimes and the like. Kuleshnyk explains the hostages response in this way, "…the hostages needs are met by the captor, who the hostage then grows fond of and begins to identify with. Basically the mechanism which worked for the hostage as a child is called upon again to help him survive as a hostage…instinctively, in order to stay alive, the hostage does feel it is necessary to behave in a certain way and does."

When I read those words, they not only clicked in my head but reached to my very soul. This explained why after the brutal beatings I clung to Aaron's legs begging for his mercy. He had control over my welfare and I needed to keep him happy enough to let me live. Any mercy he might have would be the reason for my life.

This is what we are witnessing when we see battered women return to their tormentors, defend them to authorities and bend over backward to please them. We are not witnessing female masochism but women who feel a bond so strongly that the only word they know to describe it is love. We are seeing women behave with common sense in an order to reduce their injuries, women who have the good sense to do what they need to do because they are subject to an unresponsive justice system.

My research would explain in detail how I, and so many other women, got in the position of staying with the most brutal of men. I was astounded when I ran across the chart of techniques that influenced this bond and then compared them to The Duluth Minnesota Intervention for Men Who Batter. The conditions that needed to be present for this bond to occur complemented and supported those presented by battered women's advocates to explain what battered women endure.

For Amnesty International, Albert Biderman charted the techniques and conditions necessary for the Stockholm Syndrome to occur:

Isolation
Degradation
Enforcement of Trivial Demands
Intermittent Violence
Threats
Occasional Indulgences
Exhaustion & Debilitation
The Demonstration of Omnipotence
Monopolization of Perception

What is amazing is that these conditions and techniques were compiled for POW's and traditional hostages but identically mirror the conditions of a violent domestic relationship and fit perfectly with the "Power & Control Wheel" from the Duluth Intervention Model. This is not to say that batterers go out and do research on how to get women to accept abuse. People do what works for them. The batterer only needs to backhand his intended once on the first date, to find out how quickly that will land him in jail. He has learned, one way or another, what works. Maybe he watched his parents or grandparents or maybe he has learned on his own. Either way he has learned what type of woman (appropriate victim) is more accepting of his manipulation and what techniques work. Let us now focus on the conditions present in a relationship where the Stockholm Syndrome can develop.

Isolation - Battered or not, women in relationships frequently find themselves isolated because they spend so much time focusing on their lover, the kids and the relationships. For battered women this is compounded. The saying "mother knows best" often proves true and the friends and family of battered women often don't like the batterer. He knows this and disapproves of any contact she might have with someone who could fill her head with logic, reason and truth.

Hostage-takers, prison guards and cult leaders also isolate their victims for the same reason. If there is no one else in the hostage's life then the captor is the victims only "reality check" and feedback. The captor may be the hostage's only other source of human contact. This isolation removes competing ideas or opinions and leaves only the input of the captor. The victim gets little, if any, feedback from others and will doubt their own judgment, reality and even their sanity. The isolation deprives the victim of necessary support and makes the victim more dependent on the captor.

Even if the friends and family don't know about the violence, batterers are narcissistic and do not want to compete with anyone else for attention. The battered woman also tends to isolate herself out of shame. She does not want people to know she lives in violence so she may contribute to the isolation. She is being berated for staying and is ashamed of not only the abuse but her choices. This can make contact with others quite uncomfortable.

Degradation – This happens in many different ways including verbal and emotional abuse like name calling and humiliating the victim. It happens when the victim is made to feel less than others and treated as stupid or made to perform humiliating or trivial tasks. For example, Aaron would also brag and laugh about stripping his ex-wife naked and making her crawl, and stay, under the bed. He would lay on top of the bed and threaten her with violence, telling her the only way she could stay safe was to stay under the bed.

It is not just something that one individual does to another but can be a terrible message sent to large groups of people by the community. Not until I did a victim impact group for racists did I realize the level of degradation and it's impact on blacks inherent in our society. My racist father unwittingly made sure I was always aware of, and appalled by, racism and I always took it seriously. But the young black men that I used to teach the adolescent KKK wannabes, also taught me how deeply they were affected by the constant degradation they live with because of their skin color. Even when it's subtle, like seeing women subconsciously clutch their purse as the young men walk by, the constancy of the message is overwhelming and hard to counter. And they often prevail in their lives despite it. Degradation does not only happen in interpersonal (or one-on-one) relationships. Whole groups of people (blacks, Hispanics, immigrants, the elderly, gays etc…) are often degraded and devalued by other groups.

Degradation lowers self-esteem leaving the victim to question everything from "do I bake or broil" to who they are at their very core. Women are degraded in society from birth (breast and tuna jokes, for example). Battered women are degraded in the relationship both overtly and covertly. This ranges from the batterings themselves to name calling, to the enforcement of trivial demands. She is also degraded every time someone asks her why she stays. Inherent in this question is another question, "How could you be so stupid?" And that question assumes she could actually just walk away.

Enforcement of Trivial Demands – The enforcement of trivial demands is when we are forced to do things that really aren't important, such as ironing underwear, setting a table just so or brushing his teeth. The enforcement of trivial demands serves to get the victim in the habit of saying yes. It develops a habit of compliance. Edward Levin, in his book *Negotiating Tactics* says, "You request things that you know you can get and once you have established a yes pattern the requests can become greater." This is very important in mediation and conflict resolution.

Compliance becomes a habit – toilet paper on the roll just right, dinner on time and, oh yeah, don't forget to clip my toenails tonight. The trivial demands made on battered women can be ridiculous – to the outsider. Inside the relationship they serve a purpose. These things also serve to degrade and demonstrate omnipotence, which means to demonstrate that he is all powerful. The techniques all work together to achieve compliance.

Intermittent Violence – Intermittent violence serves to keep the victim focused on the perpetrator. If we don't know what's going to happen next, we will work very hard to watch, learn and predict another person's behavior. This is called hypervigilance and we see it in a lot of situations – domestic violence, children of alcoholics, abused children, prey animals and combat veterans. The violence needs to be intermittent because if the victim can predict it, she wouldn't need to stay focused. She could just set her watch, go about her business and then deal with the assault when the alarm goes off.

Intermittent violence serves to keep the victim on their toes and ensures compliance or the yes habit. Dee Graham *et al* states that this intermittent violence, "alternating with warm friendly, kind behavior, in such a situation where there are no alternative relationships available, the victim will bond to the warmer, positive side of the abuser." And this is what we hear the victim explain as love. It is a bond to the side of him that hasn't yet killed her.

Threats – Threats can be in words, actions or even a look, and serve the purpose of compliance (getting the victim to obey). Threats cultivate anxiety and fear. Once violence is used, a threat is usually enough to achieve compliance because the victim knows the perpetrator is capable of the violence. The victim can no longer assume these are just threats.

Occasional Indulgences – These are when the victim occasionally gets pleasurable things whether they are material or emotional. The material indulgences might be flowers or jewelry and the emotional could be a hug or simply approval.

Occasional Indulgences provide something to look forward to and a reason to comply. If there wasn't hope on the victims part, for what the batterer could be, she wouldn't have stayed in the beginning. There needs to be occasional indulgences, something to hang onto. If there was no positive side to bond to, the battered woman would not bond, the cult member would not believe and it would be more difficult to control the prisoner or hostage. If the perpetrator has no redeeming or good qualities it would be easier for the victim to see the truth and resist.

Domestic violence experts refer to this state (Occasional Indulgences) of a violent domestic relationship as the honeymoon phase. In the cycle of violence apologies, gifts and promises make up this part of the cycle. When the battered woman responds, "Because I love him" to the question, "Why do you stay?" this is the part of him that she has bonded to and she clings to those occasional indulgences.

In *Negotiating Tactics*, Edward Levin talks about the importance of giving away smaller things in order to get more. In an abusive relationship the emotional and material windfalls may far outweigh those of a healthy relationship. But they come with a hefty price tag. In other words, the highs are much higher and the lows are life threatening.

Induced Debility & Exhaustion – This occurs when victims are not allowed to sleep or rest, and are overworked and over stressed. It also occurs from lack of nutrition. Most women are exhausted from daily routines and the expectations on them. This is increased for battered women. They have the stress of trying to please the batterer, predict his moods and trying to reduce their injuries. Beatings, in and of themselves, are exhausting and leave one defeated.

Exhaustion reduces the ability to resist. Two-year-olds to teenagers learn how to work this. My teenagers learned quickly that I was at my weakest late at night. Exhaustion also impairs our judgment, like trying to make a decision after your spouse has died or after you've been up for 36 hours. And the effects of chronic stress certainly effect us as seriously as exhaustion.

The Demonstration of Omnipotence – This is when someone presents themselves as all powerful. They have complete control and all of the power, like God. This happens all the time in violent domestic relationships. As her self esteem is lowered through verbal and physical abuse, his power is increased. While her value is lowered in the relationship, his is proportionately increased.

From his control over the money, the car, the beatings and his having control over whether she lives or dies, the feeling she has is that it doesn't matter what she does, he will always win. She comes to believe that resistance is futile. She can't change her situation and has no control. When he tells her he will kill her before he lets her go, not only does she believe that he will, but she believes he can. Batterers often tell the victim that they can't get away, that he will find them. And the women, justifiably, believe this.

Just because this tactic can be named and is common does not mean it is a hollow threat. The majority of battered women who are killed, are killed when they are trying to leave. We need to listen to the victims in this situation. She knows him best. After all, she has spent all of her energy focusing on him, watching him and trying to please him. SHE is the expert on what he is capable of and we have no business second-guessing her decisions.

Monopolization of Perception – This happens when a person is subject to a situation or another person requiring all of their attention. It is where the victim's entire world consists of the situation or other person. This serves to keep her focused on him. Her attention is fixed on the immediate situation and this prevents her from thinking about solutions and the future. He is her whole world and her response to this is the hypervigilance I discussed earlier. Hyper meaning overactive and vigilance meaning attention (overactive attention).

If she is focused on what he wants and how he feels, sometimes minute to minute, she is not going to be thinking about herself. She watches him and responds to his moods and feelings in an effort to keep him happy and reduce her own injuries. Her efforts to predict and control his behaviors leave her off balance and contribute to her feelings of exhaustion. And every time she fails, she feels more responsible for his violence and more powerless to stop it. And the only outcome there could be is her failure because his violence has absolutely nothing to do with her. He would beat me. He would beat the Virgin Mary. He would beat any woman he was with.

These techniques and conditions all work together and support each other. For example monopolization of perception or isolation would be tough to achieve one without the other. And degradation really contributes to achieving both. A degraded person is more likely to be, or allow, isolation. A degraded person is more likely to be willing to focus on another person. Especially if they think that other person is all powerful (omnipotent) and they believe the other person might kill them (threats). And unpredictable beatings certainly would give a person good reason to put all their focus on the perpetrator (monopolization of perception). These techniques and conditions work together like a well designed drug to give those who want it a great deal of power and control over another.

These techniques and conditions all work together and support each other to assist the victim in establishing a mindset within herself, and a relationship with a perpetrator. This victim mindset and perpetrator relationship is Traumatic Bonding and its occurrence, or lack thereof, can mean life or death for the victim.

The Implications & Necessity of Bond

The bond serves to reduce injury. This bond between victim and offender, prison guard and hostage, abusive parent and child, cult member and leader or batterer and battered woman, does not simply go one way. When the victim personalizes themselves to the perpetrator this reduces injury. In hostage situations, maybe this occurs because one particular hostage out of 10 told the captor about their children and grandchildren, showed compassion and actually listened to the captor's problems. The bond goes both ways.

Irka Kuleshnyk says, "Although positive feelings usually form in a hostage crisis it is possible that hostages may develop negative feelings of hostility and antipathy toward captors. Behavior reflecting these attitudes may intensify feelings of malevolence toward the hostage which the captor may already possess…Not surprising then, in all recorded incidents where this has occurred, detrimental consequences have come to the hostage. As is now clear, the failure of the development of positive feelings, especially when replaced by negative feelings can be extremely dangerous to the hostage."

Kuleshnyk goes on to say, "…hostage takers have demonstrated that they can develop positive feelings toward their hostages and it is primarily because of this that the major advantage of the Stockholm Syndrome is the saving of lives. In a South Moluccan terrorist case in 1975, one of the hostages picked to be executed told a fellow hostage about problems he was having with his marriage and daughter. The captors overheard him and as a result could not execute him. Unfortunately the Moluccans executed another hostage who they had not gotten to know."

It is an unwise hostage that provokes and aggravates the captor. A POW that screams racial slurs and challenges at his captors would not live long. An abused child that dared the violent offender to beat them would find their request honored. Yet we expect battered women to leave the batterer, have them arrested and testify against them. Women are supposed to do this within a system that will only remove the captor for hours, where restraining orders are all but impossible to enforce, and where the system that disrespects and blames them may later order them to share custody or participate in **joint counseling**.

Battered and formerly-battered women are left, by our legal system, in a ridiculous and dangerous situation. They know this and when they refuse to take the ill-thought-out advice they are bombarded with, we then label them as masochistic and stupid. If battered women had given in to this advice over the years we would have seen many more deaths at the hands of batterers.

B. McClure, in his 1978 book *Hostage Survival*, warns against the development of negative transference, "or the development of antipathy and even aggressive hostility toward their captors. The reasons are that such hostility liberates the captors from any guilt they may have felt in seizing the victim…it justifies and intensifies any feelings of hate which the captors may attach to the hostage…and it may wound the ego of the basically insecure captor prompting direct retaliation."

Many facilitators and counselors work hard to relieve the guilt that batterers feel. In fact, pop psychology discourages guilt. This is ludicrous. Guilt helps us to control our behavior and gives us insight into our own bad behavior. Guilt serves a good function in our lives by screaming at us that something is wrong with our behavior. Guilt tells us we are misbehaving and is an excellent tool for modifying our behavior. Perpetrator guilt has worked to save the lives of many people.

The battered woman knows that her captor has a fragile ego and her years of hypervigilance (watching him) have given her tools to keep from bruising his ego. The battered woman knows that an all-out attack on that ego could end her life. He has told her repeatedly that he would kill her before allowing anyone else to have her. Much to the dismay of law enforcement, prosecutors, advocates and loved ones, this bond discourages cooperation with authorities who are seen by the hostage and the hostage taker as the enemy. The hostage and the battered woman believe that the captor, and batterer, are simply misunderstood, persecuted, just need love and understanding and that they can be fixed. This is her only hope of escape. She believes she can not physically escape, so changing him is all she has.

It is not only the bond itself that discourages cooperation but the services and interventions that we offer battered women. The women know that if they cooperate with authorities, the authorities will not offer them the protection they need. We need to accept this bond and respect the purpose it serves and design programs and interventions with the bond in mind. Again, without this bond there would be many more dead women.

Consider the hostages who are taken during a bank robbery. Let's say they were held for two days before authorities were able to negotiate a surrender. What if we then ask the hostages to testify? But they are told that the robber would only be held overnight and that they would have to go and get a restraining order to "insure" the robber stayed away from them. Of course the hostages would not cooperate. Yet we expect women who have been in relationships with their captors for decades to do something different and then shame them when they don't. Shame on us.

Others, in addition to Biderman, have also laid out criteria or conditions and techniques for Traumatic Bonding to occur. James T. Turner, in Vol.6, No.4 of *Political Psychology* 1985, included face-to-face contact, passing of time, preexisting stereotypes, language, cultural value structure, the sophistication of the individuals and the timing of the violence.

Turner also asserts that Traumatic Bonding is not an unusual phenomenon, but is in fact "a normal psychological process that is intensified by factors related to the immediate life-threatening nature of the hostage situation." In other words, the reaction of the battered woman is normal.

Face To Face Contact - is an important element. This is why we don't see the bond in cases of rape etc... The length of time that the victim spends with the perpetrator will proportionately effect the strength of the bond. Because the bond goes both ways and serves to protect the hostage, guards are frequently rotated in an effort to prevent their bonding.

This face-to-face contact can also cause an old bond to resurface. I am a strong proponent for victim-offender mediations/ameliorations, a process that helps the victim get answers to her questions and put a face on the person that traumatized her. But I have been quite vocal in my opposition to any type of mediation, amelioration or counseling in domestic violence situations. Even child visitation can cause this bond to reoccur and can leave the victim in a lifetime of turmoil, and the offender with an endless source of power over the victim. More on this in Chapters 4 & 5.

Face-to-face contact does effect enmity (hatred, from the word "enemy"). It closes the "them and us" gap. Face-to-face contact can cause a racist to change his mind, or an animal hater to feel differently. It often allows both parties to better understand one another.

If you have a rape survivor who is having nightmares about the monster that raped her, the best thing for her might be to meet him and ask him questions. This puts a human face on him instead of allowing her imagination to continue. Yet in a domestic case the victim already empathizes with the offender to an extreme degree. In this situation we do not want the bond to reoccur.

Another example of how face-to-face contact effects the bond is with sex offenders. To perpetrate the crimes they commit they must first depersonalize or objectify their intended victims to help alleviate the guilt. For example, tuna jokes, viewing women as property and seeing women as less than they are is something they have probably done all their life. They have already depersonalized and objectified the victim.

We also see this with young men (and the rest of the society) going off to war. They depersonalize the enemy with terms like pie face, gooks etc... And this is the language that Edward Levin talks about in his book *Negotiating Tactics*. We also see this in racism (slurs my computer won't even type) and any situation where someone feels a need to justify their actions and relieve their guilt. This is one reason victim impact can be effective. Face-to-face contact makes it more difficult to dehumanize another. They learn about the other's life and personality. They see that they have more in common than not.

In victim impact, offenders learn about the harm they have caused and they see the face that endured it. They hear the heart that broke and learn of the lives they altered. They are not protected by prosecutors and the legal system from seeing the results of their behavior. The victims benefit from this face-to-face contact by seeing that this was not some abstract monster. This is a person who was also a victim that decided to create victims. The contact allows them to ask questions like why they were picked, what did they do with the ear rings, and why did the offender lock them in the trunk. Every victim that participates in my victim impact or an amelioration only regrets that it wasn't available sooner. And, as I have said repeatedly, this is not only inappropriate in domestic violence cases, but harmful to the victim and dangerous.

Timing of Violence – according to Turner, violence may accelerate the bond, "Violence during an incident can be accepted by hostages if the individual attacked has engaged in some type of provocation that threatens the stability of the situation." Remember, Turner is talking about what we traditionally think of as hostages. Yet this perfectly fits domestic violence. Doesn't leaving the batterer threaten the stability of the situation? How often do we hear women take responsibility for the beatings they endure? If we apply the theory that hostages revert to what worked for them as children, then what they want is stability. Turner goes on to say, "Hostages may justify the violence by statements such as "he deserved it."

Sophistication of Individuals – This is an interesting condition. I have read the work of researchers who assert that the bond can only occur with the less sophisticated. This is absurd. Domestic violence crosses all socioeconomic lines and a captain in the military is as susceptible to the bond as a private. In fact, the military is now teaching those who are at high risk of being taken hostage about the bond, except women. We know of few trying to get this information to women and service providers.

One thing that all the research agrees on is that the bond is in the best interest of the hostage and thus potential hostages must be educated on the issue. We have to educate our young women on this issue, especially battered women. Turner says, "A trained hostage cognizant of these factors can attempt to manipulate the captors as well. The total hostage experience and aftermath are clearly handled more effectively if the individual is prepared and trained."

Turner also warns that hostages must be able to control the identification (or bonding) in order to avoid being satellites (or tools) of their captors. In other words, if we educate them and provide them with a larger escape hatch that also offers safety, they will be more likely to cooperate with authorities. Battered women are made to feel stupid and masochistic for staying. They are buying into the self defeating explanations that they are weak and into the idea that it is their fault for staying. Until we give them information and can protect them, it is our fault. Turner says, "The hostage trained in techniques of survival can attempt to enhance the value of life by being more human in the eyes of the captor."

Without information, traumatic bonding is as perplexing to the victim as it is to onlookers. Our goal is to give women, and those who ask the question, the answer to, "Why do you stay?" This explanation is in no way intended to excuse the fact that battered women stay, but instead to explain their decision. While the explanation is not intended to excuse the fact, we can not expect them to take action against something they can not even explain. If they can't explain it how can they counter it? Rather than using this explanation to excuse the fact that battered women stay, it is intended to give them the tools they need to fight the manipulation and coercion that keeps them in the role of domestic hostage. My hope is also that answering the question, "Why do you stay?" will help those who judge and criticize the women to find compassion and to design a system that actually enables her to leave.

      While it is inappropriate for anyone to judge these women, it is appropriate for formerly-battered women, and there are many of us, to tell battered women the truth and to keep the expectation bar high. Battered women who are still disabled by the trauma have no obligation to reach out. It is absurd that victims of rape, and other violent crimes, are told that they have an obligation to cooperate with prosecution. As long as victims can become entangled in a legal system that may revictimize them, they have only an obligation to recover. Reporting the crime and assisting in prosecution is for the women who are compelled to do so and feel they can survive another trauma, because the more contact they have with service providers and the system, the more likely they are to be revictimized. Often the damage done by the system and service providers will cause more injury than the batterer.

4

Tool Box For Trauma Survivors & Those Who Love & Support Them

After the nightmare of surviving a trauma (rape, assault, woman beating etc…) a whole range of new thoughts, feelings and behaviors are thrust upon us. We find that not only are we different but we see the world differently and, in turn, the world responds to us differently. Our loved ones behave differently around us and we have fears and frustrations that we can't even verbalize. This new way of being is confusing and frustrating as we find that all the rules we were taught about being safe and good aren't true.

After a trauma the victims may find friends and family distancing themselves, because people who are going through trauma can behave in ways that are perplexing to others. It can help to keep in mind that the victim is as perplexed as anyone over her actions and reactions.

Those that support them may also be frightened and overwhelmed by the needs of the victim/survivor because they have little information and virtually no tools for coping. This goes for both the victim and their loved ones. Information on surviving trauma is not readily available and leaves both the survivor and their loved ones in turmoil. This lack of information and skills leaves the victim even more isolated. Teaching victims/survivors and those that support them can make this painful period in life smoother, providing a better opportunity for a good outcome and minimize the damage to the entire family.

This chapter, and the next, offers specific tools for victims and those that support them. These tools can work for all types of trauma survivors, secondary victims like the relatives of homicide victims and combat veterans. These tools come from decades of trial and error and are the tools that hundreds of victims have found most helpful. Just like a hammer is not designed to sand furniture, not all of these tools will work for everyone in every situation. That's why you need a large and varied tool box.

Find the tools that work for you and keep them close because recovery is a long process. Have you ever wondered why some people emerge from a trauma better, while others are left bitter? Often the difference boils down to the tools (coping skills) they have available to them as they emerge from their traumatic journey.

I am a victim-offender ameliorator, not a mediator. Inherent in the term mediation is the concept that both parties give and compromise. In the area of violent crimes, and that is the only area I work in, compromise is inappropriate. The victim has already given more than they ever consented to and it is inappropriate to ask for anything more. I teach people how to take a terrible experience and find its highest and best use.

About trauma, people often say things like "it will make you better" or "what doesn't kill you makes you better" etc... This is not true. It's just a saying that makes people feel better for a moment in time. Just because it didn't kill us doesn't mean it made us better. Many people become worse. Some people may become worse only for a short time and others may be forever scarred. If we have the option, it is ours, to become better. Again, just because a trauma didn't kill us doesn't mean we are automatically enhanced. We have to work to find the highest and best use. It doesn't just pour over us because it didn't kill us.

The experience itself does not make you better or stronger. The victim/survivor should have the opportunity to make themselves better and to learn and use the experience. But not all victims/survivors are offered this route. They are frequently left to incorporate the traumatic experience unprocessed, unexamined. This can leave them with all kinds of problems including criminal behavior, like my adolescent sex offenders. This chapter is designed to help those who want not only to survive the experience, but who want to learn as much as possible from it and possibly be enhanced by it. This chapter is for those who don't want to waste a terrible trauma. It also provides those that support the victim the information they need to do no harm, and actually even help.

People often ask me why I differentiate between a victim and a survivor. A victim is someone who either couldn't or wouldn't overcome their traumatic experience. Often this is through no fault of their own. Sometimes the physical trauma is so great that their body just couldn't survive, as with murder. Sometimes the emotional trauma was so great that their minds could not continue functioning as before, like some combat veterans. Sometimes they just refuse because they are so afraid of the pain they sedate the break-through pain in one way or another. These are victims.

Survivors are people who were physically and emotionally able to survive the trauma. They survive, maybe smarter than before, but that is all. Thrivers are people who take the experience and turn it inside out, upside down and round and round to learn what they can. They are the people who then take the experience and do something with it. They may start a grassroots movement, get laws passed, teach and support others or somehow use their horrible experience to contribute to their community. A survivor may also continue to live a quiet, productive life, and nothing more.

For example, I did a homicide amelioration where a 13-year-old boy picked up a gun and shot his 13-year-old friend in the head. After the amelioration and doing his time, he went into the schools to teach kids about the reality of guns. While he could never undo his fatal choice, he could use it to improve his community. The founder of Mothers Against Drunk Drivers (MADD) lost a child to a drunk driver. She could not bring her beloved child back, but she could change her community, and that she did! With the right mindset and tools we CAN change our world. Why do you think it is former addicts working with addicts or survivors of rape working with survivors of rape? Not only do they need to find meaning in their experience but they ARE the experts.

Just as I do not think that rape survivors have any obligation to report the crime and participate in a system that may revictimize them, you do not have to start a movement or do public speaking to be a survivor/thriver. A survivor/thriver overcomes the trauma and continues on with their life. A thriver heals themselves and then goes on to use the experience to help others in some way. They help some avoid bad experiences and teach others how to overcome them. Without them I would have had no one to teach me what was happening and why.

That does not mean that just because you heal quietly you are having no impact on your community or that you are not teaching and helping others. Some of my best teachers were quiet women, hidden away, who saw my suffering and opened their arms. They did not start a movement or do public speaking yet still had an incredible impact on their communities by opening their arms and hearts to young women that needed them. Some were good examples, no more or less.

There is no doubt that the work we do to overcome trauma is mind-bending, grueling and painful, but the rewards can not be measured. Not only do we, as the survivor, benefit. But everyone who comes in contact with us for the rest of our lives can potentially benefit from our work. Also, doing this work will help us to minimize and even avoid future traumas.

We all build toolboxes; but the difference is how we stock them. Your toolbox can be stocked with addictions, violence and bitterness, or you can stock up on insight, knowledge and experience. While it is easier in the short run just to deny the trauma and the rubbish it has left you with, in the long run this road is destructive. No good can come of it. Unfortunately this is what we see most often. The world is filled with parents who are destroying their children by sedating pain in one way or another. We have victims, raising victims, raising victims because no one has stopped to deal with and fix the "family traditions". In correctional facilities I don't just work with batterers and sex offenders. I work with crack babies, of crack babies, of fetal alcohol syndrome babies, of fetal alcohol syndrome.

Thrivers consciously choose to descend into the black abyss of the trauma in order to conquer the demons they were left with. Often they choose this descent without much faith that they will eventually rise back up and harvest any reward. These people unquestionably meet the definition of bravery. They are willing to do what they need to do, damn the fear. They choose to walk into a terrible sandstorm, shades down, and face the monsters while offering them their hand in peace. They can not slay them because the monsters must be studied, incorporated and made an ally. We can now turn to questions and comments I most frequently hear from victims and the tools I offer them. I have organized it with headings for the general topics.

God

Q: "How could God do such a thing? (How could God do this to me?)"

A: God gets blamed for everything when, in fact, all religions and science acknowledge both a negative and positive energy. Christianity speaks of God and the devil. Science notes the negative and positive energy and the Chinese Yin and Yang. God is not responsible for everything.

I would have no faith in a God who would use the types of traumas I've seen, to teach people. My God is compassionate and loving and when She sees children raped, animals tortured and man's inhumanity toward anything he can catch, She weeps with us. As a Christian (and Buddhist) I was taught that Christ died so that we could have free will and when humans use that free will to harm other beings my God is not responsible, but disgusted.

My God does not punish us or brutally take our child because "She needs another angel". Those are the acts of man. Some choose to use their free will to loot anything they can, and others use the same free will to enhance all they touch. Hearing horrible acts attributed to my loving God saddens me.

Q: *"God doesn't give us anymore than we can take."*
A: Again God does not give us trauma. And people are faced with more than they can take all the time. People "snap" and go on shooting sprees, kill their families and commit suicide all the time. "God won't give us anymore than we can take" is a nice thing to say and may provide some temporary comfort, but it just isn't true. It could actually be harmful if we leave it all to God and don't do what we need to do to support traumatized people. "God works through us" is more accurate.

How we take trauma depends a great deal on how we work to endure it and then overcome it. If we acknowledge the traumatic event and then vigilantly work to understand and ameliorate it, thriving afterwards is as close to a guarantee as we can get. If we deny the trauma, try to hide it and dismiss it, we may survive but thriving may not come.

Instincts

Q: *"I knew this was going to happen. Why didn't I listen to my gut?"*
A: Everyday, 24 hours a day, we are taking in information about ourselves, others and our environment. We are taking in so much verbal and non-verbal information that most of it is unconsciously going to our subconscious. Our brains could not possibly acknowledge everything that's coming in all the time. Regardless, the information is coming in and being filed.

When you get a gut feeling it could be an answer or a warning coming from that massive filing cabinet in your brain. We can't put logic or words to that gut feeling but we know it to be true. We can't rationally explain it and therefore we want to just dismiss it. Often we want to dismiss it because it isn't telling us what we want to hear. Maybe we tend to dismiss it because that's what we've been taught to do with things that come from our gut.

Many lives could be saved just by listening to that little voice in our head (heart or stomach, wherever yours is). Imagine a horse in the wild who gets the feeling that danger is around, but dismisses it. Instead the horse just stands there and tries to analyze why he feels a need to flee. In the time that the horse has wasted, she has probably sealed her place on the dinner menu. Horses are prey animals, which means that other animals eat them. In a world where a woman is beaten every 18 seconds and 3 out of 4 girls are sexually assaulted prior to age 18, the majority of our population also consists of prey animals. Like animals, humans are also prey and predator. Animals follow their instincts. Humans dismiss them, to their detriment.

    We are so much more than we can explain, and our capacity for knowledge and information storage is incredible. Maybe you picked up nonverbal cues from your father or boyfriend right before he beat you. You were so preoccupied with reducing your injuries that you didn't stop to intellectualize and analyze the information. And that is certainly wise. Somewhere in your brain you noticed, and filed the fact that, right before he hit you his right eye twitched. You did not have time to intellectualize then and you may not have the time now. Maybe you were only half listening to the description of the rapist that was broadcast on the news. But as this man approaches your car something inside of you is screaming. Listen!

    If you have seen something once, you have a good chance of predicting it in the future. This does not mean that if you fail to predict an assault it is your fault. Offenders can be quite resourceful and charming when it comes to picking and grooming their victims. But, if you've seen it once you certainly have an advantage. The trick IS to know you have seen it before and to react to the answer stored, without logical explanation, in your brain.

    There were reports that when the World Trade Center was attacked, people were fleeing the building when they were sent back to their offices by authority figures who told them it was safe. These peoples' instincts told them to flee the burning building. Yet many of these people set aside their instincts and common sense for a more comfortable scenario offered to them by an authority figure. This may have contributed to the deaths of many people who chose to dismiss what they knew to be true.

    For more information on gut feelings and safety read *The Gift of Fear* by Gavin DeBecker. This book is required reading for those who work with us and is a valuable tool in teaching women to be safe. One afternoon as my husband and I ran errands, I got a sharp pain in my chest and felt an urgent need to talk to Sara. Using my husband's cell phone, I began calling her father's house, trying to find her. I couldn't and we went on home.

As we walked through the door the phone was ringing and Sara was calling.
"Mom," she said, "Something is wrong with me and dad won't take me to the emergency room."
I had her put him on the phone and listened as he made one excuse after another, including that he was just getting ready to sit down to dinner. I told him that he had better take her now and used the most threatening voice I could muster. I told him where the nearest hospital was and arranged to meet him there. When we arrived they were not there. We called all around the city and found them at another hospital. It turned out that she was terribly sick. She had an infection that had gone to her lungs causing her terrible chest pains, somehow, I had sensed that.

On another occasion, after arriving home from the correctional facility, I opened the front door and let one of the dogs out to do her business. This was routine and normally not any concern. But that night, within minutes of letting her out, a panic came over me. In hindsight this is surprising because that property is laid out so that it takes minutes even to get off of the property. I told my husband and ask him to help me. Believing this was "just" another one of my panic attacks he refused. I began searching the property with no luck and went back to get help. My husband reluctantly joined me and showed his aggravation without inhibition. I was searching up by the greenhouse when I shined a light on a pair of eyes. It was Jade and, I couldn't put my finger on it but, she looked weird.

When she heard my voice, it was as if she knew she was safe and she collapsed. She is a very large dog and had apparently been hit by, and rolled under, a truck. We rushed her to the animal emergency room where she fought for life for several days. She lived, minus one leg, plus the signs of some terrible trauma.

Now when I tell my husband to slow down because I have the feeling we are going to hit a deer, he listens. His choice to listen is usually rewarded as we move up the road and find where we had just missed deer. Listening to that little voice inside of us can be extremely valuable for many reasons and serves many purposes.

Q: *"Every year I have a strong reaction to the trauma on the anniversary. What can I do?"*

A: Whether or not our mind remembers the trauma, our bodies and spirits do. In 1996 I suffered a severe brain injury as the result of a violent crime. One of the areas of my brain that sustained damage was the locus of time perception. I had no idea what year it was much less the date. I couldn't read or even tie my shoes. Yet one year to the day after the brain injury I lay curled up on the bed, crying. I felt so terribly traumatized and emotionally sloppy. I had no idea what was happening. I heard my husband's voice.

He said, "I didn't know whether or not to tell you this, but I see I have to. Today is the one-year anniversary."

Just knowing why I was so traumatized made the overwhelming emotions manageable.

Again, whether we consciously remember the anniversary or not, the memory of the trauma is stored in us. I often have this feeling of being unheard. Even when I know it isn't logical and I have been heard. This feeling can frustrate me and it has been here for as long as I can remember. I shared this with a family member who told me that as an infant I would cry and my parents would forbid anyone even to check on me much less offer comfort. I was left to cry alone, frequently and for long periods. My parents believed that this would teach me that I wasn't the center of the universe. Well, it worked. It also left me with the feeling that I was totally insignificant. If the family member hadn't shared this I still wouldn't understand the origin of this feeling and would struggle harder to heal it. Naming the source of the feeling doesn't cure it but it gives you a place to start.

Survivors have had great success with taking the anniversary of a traumatic event and making another memory or tradition. If you narrowly escaped death, celebrate a second birthday. Celebrate your survival. If you were sexually assaulted do something empowering like skydiving. If it is the death of a loved one volunteer on that date to rock crack babies or work in a children's home. You can be as creative as you like. Customize this day in the way that you need to in order to promote your own recovery. Make this a different kind of anniversary.

Facing The Problem

Q: "Why do I have to deal with this? It's over and done and I just want to move on with my life."

A: You have been physically, spiritually and emotionally wounded. You will remember it whether you want to or not. How much sense does the following scenario make to you?

You are hit by a car and an ambulance comes to take you to the hospital. Both your right arm and leg have horrible lacerations. When the doctor comes in, she stitches your injuries without first cleaning the gravel and road dirt out of the wounds. She sews you up including dirt, gravel and everything else that found its way into the wounds. You would probably stop her and insist on being tended by someone who knew what they were doing. You would, hopefully, insist that the debris be cleaned out before closing the wound because you know that if it isn't, you will get an infection. The debris might not be a problem for a day or two, maybe a week or months. Maybe you could even hold the infection at bay for years. But eventually that debris will demand that you deal with it. This is what you do for your body. You take care of it.

Your mind and spirit deserve no less. After a trauma, your mind, spirit and often your body are injured and need to be dealt with properly. Hard as you might try to ignore and conceal the debris, it will rise to the surface through addictions, sexualizing, anger, self-loathing…pick your dysfunction, and you will. Ignoring the debris will make it even more determined to be acknowledged. You can clean it now, reopen it and clean it later or spend your life fighting infection.

Hard as you might try to just move on, it's like carrying around a gigantic trash bag and every time something unpleasant happens, you shove it into the trash bag. After a while, stuffing everything in the bag just becomes habit; the good and the bad go into the bag. Instead of sorting and disposing of things as they come up, you just shove it into the trash bag. The trash bag becomes full and bulging, but you just keep toting it around, believing no one notices.

Then one day you're walking around, minding your own business with your (unnoticed) trash bag strapped to your back, when you bump the corner of the desk at work. The trash bag rips under all the stress and all of your trash comes pouring out in front of everyone. This is a point where you can deal with the issues or stuff them back into another bag. This is what we are witnessing when we see someone snap over what appears to be nothing.

Traumas give you valuable life experiences that can help others as well as yourself; give you insight and wisdom, or destroy everything they touch. You can deal with them in a controlled and constructive way similar to sorting and filing, or you can spend a lifetime cleaning up the remnants every time your overstuffed trash bag gets bumped. You can try to swallow them with food, wash them down with alcohol or sedate them with pills, but they will always resurface.

One of my adolescent offenders listened to these metaphors and analogies over and over with a blank look on his face. I was trying to find one that worked when I saw his face light up.
"I get it," he said, "It's like I have this computer program in the back of my mind running my computer. Some of the things that the program does I can see and other things I'm not even aware of. I can deny it all I want, but the program is still running my computer. All I have to do is get in there, find the program and fix it. Then I'll have control of my computer again."
"You got it."

Getting "Over" It

Q: I was ordered into counseling with the man who beat me. He denied everything and the counselors response was "There is no reality, only perception." How can this be?

A: There is no reality, only perception. Yeah, tell that one to the judge. "Your honor, there is no reality, only perception. She just thinks I raped (cheated on, assaulted, murdered) her. That's not my reality." It can't be. Anyone who is thinking clearly knows that there is reality and there is perception. While there are gray areas and misunderstandings, there are also undisputable truths and yet we are subjecting trauma survivors to this denial strategy of "I can say it ain't so, so therefore it isn't, end of discussion." Having their reality invalidated by "educated professionals" is terribly damaging to the victim/survivor.

Psychology has given many abusers an out by rewarding their denial. The message is all you have to do is deny your behavior and that's the end of that. While you sit with a blackened face and busted mouth being told it is only your perception, he has been handed denial and validation. End of discussion; because it is only your perception, according to some mental health service providers. And the offender thanks God for the out. **Find a new counselor or enlist the help of your local battered women's organization to have a stop put to the court ordered revictimization.**

Q: "Will I ever get over this?"

A: It depends on how you define "over it". You have gone through an experience that has forever changed you. You will never be the same, so forget that goal. As I said earlier you can be changed for better or worse. While the trauma may not have been your responsibility, it is your responsibility if at all possible, to squeeze as much positive out of that lemon as you can. This is not to say that your torture and trauma had a divine purpose. It is to say that you have an experience that you really do not want to be in vain. You can use it to benefit yourself and others or degrade yourself and others.

Right now the experience feels painful and awkward to you. It is new. It may feel as if you have a third arm sticking out of the middle of your chest. The arm is painful and it flops around a lot. You don't have much control over it and it causes you to cry a lot. You are, predictably, furious that you have been saddled with this third arm. You may be ashamed of and embarrassed by this seemingly ridiculous appendage and you can't seem to get control over it. You can't predict from one moment to the next what the damn thing is going to do.

You go through the stages of grief. You try to bargain with God. You deny the arm is really there and sometimes you just feel furious. But, as time goes on you get more comfortable with the arm. You just start accepting it. You are learning how to control it and all of a sudden you are noticing how many other people are also walking around with this stupid arm. In time you realize that you can use that arm to rock another baby, wipe another tear or stroke another head. While you often see people using the third arm to hurt other people, maybe they are using it to hold an extra weapon. You eventually hone your skills with it and find it to be a great asset.

You will never be the person you were before the trauma. You will be better, different or worse, but you won't be the same. You can't "unsee" what you've already seen. You can deny it but what you have seen has still been filed in your brain. They are still in your subconscious. You HAVE seen it. When we see former addicts working with addicts, formerly-battered women working with battered women and survivors of rape working with victims of rape, it is because they have learned to use their experience positively. They have developed the muscles in that third arm. "They have come to see the power in their knowledge and they chose to use it to help others."

Reaching out to others is a vital part of recovery. When we see others who have a third arm it alleviates our shame and embarrassment. When we spend time with people who have a third arm we learn skills from them. When we can help others who are struggling, our lives are enhanced immeasurably. It is very difficult to rock a baby dying of AIDS and still feel overwhelmed by our own trauma. This is not to say that we cover our own trauma with the trauma of others. Wait until you have done your own recovery and then reach out to teach and help others, especially when we have experiences and wisdom they desperately need.

The experience, like the arm, will never go away. People often say, "I need closure." Some doors always remain cracked. Not all of them can be closed. You can choose to become comfortable with it, allow it to become a part of you and eventually have a great asset. You can use the asset for peace; healing and enlightenment; for evil; or you can just let it flop around. Regardless of what you choose, the arm is yours now and forever, to do with as you please, which includes spending a lot of time and energy pretending it isn't there. Be patient with yourself. If recovery and thriving is what you seek and you are taking the steps, it will happen."

Q: "I am left with such a big hole in my life. There are things I need that my parents never gave me. How do I fill these holes?"
A: All of us have inner children. All of us actually have several inner children which represent critical periods in our lives. Inner child work can be powerful. How old were you at critical moments in your life? Do you have a neglected four-year-old? Do you have an abused ten-year-old or a raped 12-year-old? Do you find them running the show at inopportune moments?

Do you find yourself reverting to a ten-year-old after being with your family for the holidays? Does your wife complain that you act like an eight-year-old over toys? Do you experience anger that you felt when you were fifteen and the cheerleader took your boyfriend? Acknowledge these inner children, bring them into the light and give them the attention and guidance that they need. The have gone unacknowledged for far too long and as an adult you now have the power to give them what they need. Not only do you carry these inner children around with you, but you now have a more experienced, more mature adult to give them what they need to heal.

Elliot was a dangerous, 18-year-old sex offender who had been incarcerated, in one way or another, all of his life. He had gone from foster homes to group homes to the correctional facility. Elliot desperately needed help and for a long time I refused. I believed that Elliot was not sincere and that he and the staff viewed working with me as his ticket out of the facility. Whenever I thought that was the case, I refused. I am a firm believer that what I do with offenders being in addition to, not instead of, consequences imposed by the courts. Anyway, I finally agreed to help him with his lack of empathy. To do this, I had to put the trauma he experienced face-to-face with the trauma he caused.

Elliot had been so traumatized that I had to spend the first weeks teaching him to communicate so I could understand him. All of his life, anything that he may have wanted to say to the world was drowned out by his slurring, mumbling and stuttering. People usually just dismissed him as opposed to putting in the work required to understand him. Elliot progressed quickly and I soon found out that I had been right. The staff had used me to facilitate Elliot's release and I knew that I either had to get this right or step up and fight against his release. I didn't want to do the latter because my policy is not to help or hinder their release. I had to get some important information into his head quick.

"You remember a beating when you were seven?" I asked.
He nodded shyly.
"So a wounded seven-year-old is part of what you carry around?" I asked.
Again, he nodded.
"And the 14-year-old was the one who violently raped your sister. Is that right?" I asked.
Again, he simply nodded.
"And right now you have an 18-year-old who knows a lot more than the hurt seven-year-old or the angry 14-year-old," I said.
He again nodded in agreement.
"So, Elliot, what are you going to do with that seven-year-old and 14-year-old when they start wanting to run the show?" I ask.

For the first time that day I saw his facial expression change. It was clear that Elliot got my point. Prior to that day the only tools he had to control his dangerous inner child was the restraint of the guards. He was about to add one that he could control.

"I want you to close your eyes and imagine that hurt, wounded little seven-year-old. I want you to hear the horrible things your mother would say to him and the names she called him," I paused to give him time to frame up the images before I added another, "And Elliot I want you to think about that cowering position he used to take as she hits him over and over."

I could see the hurt on his face as his eyes remained closed.

"He's totally helpless, Elliot, and he has no one to protect him, does he?"

Elliot nodded as his face seemed to collapse inward. His shoulders began to slump and his hair fell back over his eyes again. I knew he was hiding. This was a response we had spent a lot of time on but now it was okay, safe for him.

"But that's not true today Elliot. Picture yourself as you look today," I paused, "You are a strong young man and your seven-year-old needs you. Imagine your 18-year-old walking into the picture and scooping the hurt seven-year-old into your arms. Hold him on your lap, really close to you, Elliot. You are no longer seven and you can protect him. You can hold him and love him and protect that hurt little baby boy for the rest of his life. That's one of the benefits of growing up. We have age, skills and tools to help us through life."

I could see the peace taking over his face. He raised his head and moved his hair back. I was surprised that he trusted me enough to really go there. So often people feel stupid or afraid to actually go to the hurt they feel. This young man wasn't and I knew his willingness to go there could be his saving grace and, quite possibly, that of others.

"Sit down with him, Elliot, and hold him in your lap. Have your 18-year-old tell him how important he is and how much you love him." Elliot's eyes opened, flooded with tears. He looked at me with gratitude and wonder.

"Elliot you no longer have to leave the seven-year-old in pain or let the 14-year-old be violent. You have an 18-year-old that can love and honor the seven-year-old and make the 14-year-old behave.

Think about it. If you were running your own business would you let one of them run the show?" I ask.

"No," he answered quickly, shocked at the prospect.

"Well you certainly can't let them run your life, because your life **is** your business. It's all you have and those two just don't have the skills to run the show. You have an 18-year-old for a reason. That seven and 14-year-old need you. And in time you will have a 23-year-old and a 30-year-old that know even more."

Elliot understood this new tool and I saw immediate results. Whether or not he was able to use it enough to make a difference, I don't know. No one asked me how I felt about him leaving the facility, I certainly felt deceived by the staff, but I felt quietly positive about his future.

Inner-child work can be used in a multitude of ways. While trying to stop smoking I imagined an addicted 14-year-old who simply wanted what she wanted, consequences be damned. I used 14 because I started smoking at 12, and 14 was probably about the time when the addiction was really strong. I also chose 14 because the determination to smoke mimics the determination that my 14-year-old had.

When the determined little addict hidden deep inside me started throwing a fit for a cigarette I imagined my firm, logical 43-year-old saying, "No."

And maybe my 14-year-old screamed, threatened, flopped across the bed and swore I was ruining her life. But the fact remained I would not let a child eat a bag of candy for dinner anymore than I would allow a 14-year-old to smoke.

I must confess that after four days that 14-year-old got the best of me. She is younger and has stamina I can't imagine ever having. One day, in the midst of the crisis du jour, I ripped the patch from my arm, flopped across the bed and started screaming, "I hate you. I hate you. You're ruining my life."

While I joke about the 14-year-old getting the best of me, the point is that we don't necessarily achieve our goals on the first try. However, practice does make perfect and eventually I will stretch that four days into the remainder of my life.

Q: "My family (ex-husband, mother, sister etc…) has hurt me deeply. Every time I go around them my problems get worse. What can I do?"

A: Relatives are the only abusers that we are expected to continue relationships with, and some judges may even order us to do so. All of our lives we are told that family is the most important thing. Sayings like, "Blood is thicker than water," often make it difficult for us to cut the ties of a toxic relationship and to move on with our lives. When someone consistently causes you harm you have no obligation to that person, blood or not. Respect is not something you have to earn. You are entitled to it and then you keep it based on your actions. I am a firm believer in no contact policies with people who repeatedly disrespect and hurt us.

Life is very short and our mental health can be fragile and tentative. Do you really have time to spin your tires in the same old ditch? A popular definition for insanity is, "Doing the same thing over and over expecting a different result."
Say you have a choice of several roads and at the end of one of them sits the home of the person who repeatedly hurts you. The road up to that house is muddy, winding and treacherous and every time you use the road you get stuck in a ditch. Do you keep using that road?

Animals have no denial. You do not see animals intentionally put themselves into situations where they will be harmed. The mouse does not curl up with the cat because he feels a need to "work it out". The cat does not befriend an aggressive dog because she believes in the dog's "potential". The zebra does not deny that the lion means them harm. If they did, it would only happen once. Yet humans will repeatedly put themselves in the same dangerous situations, denying previous experience, over and over. It is only humans that practice denial. And we think we're superior?

When we continue going into violent or abusive gatherings or relationships, we are not protecting ourselves or our inner child. We are not protecting our children, our future and we are denying ourselves the full opportunity of recovery, self respect and dignity. Every time you go back into those situations, you are saying to all of the elements of yourself that, "You don't matter. I won't protect you. You are nothing without their approval."

At 12 years old I became an "habitual runaway". I wanted to take my sister with me but, aside from the fact that she wouldn't have considered it, there was no way I could take care of her. I was only a baby myself. As our lives went on I learned and I tried not to deny what I saw. I knew education would be my ticket to the life I wanted (violence free).

My sister, on the other hand, stayed with the family trying desperately to win our father's approval. I struggled in a lot of ways but my struggles were totally different from those of my sister. All my life I had worked hard to maintain as much distance between my abusive family as I could, while my sister worked hard for our father's approval. I went 10 years without seeing them at all. My sister never quit seeking approval and I broke my 10-year no-contact policy when she died because of her choices. I felt it was appropriate for me to attend her funeral and, deep down, I hoped the family had learned something about the effect their abuse was having on the two targets (my sister and me). They hadn't and the no-contact had to be reinstated.

If someone is causing you harm your life may depend on your ability to just cut your losses and move on. Whether it is an abusive birth family or a battering husband we have no control over the behavior of others. There are times when we can't totally cut off contact with toxic people. If you have children with a batterer, the courts may make no contact impossible. Our courts have not progressed to where they need to be and I write more on this in the chapter about service providers. Situations where you can't cut off contact are good candidates for detachment.

Detachment

Detachment has been one of the most effective tools in my toolbox. The Serenity Prayer goes:
God, grant me the serenity to accept the things I cannot change
The courage to change the things I can
And the wisdom to know the difference.

This is a good starting point for detachment. Let's start with the second line. "The courage to change the things I can." When you see a man beating his dog, child or spouse, can you change that? Maybe, maybe not. But you should certainly try. We live in a world where people don't want to get involved because they are afraid of the consequences to them. This is appalling. There is nothing worse than a good person who watches suffering and does nothing.

When we walk away from the child who has just been slapped in the grocery store or turn our heads to the man beating his dog we are sending very strong messages to both the victim and the offender. To the victim we are saying at least that they are invisible, that we don't care about them and at most that we think they deserve it. To the perpetrator we are saying that their violence is acceptable to us or that we are also afraid and influenced by the willingness to use violence.

One afternoon I saw a woman standing over a stroller yelling at it and punching into the pile of blankets and the child beneath. She was using her fists and I had security confront her while I stood there. She bullied them too and they backed down. When they left she followed me through the mall screaming and threatening me. She followed me all the way to the car and, yes, I was scared. This was at least 20 years ago and I often think about that child. I do find comfort in the fact that I tried. If we turn our heads away, we also have blood on our hands. This is how we change the things we can. But after I gave it my best I had to accept what I could not change and that was that this child would experience a life of beatings. This is where detachment helps.

I do not mean detachment as in, "I don't care about you." I mean detachment as in, "I can't change this situation right now so I have to reduce it's effect on me." When you cannot change a person or situation, detachment helps you keep from getting sucked into it. If you can not physically pull yourself out of a situation, then you can emotionally do it and reduce the effect it has on you.

For example, when you have to see your battering ex-husband because of the children, you can emotionally pull yourself out of the mix. If you are no longer at physical risk you can interact with him as if he is someone else's ex. You are just there to accomplish another daily chore and cross it off your list. He is of no significance to you. Maybe you can use the image of being a bystander and watching the interaction. Maybe you can use the image of moving from the emotional right side of your brain to the logical left. Or you could interact with him as if you are a social scientist and you are interested in seeing what he does next.

View the situation as out of your control, not your responsibility, a learning opportunity and possibly even entertaining. Find an image that works for you. Instead of being a sponge that soaks up everything, how about using an image of being covered in polyurethane? Nothing can get in. If you can remove your emotions from the mix, the behaviors of others can be fascinating and educational. Keep yourself from soaking up the abusers behavior. It is possible to avoid some of the weight of his emotional and mental abuse. But remember, if he is using your children to abuse you, you have the right to report that and to protect yourself from that as best you can. It is possible, and preferable, to defend and protect yourself from a detached position.

Watching also helps you better understand them and what they might do next. If you are upside down in a vat of tar, how can you see, much less have an impact on, the world around you? Detaching from your emotions can help you to understand that their behavior has absolutely nothing to do with you and everything to do with them. When my ex calls me filthy names it is no reflection or definition of me, but of him. Another benefit of detachment is that the offender may lose all gratification if you stop responding. It might not be as much fun for your ex to call you a slut if it doesn't make you angry or cry. When behavior isn't rewarded it may stop. Try saying to yourself, "This has absolutely nothing to do with me and everything to do with him." What comes out of someone else's mouth is only a reflection of them, not a definition of you.

During the periods when I did attend family gatherings I used to walk away crushed that the event didn't go better. I so desperately wanted that human sanctuary called family. I was always shocked that they would misbehave when the true shocker would have been if they had behaved any other way. Then I learned detachment and the amusement was truly unending and the learning invaluable. This enhanced my ability to see negative family patterns and victim blaming which offered powerful insight. It's hard to see things as they are when we think it's all about us. Their behavior is about no one but them.

I remember one Thanksgiving, curled up on the couch reading as my sister worked hard to engage me in the usual argument. I continued reading as she escalated her attempts, determined to get a response. I put the book down and watched, probably more for safety reasons, but at this point the entertainment value was through the roof. Then out of nowhere I watched a head of cauliflower whiz by my head, thud against the wall and explode into a zillion flourettes. She had pitched me a fastball and from the looks of it she had been fueled by some serious drugs or anger, probably both.

For the first time I was not being pulled into the mix and it felt good. It was amazing to watch the behavior of the others in the room after spending so many years upside down in the vat of tar. For the first time I was an outsider looking in and learning a lot about the dynamics of a family that seemed to rot with age. Accumulation of grace and wisdom certainly was not a family goal. Unfortunately, my sister escalated to the point of canned goods and bringing a chandelier down on one of my daughters. That was the point when it was no longer physically safe. We packed up and drove the 120 miles home and that was when my 10 years of no contact began. That is how detachment works. Step out of yourself, watch, learn and be entertained. It has nothing to do with you and everything to do with them.

Detachment is different than dissociation which I talk about later. Whether you have been traumatized or not, detachment is a worthy skill to master. Whether it is to minimize damage to yourself or to block out things that are happening to another being, detachment can reduce trauma. With detachment you can view what is happening and live to bear witness to the events you have seen.

Q: "Why would my husband (mother, sister, brother etc...) do this to me?"

A: The most common question I hear on this subject, is in relation to child abuse. It is so sad to look at the face of a young man whose mother abused substances while he was in utero, and try to answer this question. As cold as it may sound, the answer I offer these young people is, "It was nothing personal." While abuse is very personal, it has absolutely nothing to do with the victim and everything to do with the offender. As personal as it may have felt, it was nothing personal. If I had been your mother's child she would have abused drugs. If she had given birth to Martin Luther King Jr. she would have abused drugs. If she had been carrying the baby Jesus she still would have used drugs. This had nothing to do with who you are and everything to do with your mother and her addiction.

Battered women often wonder why he beats them. As much as he blames you, it is not your fault. All of his justifications are contrived. If he had none of the justifications he recites, he would find another. Batterers always justify their violence. The violence comes before the reason. Again, if he had married me, he would have beaten me. If he had married a supermodel he would have beaten her. If he had married the virgin Mary he would have beaten her. As personal as a beating is, it has nothing to do with you.

The same goes for the child who is singled out and scapegoated by the entire family. The family was going to pick out one member to abuse. That's where all of the family's rage and anger is vented. It is hard to know why one child is singled out over another. It may be some type of a health issue or handicap. It may be the child's personality but the fact remains, if there are three children you had a 33% chance of being "it". Again, as personal as it is, it is nothing personal.

The young man who asks why his mother poisoned him in utero needs to understand that it was her addiction. The battered woman needs to realize that she is being battered out of his anger and need to control her, rather than her actions. The young girl who does not understand why she was raped by her father needs to know that he would have done that to any daughter he had been blessed with. It was not you. It was him. As personal as it was to you, it was nothing personal. While that may not offer us all of the comfort we seek it is an important answer to the question.

Post Traumatic Stress Disorder & Vicarious Trauma

***Q:** "I have been told I have Post Traumatic Stress Disorder (PTSD). What is this?"*

A: PTSD is when, after a traumatic event, the victim still suffers from the event with a number of serious problems. These include:

> overactive startle reflex
> nightmares
> night terrors
> night sweats
> panic attacks
> flashbacks of the event
> general anxiety etc...

  The victim continues reliving the event when it is plugged into or poked in some way and the symptoms of the trauma manifest themselves in their everyday life in many ways such as: generalized anxiety, overactive startle reflex and panic attacks.

  I had one doctor say that PTSD is rare and he has never seen anyone who actually has it other than a couple of combat veterans. Fortunately, I have only heard this expressed once. While many war veterans have seen horrors that most of us cannot imagine, it does not mean that others' responses to trauma are any less real. Pain is relative. I have seen people go to pieces over things I was sure they could easily handle, and I have seen people take much more trauma than I imagined possible. Comparing traumas doesn't work because pain is relative and we all experience the world differently.

  I authored a piece on medical trauma. A victim of medical malpractice compared her reaction to medical abuse to the reaction she had when she was raped. Her description was certainly consistent with the other 22 victims I took to Chicago to do victim impact with the American Medical Association. These people had been horribly tortured and traumatized. After publication I received a call from a woman in New York.

She was very upset and said, "My infant son was killed in a local hospital by malpractice and I am also a survivor of rape. There is no comparison," and to my horror and surprise she continued, "The rape was much worse."

I told her I respected her opinion but would certainly be interested in what her son thought was the more traumatic of the two. We cannot compare traumas like cars or show dogs. Pain is relative.

Panic Attacks

Q: "I have overwhelming panic attacks. What can I do?"
A: Panic attacks cause a lot of physical as well as emotional symptoms. Some of these symptoms are: stomach cramping and diarrhea; racing heart; racing mind; sweats; etc…

Carry a pen and notebook. When you feel a panic attack coming on stop what you are doing and write down what is going through your mind. This is similar to vomiting up your story except that it serves some other purposes. Writing what you are thinking will slow down your brain. Write until the panic subsides and then later go back and read it. You will get insight into the panic. You will see how ludicrous some of these fears are and you can find triggers and issues that you can deal with.

For example, after six years of no panic, after 9/11, I started having panic attacks again. Because my husband and I study the human and animal response to trauma, we are home to many rescue animals. I was afraid and panicked by everything. The fears around the animals were endless, but I will use the example of the kittens. I was afraid they would run off. This was totally irrational because the nearest neighbor is a long-distance phone call. I was afraid they would be eaten by coyotes. This was a possibility. I was also afraid they would be stepped on by horses, also highly possible. Writing about the fears helped me to figure out what was rational and what wasn't.

For a short time after 9/11, I started caging the kittens. This was not reasonable. Having managed a Humane Society I knew that this was a common practice but not by us. This is an inhumane practice. I was reducing their quality of life out of my fears. Like the rest of the nation I watched in horror as thousands of people were murdered. My panic was controlling me and caging those little kittens was no more practical than caging my daughters. The solution came in the form of a house being converted into a cattery and a great deal of detachment. The cattery was much easier to construct than the detachment. I had to do the best that I could to protect life and accept that bad things happen to innocent beings.

As you accumulate a "panic journal" you will have a record of the thoughts that are paralyzing you. Even if this doesn't help immediately, it will give you a record of your thoughts to work on. This paralysis is degrading your life. As you scrutinize your thoughts and analyze the issues behind them you can make choices with information as the meat of your decision. Choices such as: do you want to continue wasting precious time on ridiculous fears? Do you need medication? Is this or that a situation you can change or must you accept it?

Q: "Why do I get so upset over things I hear or see? I don't understand."
A: After a traumatic event, witnessing another traumatic event, whether it's happening to you or not, can bring out the initial feelings you experienced. This is called vicarious trauma and can happen whether you suffer from Post Traumatic Stress (PTS) or not. For example, seeing a cat kill a bird can provoke an intense reaction that others just don't understand. Maybe you don't even understand it, but you certainly feel it.

The trigger may be something as obvious as a friend being raped within months of your own trauma. The trigger can be as subtle as seeing a man in the grocery store wearing the same shirt your batterer wore when he beat you. You must find and be very aware of your triggers and how you react. If you are walking through life reacting to these triggers without awareness, you will feel out of control. If feelings and emotions have a reason, rhyme, pattern and explanation it is easier to say, "This isn't happening right now. I am remembering it. I'm not crazy. I am not in danger from this memory. Something has plugged into the memory."

Q: *"I am always overwhelmed by feelings that others are experiencing. What is going on?"*
A: I am frequently approached by survivors who feel constantly overwhelmed by feelings. This can be crippling. Have you been pregnant and cried, seemingly without reason, or watched a pregnant woman who cries at every television commercial? This is what these people are experiencing except it isn't tied to pregnancy. Just as I see young men who have no apparent empathy, I also see people who fall on the other end of the spectrum and are truly empathic.

Empaths are people who deeply understand and feel the feelings of others. It may only be because their own traumas are being plugged into or it may be more. The result remains the same. They can be crippled with emotional pain or they can learn to control and direct the empathy and have a profound impact on others. Often empathic people don't understand what is happening. They may be diagnosed as depressed, and they need information and support as they make sense of what is happening to them.

Feelings

Q: "How do I deal with this anger?"

A: The first thing you should do with anger, and most other feelings, is to allow them. Don't resist a moment of <u>healthy</u> anger. Anger is an intensely physical feeling and needs to be dealt with physically as well as emotionally. How many women do you know who can clean their entire house because they're angry at their husband? My mother would literally add another room onto the house if she got mad enough at my father. I think by the time they sold that house she had added on six or seven times. I dealt with anger by becoming good at shooting baskets on the court and, following in my mothers shoes, I can do a mean drywall seam. Anger is a powerful motivator. Deep anger about injustice, channeled properly, can fuel the most meaningful advocacy and social change movements.

However, the entire time we are constructively giving physical expression to anger, we need to be examining it. At the same time we are giving anger a physical outlet we need to be doing something like writing, singing or drawing so that we can understand it. Get the feelings up and out like vomiting. Tell your story over and over. Write about it until you're exhausted. The feelings, left pushed down, are toxic and like vomiting it may be uncomfortable to bring up, but you feel better afterwards. Get the feeling up and out. Anger suppressed truly will eat us alive. Do whatever it takes creatively and constructively to get the anger up and out of your body.

While we are constructively dealing with the feeling of anger we need to be examining it. I visualize anger as a slab of raw liver sitting in my hand. You want to examine every bit of it. Poke it. Watch how it responds. Turn it over and look at the other side. You want to learn everything you can about this feeling and your response to it. How do I feel when I get angry? Does my stomach churn? Do my shoulders tighten? Look at your triggers. What just happened? When did I start feeling this? Is this mine to deal with or someone else's? How am I venting this? Who is around me? Am I taking this out on my child? Do I have a taste in my mouth?

Am I hot or cold? Ask yourself all the questions you can think of to learn about yourself. There is no better investment.

Examine every side and every angle of that feeling and then slowly and gently peel the anger up and look at what's underneath it. I suspect that you will find hurt or maybe sadness. You might find feelings of inadequacy or vulnerability. Maybe there is a memory or a smell that is provoking the feeling. Anger frequently covers other feelings that we are less comfortable with or vice versa. Maybe we are more comfortable with hurt or sadness. If that's the case do the same thing with it. Allow it, examine it, feel it and then lift it up and see what it is covering. Some people are more comfortable with hurt than anger. The exercise will work on all of our feelings.

Another good tool for feelings is to put a time limit on certain behaviors. If you feel a need to go to bed and cry then allow yourself that but put a time limit on it. For example, "I will give myself three days (weeks, months) to lay in bed and cry." The time limit depends on the trauma and what you need. If your child has been killed, then three days of tears will probably not satisfy you and is an unreasonable expectation. Victims find this tool quite helpful. Put a logical time limit on any one indulgence.

You will probably have to do it over and over but each time you have to deal with the feeling it gets easier. Almost every exercise we do during recovery has to be done repeatedly. Recovery and grief is not a straight line. You go back and forth, in and out of the stages. Just because you have been through denial does not mean you are done with it and won't go back.

Q: "I find myself feeling so powerless. What can I do?"
A: A good exercise I have found for finding your power is to go back to the inner children I discussed. Scan the years and mindsets of your life and find the period when you felt powerful, unstoppable. Quietly remember that period and what it felt like to feel strong. Soak in it. Practice recreating that mindset and eventually powerless will just automatically be replaced by the thoughts you had during your powerful period.

Q: "I find myself feeling so guilty. How can I make this go away?"
A: Working with the populations that I do (victims and offenders) I have come to believe that guilt is not a feeling we should dismiss. Guilt is a "red flag" feeling. If you feel guilty about something it is probably because you need to either stop doing it or change the way you are doing it. After you have stopped or changed it and made all the amends that you can, guilt is a terrible waste of time.

Guilt is different than shame. Guilt is when you feel bad about something that you are doing. Shame is when you allow that behavior to become part of who you are and you are "ashamed" of yourself. Shame is a destructive feeling. It is akin to "I am bad" as opposed to, "my action was bad."

Q: "Just when I think I have control of my destructive behaviors, they resurface. What can I do?"
A: While recovering from a trauma we often find ourselves going over the same old feelings, the same tired behaviors and we feel like we are just going in circles. And for awhile, we are going to be going over the same old ground. For example, the stages of grief are denial, bargaining, anger etc... but just because we went through a stage doesn't mean we're done with it. We can be ambushed and feel like we're right back where we started. But it isn't so. Every time we step back a little, we go back with more experience. We can better manage the feeling because we know the terrain, we've been there before.

I do not consider crying, going back to bed, temporary withdrawal or constructive physical outlets for anger to be destructive behaviors. These are behaviors that can help us get a feeling out of our system and help us find our balance again. If you find yourself relapsing back into abusive relationships, substance abuse, sexualizing, eating disorders, shopping, gambling etc...you have not dealt with the cause. Are you trying to skip steps? Are you trying to use a band-aid on kidney failure? Or are you sewing up a laceration without cleaning it? Don't confuse symptoms with causes. You have to deal with the cause to alleviate the symptoms and deep negative beliefs about ourselves are often at the root of destructive behaviors.

This is true with some exceptions. There are many behaviors that you can just stop. If the behavior is coming from a severe trauma or a deep-seated thinking error it may reappear as something else if you don't deal with the cause. You may stop sexualizing only to find yourself drinking. Dealing with the cause of destructive behaviors is painful work and many people absolutely refuse to go there. Turning yourself inside out like a sock is one of the hardest and most rewarding things you will ever do. This is where a skilled counselor or advocate, knowledgeable about trauma, can be an essential guide and support. This is also a time when the wrong choice in counselor or advocate can do terrible damage.

Dissociation
Q: "I often have a feeling like I am not there. I notice it especially during stressful times. It's as if my mind isn't in my body. What is this?"
A: Dissociation is a tool that we use to protect our mind from traumatic experiences. We are not usually initially aware of what we are doing. Survivors of rape and assault might describe a feeling of not being there during the assault. They might describe it as projecting their mind outside of their body. They might describe it as sending their mind deep into their body to protect it. "I have no power over what is happening to my body but I can protect my mind."

Often, survivors of child abuse have blank periods in their lives that they just can't remember. Law enforcement may be totally perplexed and simply dismiss a rape survivor who can't remember details they believe should be obvious. The rape survivor may not remember what the perpetrator looked like, but have nightmares about the smell for the rest of her life. The closest I could describe it to someone who has never felt it, is day dreaming to the extreme. While this survival strategy of the mind may be quite efficient at protecting the mind it is frequently used to discredit the victims and to paint them as "crazy".

Sometimes the victim finds that she is losing time and the dissociation is continuing. This can be triggered by a memory, a smell or something else around us that leads us to believe we need to protect ourselves. While separating our mind from our body may feel more comfortable, if you are truly in danger, you need to bring everything that you have to the situation to avoid injury or minimize the damage. Dissociation could mean that you miss a cue or a chance for escape. An image I have heard used is "instead of closing your eyes, put on some dark shades." You need your mind to protect your body. Imagine one of those inner children. Would you leave them alone in a dangerous situation? No, you wouldn't. Then don't do it to yourself now.

The "F" Word (forgiveness)

Q: "My abuser wants forgiveness. Why do I have to forgive him?"

A: You don't have to forgive anyone. For a perpetrator to even ask for forgiveness is inappropriate and out of line. You should not be asked to give anything to the perpetrator. You have already given more than you ever consented to. It is appropriate and even expected that the offender apologize. That's it. They should not ask for forgiveness. The state of your forgiveness, like your uterus, is between you, your best friend, your doctor and your God. But it is important that you "let go" and move on when you can. This has become the popular definition for forgiveness.

I detest the word forgiveness because so many people believe that they are entitled to it and that they can do as they please and then ask for forgiveness. There is a saying, "Better to ask forgiveness than to ask permission." Unfortunately many offenders and abusers live by that code. People not only do this with their day-to-day life but with their conscience and higher power. They live a self serving life and then, on their death beds, ask for forgiveness. They believe they can walk through life leaving a trail of destruction and then say the magic word (the "F" word) and have the slate wiped clean. This is not the case with our day-to-day relationships, nor do I believe it's the case with our souls.

Since, after someone hurts us, this is a predictable request, I want to define the word. I do not see the word the way it is used in pop psychology. I do not see it as simply letting go. I do not see the word as saying, "What you did to me is okay," either. Nor does forgiveness mean that you will ever forget what that person is capable of. In fact, it is imperative that you never forget. If they did it to you once, chances are pretty good they will do it to you again. The biggest predictor of future behavior is past behavior.

    I remember the day I told my father that I forgave him. In a tone of righteous indignation he said, "I don't need your forgiveness."
I said, "I know you don't, but I need to forgive you."
What I was saying to him was that what he did was not okay. I would never forget how he was capable of treating me. But I do realize he is human and will make mistakes and I accept this. I may never see him again because of the unhealthy nature of the relationship. I may never speak to him again because of the hurt I feel when I do, but I do accept that he is human and has done these things to me.

    That is what it means when I say, "I forgive you." No more. No less. The person that harmed you may be totally oblivious and unaffected by your forgiveness or statement. They were oblivious to your feelings before or they never would have harmed you. Don't expect anything. You are not "forgiving" to aid their recovery, in fact that probably doesn't exist. You are saying, "I accept that you are human and humans disappoint and often hurt each other."

Q: "But I want to do more than just accept. The person that hurt me is really remorseful and I want to forgive them. How do I do this?"
A: If the person that harmed you is someone close to you then you are probably aware of their childhood. While my mother shared little about herself with me I had enough information to form a picture of her as a child in my mind. Although my mother has never even admitted she hurt me, much less asked for forgiveness, I needed to understand and make sense of how she treated me.

    Virginia (my mother) was raised by her grandmother in a household with 16 aunts and uncles. A number of those in the household had been diagnosed with paranoid schizophrenia and I had seen enough of their behaviors to understand what that meant.

Virginia was born out of wedlock and openly referred to as the "little bastard."

I sat back and pictured her as a little girl. She told of the school bus pulling up to her house and to her horror, and the other childrens' amusement, her aunt sat on the porch with paper bags covering her hands, feet and head. She told of her grandmother backhanding her and bloodying her mouth and nose. I pictured the pain of a little girl hated because she was born out of wedlock and scapegoated by all of the people she loved and counted on. I knew that if these were the things she remembered and would share, what were the horrors she refused to share or totally blocked out?

This image, of someone who actively and viciously set out to cause me pain, went a long way toward forgiveness. This does not mean that I can allow her access to me. While intellectually I know that she scapegoated me because of her own history, the emotionally wounded inner child still struggles with hurt. But the image of this abused little girl put my mother's actions in perspective. It had nothing to do with me and everything to do with her. To protect ourselves we must never forget who is who and what they are capable of.

Q: "I know I was not responsible for the abuse I suffered. But deep inside of me I still feel guilty and ashamed. How do I forgive myself?"

A: Battered women are not only blamed for the abuse by the batterer but by society. Every time they are asked why they stay there is an implicit statement that they could leave. The same with rape and sexual assault. Young children naturally think everything is their fault. These are the reasons that "forgiving" ourselves can be so difficult.

Think about one of the significant incidents of abuse that you survived. How old were you? If you were four, picture yourself in all of your childish glory. If you were 14, imagine the awkward age. Did you wear heavy glasses? Were you overweight? Get out a picture of yourself to help you remember yourself at the time of the abuse. Were you 22 when he beat you or were you 22 to 56? Take a few deep breaths and quietly listen to all the chatter that surrounds your abused self. It may sound something like, "You're a piece of shit. You caused this. It's your fault. You don't deserve to live," and on and on.... Listen to all the self blame.

Now I want you to get a mental image of someone that you love and cherish who is the same age as you were at the time of your abuse. Is it your 22-year-old daughter? Is it your four-year-old niece? Picture this beloved person in your mind. Now imagine them being in the same abusive situation you were. Take your time. Imagine your 22-year-old daughter being beaten or your four-year-old niece being sexually assaulted. Imagine that they confide in you, the tears streaming down their face and the shame in their heart. Would you say to them the same thing that you say to yourself? "You are a piece of shit. It's all you fault..." No, you wouldn't. I am certain you would not burden them with the same worn out, shame-ridden tapes that you play in your own head. Would you pull the four-year-old into your lap and offer love, compassion and protection? Would you hold your daughter and reassure her that it wasn't her fault and she didn't deserve it? Of course you would.

Now I want you to go back to the image of yourself at the time of your trauma. Offer yourself the reassurance and comfort that you would offer another. Be kind and gentle with the traumatized age you carry. Protect yourself from the constant guilt-ridden, shame based chiding that she has heard for so long. Do this frequently. Practice nurturing yourself. I promise that if you do, it will change you.

<u>Trust</u>

Q: " I just don't trust people. How do I let them get close enough to have a relationship?"
A: First of all, if you haven't done the other exercises then maybe you aren't ready to enter into any type of a relationship. But if you have, you may have honed the skills you need to recognize people who intend to hurt you. Once you have the skills to weed out the truly harmful and dangerous people, it then turns into *pick your neurosis*.

People will all have faults, disappoint you and let you down and we need to understand this. People just can't be perfect. Have you ever let someone down even though you truly meant no harm? Of course you have and you will again. I'm not talking about falling short in the eyes of your mother-in-law who you just can't please or someone who is simply critical. I am talking about the feeling you have when you know you just weren't the best mother (friend, sister etc…) that you could have been. Humans will always make mistakes and people will always be human.

So now that you have skills to protect yourself and reasonable expectations of the people around you, move slowly. As Dr. Phil McGraw says, "Don't risk more than you can afford to lose." Only go into situations where you know that if the other person lets you down you can handle it. How people let us down and whether we keep them in our lives depends on a lot of things. It's a matter of degree, motives and what is acceptable to you. You will never find the perfect person. But addictions, affairs and abuse are always non-negotiable. Game over. And even with affairs, that is only non-negotiable if it offends your sensibilities. We all negotiate different relationships and if an open marriage is what you and your partner want, or both parties can salvage the relationship after an affair then affairs falls into the category of "what you will tolerate". But there are many areas that are not so cut and dried.

Why Me?

Q: "Why me?"
A: We all experience trauma. If you're alive then you've survived. We live in a world full of survivors. We walk with cancer survivors, domestic violence survivors, child abuse and incest survivors and survivors of white coat, white collar crimes every day. That we will experience trauma, at some time or another, in our life is a given. It's just a matter of what type of experiences, when they will occur and how we handle them. The reason for the types of experiences are as varied as the experiences themselves. For example, a cancer survivor might be able to answer the "why me" question with genetics or lifestyle, like smoking.

Some people believe that before they are born they chose what lessons they needed to learn and then their life experiences set about to teach them these lessons. Other people believe in karma and think that they are reaping what they have sown in past lives. Still others believe that God is teaching them lessons which I think is a very destructive belief because they are then left with a hurtful, mean "higher power."

Many times we truly can say that an event was thrust upon us. We were the victims of someone else's bad choice or violent action; for example, the woman whose child is killed by a drunk driver or the man whose entire family is killed when a car runs through the window of the restaurant where they are dining.

In the case of child abuse, alcoholism etc… there is a strong generational pattern and we can explain the "why me" question this way. More often than not the parents who beat or sexually abuse their children grew up that way, and so did their parents and grandparents. You can literally say, "It's a family tradition." Not all victims become offenders but all offenders were victims. The fact that it is generational does not excuse it, but does offer insight into why some parents don't react to, or even seem to see, the signs of abuse. It can be so obvious to others outside of the family because they are detached, not upside down in a vat of tar. This clarity is available to you too.

These patterns are not conscious avoidance but behaviors/feelings/instincts that the person has been taught through experience to ignore. Often what helps us survive our own victimization as a child is a blind spot for us in protecting our own children later. For example, my mother was targeted and scapegoated as a child and later did the same to me, seemingly unaware of what she was doing or why. As a child,; She survived by not acknowledging the full truth and was not able to do it as an adult either, at least not that her children saw. People who were sexually assaulted as children may suppress that experience or never really examine it. If the same perpetrator or another then assaults their child, the parent has "experience", if you will, at suppressing the signs and not "seeing" what they have seen.

There is also a lot of pressure to keep family secrets and to discount the negative effects when there are numerous victims within an extended family. This can be especially true when the abuse has stopped and victims are given the message to "move on, it's over, get over it" or that family member is sorry so they need forgiveness instead of accountability.

Often we must look at our choices to understand the question, "Why". Especially if we are seeing a repeating pattern. If you find yourself in your fifth violent relationship you need to do some serious self examination. This does not mean your actions cause him to beat you. It means maybe you shouldn't look for your mate in a bar. It means maybe you are subconsciously choosing a mate like your father. Maybe you have bought into the notion of bad boys as sexy. I don't know what the answer for you will be. I do know that if you are seeing the same thing over and over in your life, you will only understand why by examining your own self and the reason for your choices. If you were constantly walking into walls you would get your eyes checked. Our emotional well-being deserves no less.

We can look back and say 'if only I had done this or that.' Someone said, "Hindsight is like a soaking rain after the crops have already withered in the fields." This is not true. We can certainly use hindsight to help prevent further victimization. In fact, when victims find themselves being revictimized, they may not have conducted full autopsies on the traumas they have survived. They may not be fully examining their childhood or any cues they may be sending that say to offenders, "I am an easy target." Hindsight would help them do this.

Q: "Why does this keep happening to me?"
A: As a young woman, I used to believe that I could do anything I wanted, go anywhere I wanted and dress any way I wanted and if men responded in a violent or negative way well, that just wasn't my fault. And technically I was right. We are all responsible for our own behavior. When a man rapes a woman, only he is responsible. When a man beats a woman, only he is to blame. But that is little consolation when you are lying on a hospital table during a rape examination or when you are sitting in the battered women's shelter

for the third time this year. Being politically or morally right does not keep us safe.

Perpetrators are all responsible for their actions. And so are the rest of us. In my younger years, my girlfriends and I would get dressed up and go out "trolling". We stayed in a group because we knew that one of the potential consequences of our behavior could be rape. It was harmless. We were playing "dress-up" and having fun. However, not all people think the way we did. While the rapist is guilty of rape and that is a crime, you may be guilty of seriously poor judgment and that is dangerous.

Again, we can be politically and morally correct all we want, but that won't save our life. Until we start telling females the truth we can't expect to have a significant impact on their ability to protect themselves. There are many things that we can do to lessen the likelihood of being a target. For example: animals travel in herds or packs. It is harder to assault or abduct a single member of the group; be like the zebra and don't stand out, be like the stray dog and stay out of the reach of a stranger, be like the horse and stay vigilant and don't impair your senses. Offenders can behave like animals and to survive you need to do the same. The prey animals have learned to survive and will teach us how to do the same, if we will only listen.

When pedophiles choose a victim they frequently choose children who have single parents, parents that abuse substances and parents that are not involved. They pick out children who they perceive to be more vulnerable, children who don't have a high level of protection. This does not mean that the harried, single mother is to blame for her child's victimization. It does, however, mean that the more vulnerable your child is seen to be, the more likely your precious child is of being "picked". When trying to figure out how to stay safe, think of the animal kingdom and prey animals. I have listened to one offender after another tell me why they pick one victim over another. During my groups perpetrators go into detail about picking victims. Some of the things I've heard:

"Bobby had her. I figured I could too."

"She talked to me. She was really nice. I know she wanted it."

"His mom and dad really didn't pay much attention at all."
"He was so needy. I know he liked it."
"Looked like she was advertising to me."

Revictimization occurs when a person finds that they are being hurt by others over and over. They see repeating patterns of trauma in their life. This is devastating to the victim and those around them and the shame can be unbearable. The thinking is that since it keeps happening to this one particular person then it must be their fault. There are a number of reasons that revictimization occurs, none of which the victim is responsible for, but some of which she can influence.

When a being has been injured it shows. We may have convinced ourselves that our emotional injuries don't show, but they do. Just because we do not see them does not mean others can not, like a fly in the middle of our back. Just because an event does not seem real to us does not mean the rest of the world shares our perception. In fact, perpetrators have often perfected seeing these things and this is another example that magnifies the fallacy of "there is no reality only perception." Just because you have chosen to lie to yourself does not mean others can't see the truth. For example:
- The newly widowed may be lonely
- The incest survivor may keep her secret but sexualize her relationships
- The stoic POW may drink himself into a stupor daily but refuse to talk
- The formerly-battered woman may reek of low self esteem

As much as we want to convince ourselves that emotional injuries don't show, they do. And it is amazing how well these subtle (or not so) characteristics can be picked up by offenders. Like a lion looking at a herd, they know what they're looking at. They know who is weaker and injured. This is why young girls are often incested by more than one family member, widows are often scammed, and one of the reasons battered women get out of one violent relationship and into another. A weakened state leaves you open to perpetrators.

After being traumatized it is in your best interest to:
-Use your hindsight and examine what choices may have put you at risk
-Ask yourself what gut feelings you had that you ignored
-Are there any patterns? Has this happened before?
-What, if anything, could you have done to prevent the trauma
-Thoroughly examine how the attack or event has effected you
- What symptoms are you left with? How is the trauma showing?
-Examine yourself for any actions that make you stand out as a weaker member of the herd, more vulnerable.
-Seek out an honest, compassionate and wise third party for information you may not see.
-Take extra precautions during your vulnerable time
- Don't use mind altering substances that leave you impaired. An obviously drunk or high woman is an easy target.
- Examine the dynamics of, and reason for, the failure of your previous relationships. If you have just left a batterer you may not see the next one coming.
- Surround yourself with supportive, emotionally healthy people who will be honest with you. If you have to "fire" everyone in your life, do it.
- Listen to your gut instincts and follow them. If you have survived a trauma you have a lot of important information filed away in your brain.

Some safety precautions are general while others are specific to the crime. For example, when a battered woman leaves the batterer she needs an entirely different checklist.

Some Things That Perpetrators Look For:
- Anything that makes you stand out (sexy clothes etc...)
- Impaired senses (drunk, drugged etc...)
- Neediness
- Low self esteem, need for approval
- Opportunity (victim walking in alley, unlocked doors etc...)
- Absence of male figure
- Kindness
- Lack of assertiveness, fear of being rude

- Lack of healthy boundaries (not assertive, afraid to say no)

A young girl who grows up with domestic violence is not equipped to see control and isolation as a problem. Early on, it feels like protection, attention and bonding. An abuser or batterer gathers information about the other person and only gradually begins to display the negative side of his need for power and control. If you grew up with abuse, then those early signs the batterer is showing may still be compared to her father, and seem mild enough not to raise fears or reactions.

We often seek out what is familiar to us. For example, a young girl who grows up with domestic violence is not likely to be equipped to see control as a problem and therefore protect herself from that type of relationship. Consciously or not it is familiar to her. I was 18-years old when I found out that not all men beat women. I grew up thinking it was just the nature of the beast. It was wonderful to find out that some were not beasts. My point is, she may see violence in the home as normal and a man that is not aggressive may not fit her definition of a man.

Another example of seeking familiarity is when a child who has been sexually assaulted all of their life sees sexual overtures as a show of love and affection, perfectly normal. The young men that I work with often don't see having sex with children as abnormal because they were being assaulted as children. It was as normal as dinner hour.

It isn't just a matter of protecting ourselves, rather it's a matter of understanding that we have a value and we are worth protecting. Understanding that we don't deserve to be hit, that we are not shit, and that we do deserve love and kindness is important in preventing revictimization. It is not as simple as just knowing these things intellectually. We must teach that inner child who we catch, on occasion, running the show.

Helping Our Kids
&
Breaking The Cycle

Q: *"My husband is beating me and was arrested for domestic violence. The courts ordered us to do joint counseling. I am not able to be honest out of fear of him. Is this normal? What can I do?"*

A: It is inappropriate and dangerous for battered women to do counseling with the man that is (or was) beating them. This can heighten the danger. I suggest that you contact your local battered women's organizations to see if they can intervene on your behalf and educate this judge. If you are not able to get the help you need locally we have a collection of position statements available.

Q: *"My husband says that he will go to anger management classes? Are these successful?"*

A: While these groups can be potentially helpful, they can leave the battered woman with a false sense of security. I would not bet my life on them helping him to change his behavior. This may be another manipulation on his part to make you stay. The results that these groups get are as varied as the groups themselves and I don't think anyone can give you much reassurance about the outcome. You need to live separately and do your own self examination while he does groups and if, after he has truly changed, you want to have a relationship, then consider it when you can see more clearly.

Q: *" I was finally able to get away from the man who was beating me. He is now using the kids to hurt me. What do I do?"*

A: Batterers will use any weapon they can find and if the kids are what they have they have no inhibitions about doing so. I have gone into detail about this problem in Chapter 5, *Service Providers*.

Q: *"My children watched their father beat me for years. We have been out of the violence for just as long but they are terribly hurt. The drug counselors say I have to let them hit bottom. Do I have other choices?"*

A: Assuming that you and your children are doing the counseling and other necessary things to promote your recovery and mental health, there are other things you can do besides watch your children freefall. Generally, trying to control others is a waste of time and resources.

We can try to teach people, but we really can't make our boyfriends, husbands, mothers and sisters behave. When it comes to minor children we have at least a moral obligation to try to teach them to be good, responsible citizens who are not a burden to society. Having been a single parent for many years, I share the following stories without judgment of other parents and with an understanding that I was in a blessed situation to be able to do these things.

After the brain injury we had to send the girls to their father because I couldn't even take care of myself. Within about a year, I had that much neurorehab under my belt and we found out that the girls were behaving badly. At 12 and 14 they were running with adult males, drinking, driving, drugging and partying for days while their father was on the road. One 18-year-old boy was beating both of them and one of the girls was using inhalants. They had also witnessed years of "mother beating" as they would put it.

Scott and I brought them home and put them in rehab. We were given the same advice, "They have to hit bottom." I knew there had to be an alternative but wasn't offered any other options. I knew that "the bottom" of gun toting men and inhalants could easily be a grave. One night the PSA with Carroll O'Connor came on TV. I had seen it a zillion times but this time I actually heard it, "Do whatever it takes to come between your kids and drugs." Now that made a hell of a lot more sense than watching them be lowered six feet under.

It hit me! Rather than helplessly standing by and watching my daughters die or at least destroy their brains, there was something I could do. In fact, as the devious parts of my mind wandered, I realized I was in a position to do quite a bit. I knew I could stop those little kamikazes from sedating any and every thought that came across them.

I began following my daughters. Soon their friends knew that if they were at the party, their mom wasn't far behind and close behind me would be a sheriff's deputy. I let them use my vehicle and then went to local law enforcement and gave them permission to search it at any time. I literally stalked them and interfered with most of the bad behavior they could conjure. As they developed new ways around me, I designed new tricks to make sure nothing paid off for them. In time they decided it just didn't pay to be a bad citizen.

Some Other Issues

Family & Friends

As far as family members are concerned, a batterer will work long and hard to isolate his victim from you. You are one of the greatest threats to his control over the victim. This alone speaks volumes. Friends, family and law enforcement are in the best of positions to help break the cycle. Law enforcement is effective because arrest sends the message that domestic violence is a crime.

Friends and family are effective because they can give the victim the support she needs to maintain her sense of self and her reality when she's ready to leave, and offer her a different perception or "reality check" when she's ready. As family and friends we can also do a great deal of damage.

As a young girl I was embarrassed by what my uncle had done to me and the fact that the entire family knew about it made the embarrassment so much worse. That would not be the worst of it. I was mortified and betrayed to find that my uncle had not accepted responsibility for what he did to me, lied about me and blamed me by saying, among other things, that I had seduced him. That would not be the worst of it.

To hear friends and family, especially my aunts, repeat his stories back to me, in graphic detail, about how he had described the imagined seduction, would forever change me. My aunts had broken my heart like no man ever could have. That still would not be the worst of it. For them to believe him and blame me for my own victimization and the disruption in the family, would be the worst of it and a betrayal that would close a young girl up to humans and the heartache they transmitted like infected parasites.

I lived with that shame for so long and even though it doesn't effect me much now, at 47 I am still reminded that I "slept" with my uncle and still live with the disrespect my family heaped on me to avoid their own culpability.

I had protested loudly when told I would be training with sex offenders. Yet so many things became clear. I listened to the lies the offenders told to in an effort to avoid being exposed. I realized my uncle was doing what sex offenders do, and his sisters the same. The following excuses clarified their behavior for me:
"She had a tampon stuck and he had to pull it out"
"She had a vaginal infection and he had to check her"
"She was obsessed with nudity and he thought by ignoring her desire to run around naked that would stop it."
And my favorite – "as I was tucking her in I tripped, fell on top of her and my finger went up her vagina."

The above quotes did not come from my family. Nor did they come from the offenders. These are the words of family entrusted to protect the young victims I have worked with over the years. They look for any way possible to avoid the truth and dismiss the "troublemaker".

Children of Victims/Survivors

Some of the most furious people I have seen are the adult children of battered women, and I'm not just talking about my own. Unfortunately that fury is often directed at their mothers. They are mad at her for staying. They are mad at her for leaving. They are just flat out mad at their mothers. They are mad at her for all the changes her leaving created. They are mad at her for forcing them into poverty. They are mad at the parent they feel most safe with, the parent they counted on to keep them safe, which she couldn't do.

Children of battered women have been exposed to the mother's repeated attempts to leave. They've been exposed to a mother believing him time after time. They've been exposed to a mother minimizing his violence because she misinterprets the bond as love. They've been exposed to a mother that was unable to protect them from his emotional or physical violence. They have been robbed of a calm, loving, focused mother that can act in their best interest, and they have a right to be angry. Young men hate men's violent behavior toward their mother but they learn it. Young women hate men's violence toward their mother too but they learn it, accept it and may live it.

Why Children May Lie

Depending on a child's age there are a multitude of reasons that they might not be able to tell the truth when asked about their parents by the courts, law enforcement, relatives etc... Twenty years ago the notion of a child lying about abuse was frowned upon by children's advocates but we now have a greater understanding of the dynamics within an abusive family and we now recognize that there are a number of reasons why children may be unable to be honest about what is, or has gone on.

Children often feel it is necessary to align themselves with the most powerful parent. They may be confused, taking parents' actions out of context or misunderstanding what has taken place. They may feel fearful, threatened or coerced and intimidated. They may be fearful of a parent going to jail or trying to win the approval of the neglectful parent. Children may be incorporating stories they have heard into their memories. Like the battered women, children can be terribly vulnerable and a charming and manipulative abuser is not likely to waste the valuable tool in a child.

It is important to remember that children are often used as pawns by angry people and this is especially so in domestic violence cases. This is child abuse and this is an area where victim impact could be successfully utilized, not only to the benefit of divorcing parents and their children but to the adult children of divorce that could find a higher purpose for the abuse they suffered.

5

Service Providers & The System

The Batterers Use Of the System, Society and Service Providers As Weapons

This chapter is not meant as a training manual for service providers of batterer's groups (please contact the Domestic Abuse Intervention Project, DAIP, for that) rather it is a guide for the victims who will come in contact with the service providers and are trusting their judgment and skill, sometimes with their lives.

I stopped doing batterer's groups some 20 years ago, so some of this information will not reflect the evolution that responsible groups have undergone in that time. Still, if there was a policy or procedure in place 20 years ago, there likely are groups, their facilitators, counselors and other service providers who are still married to those same, unevolved policies and procedures.

This chapter is intended as a measuring device for victims who are trusting facilitators and service providers with their safety and their fragile belief in human nature. This chapter is intended to help victims/survivors judge the services they are receiving and to help validate their "gut" when they know something just isn't right. This chapter is also intended to help service providers understand, if they want, the things they are doing that helps victims/survivors and those that cause further harm.

This chapter will present proven methods of genuinely helping the victim and deflecting the manipulations offenders use to avoid responsibility. This chapter is not meant to be used instead of the previous chapter but as a complement to it.

It is also intended to provide victims/survivors with standards with which to judge the services they receive. A woman who has been raped is about to be introduced to a multitude of services she knows nothing about. It takes only one judge, counselor or police officer to leave her doubting everything she knew to be true, or to cost her her life. It may take only one "expert" to cause further damage and push her deeper into a cycle of shame and self-blame, or worse.

This chapter can clarify for the victims what they should and should not be seeing in the people and systems they have now been thrust into and help them to identify when things are going wrong. An uneducated service provider can set off our gut alarm and this chapter can help the victim to validate that warning.

This chapter not only includes information about battered women but other types of crimes. That is because it is assumed that if someone is in a position to come in contact with battered women they will also encounter victims/survivors of other types of crimes. I have also included other types of crimes because battered women are at high risk of being revictimized.

Once a battered woman has successfully escaped her batterer, his need to dominate and control her does not just dissipate. His need for control becomes more intense as his ability to control her, keep her isolated, quiet and confused (i.e. unable to act in her own best interest) is lessened. Her change in attitude and the fact that she has left constitute a real crisis for him that can, and often does, escalate his controlling behavior. As with the honeymoon phase, he may "get religion"; bring gifts; get counseling; cry; apologize and, when that doesn't work, he may quickly escalate into negative behaviors like manipulation, stalking and violence. His manipulative behavior does not simply subside.

This is often the point where, if there are children, they can become one of his best weapons, and he has no inhibitions about using them. After all, it's not as if we are dealing with a selfless being who has been putting the children first all of this time. What better weapon to use against a woman than her love and protective instincts for her children?

Unfortunately, the courts are often all too willing to oblige the batterer and his use of the children as weapons. In this state the courts separate the issue of fitness to parent from beating the child's mother. In other words, as an attorney explained, just because they beat the mother does not make them a bad parent. They believe that a man who beats and terrorizes the children's primary care giver can still be the best parent to raise them.

Sadly, it is often those with the most money who can, and will, sustain a lengthy court battle (which becomes a battle of attrition). With women still making less money than men, it is often the batterer who has the most money, and he has already made it clear that if she tries to leave he will take her children. He has threatened her with this from the day he realized just how valuable they were as a weapon. Many women live under the constant fear of him following through on his threats to hurt her or the children, steal the children or, call child welfare authorities. Using this form of harassment to wear her down is common and effective.

If the relationship with the victim and her family is fragile, they may actually be won over by the variety of manipulative tactics the batterer employs, and side with him, even to the point of testifying against her. This is not as uncommon as we would hope and that is because of the charm and manipulation that the batterer has become so skilled at wielding, continued victim blaming and an uneducated system.

If they attend a church that is silent on the issue of abuse, she may be judged by the congregation because of their lack of understanding the dynamics of abusive relationships. He may begin counseling with the pastor, presenting his wish to change, be forgiven and "keep the family together". If she does not give in, her church community may be lost to her at a time when supportive community is important.

During my relationship with Aaron I was the church goer. When I left him he began coming to my church. He worked hard to snuggle up into the armpit of God and went as far as to go to "preacher school" for the church I so desperately needed. When this started, I had to walk away, and he is now a "preacher" for them.

Twenty five years ago, while working with battered women, I had not heard of the batterer using the children once she left. At that time we were not warned, nor were we warning women. The thinking was that once she broke away the only thing left was to deal with the residual trauma.

When we look at the residual trauma, we see a complicated set of obstacles for the victims and their children to overcome. In a household where there is violence and disrespect for one parent, when the "controlling parent" leaves, the children often feel they have been "let loose" and do not have to listen to the parent who has always been discounted. In a household where the victim has not worked outside the home or has been isolated from supportive family and community resources, landing on your feet can be very difficult.

Children with serious emotional/behavioral problems (often caused when witnessing violence in the home) require time, money and attention. Time, money and the ability to give everyone individual attention can be nearly impossible when a parent is also learning a new job, trying to figure out the bus system, fighting an expensive custody battle and looking for a place to live. And if the victim is using substances to sedate her own trauma (and even if she's not) she is still dealing with trauma issues. These things impair her ability to help all family members recover, and the batterer knows this. These are only a few of the reasons we need to look at the system and what service providers can, and must, be aware of to safely and respectfully respond to the mothers and children healing from violence in their home.

Over time it became apparent that batterers were using the children as weapons and that they hated the women more than they loved their children. This is not information that the women offer. I had to carefully and specifically seek the information regarding how her children were behaving and what they were believing because, like revictimization, the women felt that if even her children felt that way and treated her badly then she must deserve it. It must be her fault. The shame around this issue was the most intense I had seen, which was why the women didn't volunteer any of this. The damage done to the women and children is often profound and life long.

Like many battered and formerly-battered women, I had suffered terrible abuse at the hands of a parade of men, which often starts with our fathers. I was lucky that the injuries were as minor as they were, even though I ended up spending years in a wheel chair and another year totally bedridden due to the damage that Aaron and Larry had done to my spine. Many women die at the hands of their batterer. I was left only with disabilities.

It isn't that victims aren't reaching out. It's that unless they reach out to a formerly-battered woman, an agency designed for battered women, or they are referred to one of those, they are more likely than not to be revictimized by the person they have turned to for help. Not because that is the helper's intent, rather because of ignorance.

When, and if, battered women do reach out, it is to a friend, family member, spiritual leader, counselor, law enforcement or the justice system. These are the people who can be the first step in helping battered women to build the connections and trust in others that has been so badly undermined and damaged by the batterer. All too often her lack of trust is reinforced because she has reached out and is then berated and judged for staying, even though the person judging her will readily admit they don't understand why she "stays". Those women who never reach out are aware of, or justifiably fearful of, how society will treat them.

It takes so little to silence a person who has been taught to submit. It is so easy to discourage and isolate a person who has learned that every seemingly positive gesture is hiding a negative or humiliating intent. Like with occasional indulgences and the honeymoon phase, she has come to see any kind or positive gesture as preceding something terrible. It is not just silencing these victims that we run the risk of when we say something insensitive or uninformed. With a few words or even a look (because she has become an expert at decoding nonverbal in order to reduce her injuries) we can send these fragile victims into a downward spiral without having any idea how we did it. This is why I advise battered women to use only counselors affiliated with organizations for battered women and even more specifically those that share the philosophy of the Domestic Abuse Intervention Project (DAIP).

People seem to have difficulty simply saying, "I don't know" or taking a neutral position. They often fail to recognize the danger of offering uninformed advice. We all love to "rescue" but it is seldom more dangerous than when we begin to TELL a battered woman what she should do or say, especially if we are not experienced in dealing with violent relationship issues.

Too often people feel like they have to have a position or an opinion. Someone asked me one time what I thought about NAFTA. I said I didn't have the information I needed to have an opinion, and they were shocked, like I was unpatriotic or something. It was as if they thought I had an obligation to have an opinion. Unfortunately, people often feel it is better to have an uninformed position than to have no position at all.

Battered and formerly-battered women face a world of ignorant positions and opinions. People feel free to jump on the band wagon and berate and degrade her, as if the batterer and she, herself don't do a good enough job at that. They have their own ill-thought-out opinions on why she stays, how she got into the relationship, what she should do, and any other issue in her life that they can piecemeal into a position. It is so easy, in the name of "just trying to help," to add to the battered woman's self criticism and shame. Anyone who has been abused is especially vulnerable to taking in opinions and judgments, no matter how ill advised or blaming. There was a point in my life when a cashier at the local grocery store could leave me questioning my entire purpose and value because she was having a bad day. While this is no longer the case, I still have to work to "tune out" the nonverbal I learned so well to read for safety's sake. Those who wish to help must remember that the battered woman has been trained to accept her batterer's reality and to deny her own. Even those who are well meaning can add to her confusion.

With a mother being beaten and degraded, not only in the home, but by anyone else who feels an obligation to have an opinion, what happens to the children of battered women? After they've found the courage to leave their tormentor and probably gone through the humiliating, degrading and victim blaming system that's supposed to protect them, does the batterer then just stop his coercion, manipulation and efforts to control her? Does his need to get even and to make her pay for her perceived crimes against him simply dissipate? Has he learned a lesson? Does his manipulative and coercive nature simply end because she is gone? She may be physically free of the batterer, but where does all that destructive energy he directed toward her go? Does he move on with his life or does he find another victim?

Remember, abusive individuals do not always recognize or acknowledge their violent and controlling behaviors. Rather they perceive themselves as the victims. When someone tells himself he is the victim, it is easy to justify using whatever power he has at his disposal to fight back at his "victimizer". It is this perception of being the victim that makes batterers so dangerous and destructive.

Remember, all along he has portrayed himself as the victim of a crazy, controlling, addicted, ad nauseum …woman. Based on his theory, she is the problem and the reason for the dysfunction in the home so, based on his logic, once she is out of the picture, he would function as a normal healthy male. But, that is just not the case.

We now have decades of experience working with formerly-battered women and their children to answer the question, "Where does all that destructive energy go if she escapes?" And while the battered women talk of parental alienation and having the batterer use the children against them, the children now prove the mother's years of allegations with their contempt and the continued abuse of their mothers. Whether the children's anger is for staying, leaving or sedating the pain, the children have been manipulated by the batterer into continuing the abuse where he left off - to tread into territory that restraining orders and miles have prevented him from entering.

Battered women must draw on a deep reserve of strength and hope, to be able to leave with the children. We ask her to do this at a time when she has been, perhaps for years, subjected to behavior targeted specifically at stripping her of her self worth, her confidence, her support system/family, her job and her friends. We call on her to step out into a community and criminal justice system that offers her no guarantee of safety. We call on her to lean on her church community, her family and the social service network - all of which have a long history of limited assistance if not actual blame for her situation.

While most are well meaning and open to women presenting their problems, our system of providing meaningful intervention and help has huge gaps that can leave a victim/survivor hanging by her fingernails. Far too often, the children have become satellites of the batterer through his redirection of terribly destructive energy, more specifically modeling disrespect, discounting their mother, misuse of power within the family and blaming.

Children learn what they live and if one person in the family gets their way by using threats, coercion and other forms of abuse children, both male and female, can learn to use the same behaviors as a way of getting what they want. Boys and girls can both hate what abusers do but end up replicating abuser or victim behavior because it is all they know.

She has removed herself and her children from the home, but that doesn't always end the role modeling of abuse of their mother. The children may see her birth family abuse and disrespect their mother. They are often present while law enforcement interrogates her about why she stays, or worse, arrest her for fighting back. They see the courts often side with the batterers and, when she reaches out to counselors, the children often see these authority figures discount and fail to take their mother seriously.

The criticisms, disrespect, judgment and abuse of the mother by not only the batterer but counselors, judges, law enforcement, and family have been witnessed by the children their entire life. While the abuse by all others may fade, the children often vent their contempt and judgments toward their mothers and this does not fade. Batterers often find satisfaction in knowing they have caused the ultimate pain when they can damage or destroy their victims relationship with her children.

Often, with the years of angry, difficult behavior and the expense of extended therapy and all that goes along with that process, a woman experiences little of the freedom and peace she had hoped would come from leaving an abusive partner. When abusers consciously or unconsciously use children as tools against the mother, both the mother and children lose as he tries one more time to regain power and control.

If service providers, and the family and friends would support the women in an appropriate way, her children would never become tools, because the batterer would lack support. The children would see him as the sole abuser and therefore not the standard of behavior. They would at least be offered an experience of seeing their mother being validated, which would counter the abusive dynamics she has tried to change in her family. In support groups for battered women, they often agonize that they leave one abuser only to take another with them. Feeling the full extent of the generational aspects of violence in the home can be an overwhelming realization for a woman who finally found the strength to leave - "for the children".

The victim experiences the initial trauma at the hands of the offender. This leaves her open to a parade of disappointments, insults and more trauma. While service providers and our current system have made great strides in learning about the response to trauma, far too often they are still revictimizing trauma survivors. The efforts we made in our early years to educate people on the responses and behaviors of victims were productive, but while a few individuals have made advances the systems as a whole remain the same. While it is now possible to find someone in a given field who understands the victim's behavior, finding a service provider who is sensitive to the issues victims face is not common and won't be easy.

When the survivor of a violent crime reaches out for help, they are making themselves and their children vulnerable to the insensitivity and judgments of those from whom she has asked for help. While the victim may think that the officer at the door or the counselor in the phone book is safe for them to reach out to, that is not necessarily the case. Victims may think that these service providers meet some minimum standard or have been taught how to help them. That is not necessarily the case either.

Even when victims seek out highly educated people, they are not guaranteed to have any training in domestic violence or other types of victimology. The title of Psychiatrist or Psychologist does not mean that the service provider has training or understanding about the reality of victims or the behaviors and motivations of offenders. I recommend to the women I work with that they not reach out to anyone not affiliated with a victim's rights organization. The potential for damage is far too great.

Often people get into the field because they have first-hand experience. These people are the most helpful. The former addict that becomes an addictions counselor has a good feel for the issues. The survivor of a rape knows what a rape victim feels. But more often the service provider is there because it is part of their job. For convenience I am referring to law enforcement, medical providers, judges etc… as service providers. These are all groups that battered women are likely to come into contact with as they try to maintain, or improve, their lives.

While the offender causes the initial trauma, a service provider can take that trauma and compound it. This is done out of a lack of accurate information and training. This is not malicious on the part of service providers. People go into this field because they want to help people. They did not get into the helping professions because of money. Most are paid very little. Like the victims they have just not been given accurate information or they may be working out their own traumas.

There are service providers who have had the training they need. Organizations that specialize in victims usually get great reviews from the victims. Many law enforcement agencies are providing special training, and some batterer's groups are well aware of the dynamics in violent relationships.

Victims and service providers need information on the behaviors of offenders to make sense of what has happened and to work against the manipulations of the offender. But they also need information on the victims themselves, and they are not getting it. But, often a sensitive approach is as easy as applying logic to the situation. For example, the age old defense of calling the victim crazy can be handled with logic. While it is unlikely that she actually is "crazy" so what if she is? It's still not okay to beat or rape her. Unfortunately teaching people to think logically hasn't been much of a priority.

Not only do we run the risk of further traumatizing the victim during an intervention, but can actually put the victim at greater physical risk. Intervening in violent domestic situations inappropriately can cause the victim to be beaten again or even killed.

Like other types of hostages it is rare that the domestic hostage has the opportunity for outside perspectives. These precious and rare moments provide an opportunity to offer the victim a glimpse of another reality. Contacts that the domestic hostage has with people outside of the violent relationship should not be squandered. Because these moments offer such great opportunity for trust building and are also moments of great vulnerability for the victim/survivor, this is a time when great harm or great healing can occur.

We are not asking the right questions - the first step to solving a problem. If we don't get the question right, we can't possibly come to the right answer. What if, instead of "Why does she stay?", we ask, "Why doesn't she leave? What stops her from leaving? What's in her way?" And there are so many other questions that we aren't even asking - like what happens to battered women and their children after they do find a way out.

Throughout their relationship the children have been a tool and her greatest weakness. During the relationship, battered women work hard to act as a buffer, to keep the batterer from focusing on the children. When a battered woman leaves, the children may be the only access he has to the woman that he wants to control, and he escalates his efforts. More often than not, to leave, she has had to immerse herself and her children in a defective system. This provides the batterer with a great opportunity, and he won't miss a beat.

Battered women must fight custody battles with the offenders. They may be ordered into counseling or mediation with their attackers. Law enforcement is often involved in domestics, and many battered women are arrested for "mutual combat" or defending themselves. Not only are women, law enforcement and the courts manipulated by batterers, so are counselors. Teaching about the charming and manipulative nature of batterers, as opposed to the fearful, closed and apparently uncooperative nature of battered women is not standard.

Now that the battered women's movement and advocates are seeing at least a generation of children of battered women that have grown-up, we are seeing that these children grew up with not only violence but terrible custody battles, listening to their mothers being lied about and degraded and watching a system that blamed her. We find many grown children who have little respect for their formerly-battered mothers due to parental alienation combined with the anger and blame that the adult children feel for a mother who did not leave sooner, did leave, or was unable to protect them from the abuser.

Hereinafter Referred to as Mother

I was no different than many battered women and, through my own bad choices, and being vulnerable to every type of predator on the prowl, I suffered one type of revictimization after another. Unfortunately, it wasn't just me that was hurt. Whenever the mother is traumatized, so are the children. In 1996 I was injured to the point of being unable to take care of my children.

This was an injury that directly stemmed from the spinal damage from being battered, slammed and rolled like an inconsequential piece of carpeting. I was left drooling, unable to read or tie my shoes from a brain injury. Now it wasn't only my body that was effected but my brain, and I needed to focus on neurorehabilitation, physical therapy and relearning even the simplest of tasks.

My husband was overwhelmed with the task of taking care of a woman that couldn't even feed herself and wasn't expected to live. We made the difficult and heart wrenching decision to send my daughters to their father. While I recovered from this terrible brain injury and a heart surgery their father was expected to do just that, father.

Unfortunately, more than a decade after our divorce, he saw this as another opportunity to hurt me, and he didn't waste it. After sending my daughters to live with him, my nephew and his girlfriend came to me and told me that my daughters were in serious trouble. This would turn out to be another time when service providers had an opportunity to shine or do terrible damage.

VERIFIED EMERGENCY EX PARTE PETITION FOR TEMPORARY CUSTODY PENDING HEARING ON PERMANENT CHANGE IN CUSTODY

Comes now the petitioner, Jasper Jameson, in person and by counsel, after being duly sworn upon her oath, and for her Verified Emergency Ex Parte Petition for Temporary Custody Pending Hearing on Permanent Change of Custody and favors as follows:

1. Petitioner, Jasper Jameson (hereinafter referred to as "mother"), and respondent, Larry J. Stene (hereinafter referred to as "husband"), were divorced by decree For Dissolution of Marriage on November 19, 1986.

2. Pursuant to said Decree, Mother was awarded custody of the two minor children, namely Sara, currently 17 years of age, and Amanda, currently 15 years of age.

3. On or about February 6, 1996, Mother suffered a brain injury. Shortly after being released from the hospital, Mother was forced to send children to live with father. Father immediately filed for a change in custody. The children were 14 and 11 when they went to live with their father. They had resided with Mother for the previous years. Mother was forced to send children to live with father because Mother could not care for the children and had a significant amount of healing and rehabilitation to do. Mother had no memory, had no control of her motor skills, was violent and inappropriate. She did not believe it was in the children's best interests to live with her while she was rehabilitating. Mother is now fully recovered and thriving.

4. Prior to the girls going to live with their father they were active girls, enrolled in school and not into drugs or alcohol. Amanda was on the softball team, and played the clarinet. She was a C student at Henderson Heights. Once going to live with her father she was enrolled in Decatur township schools. She no longer played softball, and no longer played the clarinet as the father refused to take her to practice. Sara is no longer even enrolled in school. Both girls are heavily involved in drugs, and both girls are sexually active in abusive relationships. Father is never at home and allows the girls all the freedom they desire which has proven to be extremely detrimental, and could prove to be fatal. Mother has just learned

that the children are exposed to assault weapons on a regular basis. Seventeen years ago a friend of the parties shot himself in the head with a loaded weapon of Father's while staying with the parties. The parties have first-hand experience with the dangers of loaded weapons in the house. Nevertheless, father maintains a host of guns in his home and leaves them accessible to the girls and their friends while he is not home.

5. After going to live with father, Sara returned to live with mother for approximately one year. Father sent Sara home to live with Mother as she had gotten into drugs during her stay at fathers home, had continuously "cut" school, and had also gotten in trouble with the law. When Sara returned to live with mother, Mother placed her into an in-patient treatment center. Mother began to take her to counseling with Pam Dole in Henderson Co. Ms. Dole noted that there was a lack of supervision and accountability at father's house as compared to mother's. See affidavit of Pam Dole, attached hereto as Exhibit A.

6. On May 30, 1997, by order of the court, Father was awarded sole custody of Amanda, and mother was awarded sole custody of Sara. At mother's request, Amanda was order to undergo counseling with Mother to facilitate the improvement of the relationship between mother and Amanda. Father did not encourage counseling or visitation, and in fact sought to alienate Mother from the children. Amanda is no longer in counseling.

7. Since the change in custody, Sara decided to voluntarily return to father's house, after she finished drug rehabilitation and therapy. Due to Mother's condition, she could not fight Sara's voluntary choice to live with father. Both girls prefer to live at father's house as mother sets limits and is home during the day and evening. Father is a truck driver and works evenings. There are no limits at fathers and no supervision.

8. Since the change in custody the behavior and status of the girls has greatly deteriorated. Amanda has gone from an average student to receiving 5 F's on her most recent report card. See Exhibit B attached hereto. Sara in essence dropped out of school. Decatur township threatened to file educational neglect against the father. Due to the amount of school missed mother was forced to enroll

Sara in an alternative school. To mothers knowledge Sara has not attended the alternative school. Mother desperately wanted custody of Sara and Amanda back; however, the children do not wish to live with mother and father has prohibited their relationship. Sara had no desire to return to school or rules; consequently, she would not return to her mother's home.

9. Mother suffered major disabilities as a result of the brain injury; however she has come a long way in the last 3 years. She is left with no disabilities that will effect her parenting. She is ready willing and able to assume sole custody of the girls.

10. Mother recently learned some very disturbing information regarding the children that justifies exigent circumstances supporting the need for an immediate change of custody of Amanda to mother, ex parte, pending a hearing on the matter. As a result of the news mother has learned, Mother has already retrieved custody of Sara by bringing the Sheriff over to the father's house and taking Sara. Sara is now enrolled in intensive drug treatment for illicit drugs, including heroine, crack, methamphetamine, vicodin and valium. See affidavit of Christine Good attached hereto as Exhibit "C".

11. Mother had her suspicions that the children were unsupervised and doing drugs. What she recently learned, however, is far worse than she could have ever imagined. Sara and Amanda's cousin Christina Marie Good, confided in mother when she became fearful that the girls were in danger of being murdered in gang related activity. Ms. Good reported that:

"Mr. Stene is gone most every night and the girls are there without supervision. They are out until late hours. Amanda is using pot, alcohol and crack. Sara abuses about anything she can get her hands on including heroine, methamphetamine, crack, vicodin and valium. Both girls are involved in situations involving weapons and one of the weapons is a gun belonging to Sara and purchased for her by her father. I have seen weapons laying out unsecured in Mr. Stene's house. Sara has handled guns with no adults in the house. While Mr. Stene is gone, they party in the house, including on school nights. They are known to party until 2 a.m. with adult males and alcohol. They have been partying with drugs and alcohol most every night for the last year. Education is not encouraged. Amanda gets little sleep and does not focus on school. Mr. Stene buys both girls their cigarettes."

See affidavit hereto attached as Exhibit "C". The father of Ms. Good's baby, Chris Miller, also contacted Mother regarding these same matters and reported as follows:

"Sara and Amanda are left unsupervised 5 out of 7 nights a week. They are out cruising the streets and partying until late hours. Amanda uses alcohol, pot, and tobacco. Sara uses Ecstasy, vicodin, valium, alcohol and crack. Sara has driven drunk and on valium. I tried to remove Amanda from an apartment full of drunk people, unsuccessfully late at night. There were weapons at that party that night. Amanda's boyfriend pulled a knife on Sara's boyfriend. I have knowledge that the girls have received death threats. Mr. Stene's house is a party spot at night during school nights. The girls have been partying most every night for at least the last year. I have observed weapons (one appeared to be a machine gun) laying out unsecured at Mr. Stene's house while he is not there. Sara has brought out guns and shown them to teenagers (one has a gold trigger, a 380 berretta). She claims that the guns were purchased for her by her father. Guns are readily available to partying teenagers in Mr. Stene's house.

See affidavit of Chris Miller attached hereto as Exhibit "D".

12. As a result of the telephone call from Good and Miller, Mother immediately contacted Sheriffs Department. Mother went to the father's house in the middle of the night, and found the girls there, father absent. Amanda let mother in. Sara was asleep in father's bed with another girl. Father's brother was passed out drunk on the couch. There were guns in the house, and an assault rifle propped in the corner of Father's bedroom with the three teenage girls having access. The police officer broke down the assault weapon, and turned Sara over to Mother since Mother, by court order, has sole custody. Mother took Sara straight to drug rehab where she has been locked down for drugs. Mother and her husband anticipate participating fully and daily in Sara's drug rehabilitation, as they did in the past. Currently, while Sara is in in-patient detoxification, the family counseling is limited. Sara has been doing

well thus far in counseling. Father has been notably absent since Sara's admission. A copy of the police report evidencing the events is attached hereto as Exhibit "E".

13. The allegations of Ms. Good and Mr. Miller are corroborated by a next door neighbor to father who has eye witnessed the decline of the Stene girls. In her words, she has watched the girls go from adorable little girls to hellions. The neighbor, Ms. Smyth, will testify as follows:

I observed an 18-year-old man enter Mr. Stene's house while he was away. I found condoms outside Sara's bedroom window. I relayed my concerns to Mr. Stene that his 14-year-old daughter was having sex; however, he refused to hear me and called me a liar. When I tried to tell Mr. Stene what the girls were doing while he was gone Mr. Stene refused to listen, cussed me out and walked off. The girls are totally unsupervised. There are more men and boys in and out of that house than I can count on two hands. There is traffic in and out of the house all night. I rarely see Mr. Stene over there. It is my understanding that he has allowed Amanda to smoke for the last two years. I have seen both girls smoke marijuana. On one occasion, I walked in to retrieve my own daughter and the house smelled of marijuana.

See Affidavit of Terry Smyth attached hereto as Exhibit "F".

14. Sara has been removed from father's house. Amanda remains in imminent danger if she continues to reside there. According to her cousin, she has recently been involved in gang activity and received death threats. Mother has reason to believe that if an immediate order is not issued, ex parte, and Amanda receives notice of this action from her father, that Amanda will run, which could end up being even more damaging than her current situation. Mother acknowledges that Amanda does not wish to reside with her. Of course, Amanda has become accustomed to a lack of rules and no supervision and an illicit lifestyle. Accordingly she does not wish to have limitations and supervision imposed on her. Mother spoke to father over the weekend to determine his position with regard to these events. During the conversation father acknowledged that when Sara, the oldest, was 14 that she was having sex with an 18-year-old, and that this 18-year-old was physically abusing both girls.

He also exhibited a laissez-faire attitude with regard to education, supervision and drugs. See transcription of conversation between mother and father from February 27, 1999 attached hereto as Exhibit "G".

15. It is in the best interest of Amanda that her custody be immediately transferred to Mother, ex parte, pending hearing and assessment of parties. Additionally there has been a significant change in one or more of the factors that the court initially considered in it's determination of custody. More particularly, Amanda is at a critical age. If she is going to graduate from school, immediate action must be taken. Amanda's current living arrangement is having a negative impact on her upbringing. Mother's home and the County schools and community would have a significant positive impact on Amanda. Even though Amanda does not desire to live with mother, little weight, if any, should be given to Amanda's desires based upon her current situation where she is completely unsupervised, is failing school and may be addicted to illicit drugs. Mother needs immediate custody of Amanda so that she can immediately obtain drug treatment for Amanda. Father has demonstrated his unwillingness to help the girls. His lack of supervision and caring has resulted in severely drug addicted and at-risk children. Father does not place any emphasis on school, and his continued non-involvement is detrimental to Amanda's upbringing.

16. It is requested that an immediate order be issued, exparte, granting Mother custody of Amanda pending hearing, that this matter be set for a hearing on a permanent modification of custody, and that the parties be ordered to participate in a evaluation to be performed by the Domestic Relations Counseling Bureau, and for attorney fees for the prosecution of this action. It is not anticipated that this matter can be heard on courts regularly scheduled docket. It is believed that at least one hour is needed for the emergency hearing regarding temporary custody, and that the permanent modification hearing will take one full day.

Wherefore, Petitioner, Jasper Jameson, prays for an immediate ex parte order granting her custody of Amanda pending hearing, so that the petitioner can immediately secure for her drug treatment therapy and remove her from a potentially life-threatening situation.

The court ordered the emergency custody transfer of Amanda back to me and ordered the Domestic Relations Counseling Bureau (DRCB) to again evaluate both parents and to make a recommendation as to custody.

We left the court and went directly to the fetus beater's house to pick up my cherished little girl who had morphed into someone I did not recognize. I looked in the rear view mirror at the ghost like face of my husband, who followed in another car. I wondered if I was showing the stress as seriously as he was. There had been a great deal of discussion on how to retrieve Amanda and we had what we thought, was a pretty good plan.

Of course there are few plans that can adequately predict the behaviors of a violent, vindictive ex-husband. When I pulled up to his house to get Amanda he ran out the door determined to "bust my ass". He knew why I was there because I had repeatedly warned him and both of my daughters that if citizenship, education and mental health did not become part of their agenda, I would be forced to intervene.

Scott was parked down the road, out of sight. Due to good locks on the car doors, and he tried them all, my ex had to settle for an all out assault on the vehicle. As he yelled, threatened, pounded and threw snot like an angry Rottweiler, his neighbors called the police. As it turned out, Amanda was still at the school.

As we pulled into the main parking lot of the school, we saw the patrol cars. There were probably ten, and I wondered why they would need so many for a 100 pound, teenage girl. I feared the answer to that question lay somewhere in the words "teenage girl." But knew how dangerous it could be to combine bored cops with angry and disrespectful adolescents.

Quickly walking to the door my husband and I could see the uniformed officers through the large plate glass windows that lined the front of the building. It was clear they were encircling something but just what was not yet apparent. My husband grabbed the large heavy door, the likes of which I hadn't been able to open for years.

Of course, it was my daughter they had trapped like an animal. I hadn't seen her in two years and she looked just like me, minus the wrinkles, which, for the record, she had contributed to. She hid her fear with fury, as she hissed, spit and spewed profanities. I noticed that while she had the mind of a child and the mouth of a truck driver, her womanhood had erupted. Her large breasts were covered only by a tiny, tight, low cut half shirt and her flat stomach was exposed. She had inherited a bittersweet beauty that had both opened and closed doors for me. Her long, thick, brown hair flew as she screamed profanities at me. I watched the deputies, watch me.

"You stupid whore. I knew you were going to pull something like this."

"Honey, I warned you. I warned you all. You had the power to stop this," I responded.

"You fucking bitch. You have no right. You're nothing but a dirty, drunken whore," she screamed.

While it was clear she got my looks, I now saw with sickening clarity how ingrained her fathers thinking was in her. I had not had a drink in years and, for the first time, my determination to stay sober was tested as I watched a younger version of me, screaming those things at me. It was a real reflection of my feelings. While she screamed profanities at me, it was like hearing out loud the tapes that go on in my head. I had heard it for so long from my abusive family and the men that followed, that it had played like a loop in my mind for years, and now from the lips of my child.

With every foul name, my child and my inner child collided, converged, and cooperated to crush any notion that I was worthy of air, never mind respect. She was not only my child and my inner child but her father's daughter, satellite and protégé. While those words, coming from the mouth I had nursed, hurt worse than any beating, I assured myself that, with time, counseling and information she would come to understand. I held my tears believing that she would learn about battered women somehow other than firsthand and would understand why I had struggled so hard.

This beautiful mini version of me sounded like the ignorant abusive man I had left 13 years earlier. I wondered if she hated blacks and women the way he did. I wondered if she was cruel to animals and advocated violence. It didn't matter. I spent my time trying to change bigots, woman beaters, and sex offenders. This precious child was worth my time.
"You stinking cunt. I will get you for this."
My husband stood silent. One of the deputies broke the ring of authority and stepped toward her.
"Your mother may be willing to let you go on like this but I've heard enough. I have no idea what the issues are here but this is the only mother you will ever have. If you call her any more names I will take your little ass to jail. You are obviously nothing but a little punk and this woman is willing to work with you."

I watched her big brown eyes swell with tears as she swallowed her fury. I silently prayed for her silence. My broken heart cried for so many things, but most importantly, this child I no longer knew. I did not want to see them assert their authority. I had seen cops do that before and knew it would only make her more angry. I knew she would only blame me and I didn't want to see her humiliated.

Even though I had raised my daughter for the first 11 years of her life I did not know her. I don't mean that she had changed and I no longer knew the person she had become, but rather I did not remember her. I had no memory of raising her. I had a tradition of telling them the story about the day they were born, every year, on their birthday. I no longer knew her birthday story.

Sizing up the spitting adolescent, then me, then my six foot four husband the officer asked, "Where are you taking her from here?"
"A substance abuse assessment," I answered.
"Do you REALLY think you can transport her?"
"I think so," I answered.

Transporting her proved to be much easier than I expected. It was as if the demonstration at the school was just to humiliate me and let the world know I fell short as a mother. She no longer had an audience. There was the occasional threat or name hurled across the front seat but nothing as dramatic as the fury she spewed in the lobby of the high school.

Once inside the rehab facility I left my hissing, spitting baby girl, along with a copy of the Petition For Emergency Custody Order, with the woman who would do the assessment. The Petition explained a lot more than I could choke up. At this point all the abuse of mother figures, father figures and lover imitators were defining me. I don't think I could have choked up the word "fire" had I been consumed by it.

I waited in the private room for my daughter's counselor to bring her in. We were going to do a session with just Amanda and me. My stomach turned as usual. The night that I picked her up and brought her here for an assessment, they decided that Amanda would be best treated as an outpatient. I took her home to sleep and then drove the 40 miles one way, everyday, to bring her back for treatment. Life would have been so much easier, in so many ways, had they kept her.

The first night we took her home was heart-breaking. I watched as she went through a sped-up version of the stages of grief. I watched her deny that it was really happening. She tried bargaining.
"If you will just take me home now I will get good grades, never use again and respect you," she pleaded.
On the outside I stood steady as she threatened me, spewed more anger, begged, denied, bargained, and finally fell asleep. It was the first time we had ever used our alarm system to keep someone in the house. It would not be the last.

The counselor walked through the door with my little troll. I had known Cathy for a few years now. She was Sara's counselor every time Sara came back. This was Amanda's first time in rehab but Sara had just finished her fourth round. There was no doubt that I was in for a tough ride today. Amanda's eyes were swollen from crying and her body was tense. I prepared myself to take full responsibility when appropriate and to defend myself when appropriate. She sat down across the table from me without making eye contact.

"I hate you. You are a fucking whore. Dad said you guys got divorced because you were a whore and slept with a thousand men..." she accused.
This wasn't new. I had heard this one from her sister.
"No," I interrupted, "I never cheated on your father."
"Don't you call my dad a liar," she screamed, "He was there for me when you just walked away."
"Amanda, I didn't abandon you. I remember when you called and said that your dad told you that I didn't love you any more so I was giving you to him and adopting other children. Do you remember what I said then?"
"Don't call him a liar," she screamed and cupped her hands over her ears. She began humming out loud, fingers in her ears. Had she been listening to me she would have realized that I had stopped talking. I was shocked at her determination not to hear me. That's when I realized that she might never hear the truth. That's when I realized that it may be too late.

  The counselor led Amanda out of the room. Her hands were still cupped over her ears and she hummed all the way. The counselor returned with another woman.
"Jasper, this is Amy and she will be Amanda's counselor," Cathy said, "Since I am working with Sara someone else needs to work with Amanda. I will leave you two alone."
Amy didn't speak for a few long seconds, "I have met Amanda. Can you tell me how this happened?"

  Speechless was now a frequent condition for me. I made no excuses or apologies. Anyone paying any attention, with any sensitivity should understand it, I thought. I silently stared passed the tall, thin woman who could have been Amanda if you just stretched Amanda's physique.
"How did this happen?" I thought to myself.

  There are certain concepts people don't want to hear. And those are facts and theories they will not hear and then mock you for, but only after they've turned away. I had explained endlessly, why battered women stay and the only ones who accept the answer is battered women. They are happy when you give them a language to discuss what has happened. No one else wants to hear it, yet continue to ask the question.

People had accepted cult brainwashing but couldn't stomach the idea that "brainwashing" is an every day occurrence and, whether we call it religion, education, propaganda, brainwashing, or simply hogwash depends on whether we like the results it produces. "How did this happen?" Amy asked.

How did it come to be that the beautiful babies I had protected with my own body behaved like batterers?

"This happened because I came back from Phoenix, Arizona," I finally answered.

Amy looked perplexed and I simply shrugged, "It's a long story."

As I have said, I was born into a terribly violent, dysfunctional family. As young children, spilling your milk got you knocked to the floor by a large man with military and police training. I was in battered woman training. Starting at the age of twelve I only lived at home intermittently, frequently finding the streets a safer place to be.

At about fourteen, during one of the periods I was in my parents' home, they offered sanctuary to my father's sex offending brother who was being sought by German authorities for child molestation. I later found out they knew this when they allowed him into their home with their four children.

I then became his focus, and after a brutal sexual assault I told my mother. The entire family blamed me for this assault despite the fact that I was only one in a parade of child victims. I was in battered woman training. My parents and beloved aunts lined up with other family members in holding me responsible.

At sixteen years, two weeks and one day a friend's father went before a judge so that I could marry. This man may have saved my life. I chose a twenty something engineer so that I could focus on school. I graduated in the top 10% of my class, and at the age of eighteen I loaded up my Volkswagen Van and drove to Phoenix with nothing but my Great Dane and a 12 gauge shot gun. For a few years, I waited tables around Phoenix and Scottsdale, and when Iran took the hostages I was afraid that my brother would be sent to war. I loaded up my van and came home – big mistake # 1.

Back home, things had only gotten worse. Rena was struggling seriously with mental health. There was no question as to why. As I walked in the door after a 1750-mile drive straight through, it was dinner time. Always an opportunity for violence, never squandered, my sister was curled up in the fetal position on the floor. Jim, our father, was kicking her while the other siblings sat silently at the table. I could hear Virginia, our mother, sobbing in another room. My father had only gotten drunker and meaner. My mother's head was buried further up her ass and my presence, after years away, wasn't even noticed. I moved in with them and the old shit was back up in my face.

Upon returning home, seeing my sister curled up like an animal, protecting her tender underbelly, I realized I had made some incredibly good choices for myself. I know that many young girls who have to spend time on the streets are badly hurt. I know that girls who marry early can be hurt. As that bastard kicked my sister over and over, it had never been more clear how much I had escaped by turning to the streets. I had often been hungry and slept in many an abandoned (or not) vehicle. But those were a mere inconvenience, given the alternative. Seeing my sister take her beating without shedding a tear, as her big sister had done, I never felt more overwhelmed by guilt at having been unable to protect her too.

Anyway – living back in that sick mess was again taking its toll. I couldn't get a job to save my life (in this scenario that is not a figure of speech) and knew I needed to get out of there. When I turned 21, the brother of my aunt's husband had a semi and offered to train me to drive coast to coast. He said he would pay me $400.00 a week. I happily accepted. I loved to travel and needed the money to get a place of my own. I also figured since he was connected to the family I might be safer – big mistake # 2. My own uncle wasn't safe for me, why would this man be?

His name was Larry and his entrance onto the stage of my life would be the beginning of a string of bad choices that would forever degrade my life. Growing up, we had always seen him sitting around and hear the adults talking about him. They would say that he had bad problems with women. He was considered really weird and people would talk about his tragic childhood. All of my life whenever I would see him, he was just sitting and staring. He wouldn't speak when spoken to and went to great lengths to hide from people. It didn't matter. I was going to learn to drive a semi and make, what was considered at the time to be, good money.

I got on the truck with him and at about Oklahoma he cleared his throat and told me that he wasn't going to be able to spend a lot of time with a female like me without having sex. That was all he said, and the message was clear. It was in a truck stop in Texas that my oldest child was conceived. Big mistake #?, well, I'm starting to loose track here. He paid me once and I gave that money to my mother for an engine she had put in my van when it seized up, earlier, somewhere in Texas. There were plenty of red flags but, coming from my background, I didn't see the flags, much less RECOGNIZE them as such.

Luck (or choices) have it, I was pregnant. My plan was to have the baby and raise her as a single parent. My father was not going to stand for that. He would not allow me to make that choice. Every night he would sit me, and sometimes Larry, down at the kitchen table and lecture, threaten etc... By evening my father is always showing his alcohol intake. When I was three months pregnant, I married a misogynist, under the pressure of a misogynist.

The father of my child immediately started beating me and my training to be a battered woman was now being realized. The first time he beat me I was three months pregnant, and it took two friends to pull him off of me. I always had bruises and knots on my head. Once my baby was born, alcohol became my escape from a life filled with misogynists, which included my mother.

One day we went fishing and camping at Patoka. We weren't catching anything, and I watched his mood change with every shot he took. He had a half a gallon of whisky and sat on the bank drinking and, against my protests, one worm at a time, he threw them into the lake to feed the fish. He said he didn't need to mess with putting it on a hook. When it started getting dark, I went to the tent, got undressed, and went to sleep. He came into the tent and we got into an argument over something, nothing, I'm sure. He started hitting me, and I ran from the tent. I was naked and he followed me into the woods and the black night.

As I fled barefoot through the woods crying and terrified, I tripped and fell into, what turned out to be, a ravine beside a road. Larry jumped on top of me and continued hitting me. At one point I looked up to see a young boy standing there. Larry got off of me and I saw a father looking down into the ditch. He was holding a fishing pole and simply said to his son, "Let's go." Even though they didn't offer assistance their presence had caused Larry to stop-possibly saving my life.

The physical abuse was only a part of it. The mental abuse was constant. He would get mad at me and say that I had slept with my uncle or he would call me any name he could think of. One time he bought me lingerie, a teddy. When I put it on he sat on the couch eating brownies and ridiculing me - my breasts were too little, my legs too short. I never did that again. He ridiculed me for reading. Said I had no mind of my own and needed someone else to tell me how and what to think. I still always knew that I would go to college.

I knew the relationship was a brutal mistake. When my first child, Sara was a few days old I loaded the Celica and drove to Phoenix. Sara had "colic" and screamed the whole way, and she would not stop screaming until sometime after her 21st birthday. To this day I believe that she screamed because she had repeatedly been beaten in utero. Anyway - Somewhere around Texas, I stopped at a hospital. They examined my precious, screaming baby, and then the kind nurses took care of her for a few hours while I slept. I then drove on to Phoenix.

I arrived in the desert valley crying and certainly suffering from postpartum depression about which, at that time, I knew nothing. I had no idea what I was doing or why. In hindsight, I know that I was trying to save my baby in the only way I knew how: fleeing. I had done that since I was twelve. In Phoenix, I got a room but never slept. My infant and I cried together for a few hours, I got back in the car and drove straight through to my home town. This time there was no hospital stop, nothing. She screamed,

I drove. So, when Amy looked at my daughter's contempt and asked, "How did this happen?" the answer really is, "I came back from Phoenix."

I returned to my batterer. My body was flooded with hormones and fear. I was overwhelmed by the screaming child, a battering husband, a vicious mother and a father that would rather see me dead at the hands of a batterer then to see me as a single parent – shaming the family. Fear was eating me so bad that I literally didn't know whether to come or go, and I returned to my batterer.

A couple of years and another baby passed. I was into the mom thing. I took them to the zoo and art museum, monitored their diets and read to them. Larry used to sit at the kitchen table drinking whisky and give them shots out of the cap. Amanda was just learning to stand, and she was thrilled to stand next to her daddy no matter what he was feeding her. The violence continued and after the incident with the rifle, I told him I was leaving him. He promised to prove me unfit and, one way or another, he would take my kids. Before I could collect our belongings he locked us out without clothes, diapers or bottles.

Along with the stress of the batterer I was suffering more of the consequences of speaking the truth. With the birth of little girls, childhood issues were surfacing and I was honestly confronting those. Since the abuse was no secret inside the home I expected that my brother and youngest sister would support me and gently encourage our parents to be honest and deal with the issues.

I now know that is not how it goes. Not only were they not going to support my efforts to recover from the abuse but they fell in line. I was the trouble maker and was used to set an example of what happens if you tell too much of the truth.

I believe the two youngest siblings actually preferred the way it was. At times, they contributed to the malevolent feelings and abuse of Rena and me because it kept attention focused away from them. They reaped the rewards of having all of the negative family energy directed toward us and the positive energy including money, time and attention focused on them. In their younger years I could understand how they would take advantage of this but, as they grew older they had a responsibility to step up. To this day, they believe their two older sisters deserved whatever they got.

Batterers Use of Counselors & Mediators as a Weapon

Now, more than a decade later and despite the evidence the courts had, I was subjected to a two or three year custody battle that cost between twenty to thirty thousand dollars. The courts were easily another weapon for my batterer and, at our request, the courts ordered that my ex-husband participate in counseling with me. I was tired of his years of trying to hurt me, knew that we had a lifetime to go and hoped that a counselor could help to alleviate some of his need to hurt and control me.

At this point I had many years experience working with other battered women, ten years experience teaching service providers about battered women and was an expert witness in these cases. I would have, and did, protest loudly over court-ordered mediation or counseling between a battered or formerly-battered woman and her perpetrator. But I believed I was somehow different. Somehow I thought that, because I had information and was aware of the dynamics, that I could take it. I thought that the information about the dynamics between me and the man that beat me could keep me from experiencing the problems that other battered women have when forced into counseling or mediation with the batterer. I was terribly wrong.

Prior to my understanding those dynamics I had been hurt by many counselors. Batterers are not just charming and manipulative with "their" women. They are also good at charming anyone else who can also influence, control or hurt the object of their "affection".

Aaron dragged me from counselor to counselor in an effort to fix me and while there were a number of times I was hurt, two instances were particularly hurtful. One night, after a lot of resistance, I agreed to attend an AA group with Aaron. He introduced me to the facilitator, Heather, and we all took our seat in the circle. I thought I was there as an observer. I had never attended an AA meeting but this one did not seem to be unfolding in the same way that I thought the meetings were intended. I thought I was there as an observer especially given that I was a first timer.

I was embarrassed as a lot of pressure was put on me to talk. The group of about twenty people were not pressuring me to talk about my drinking or any other type of addiction. I was being pressured into talking about my relationship with Aaron, who had been doing these groups for quite a while and had a close relationship with those encircling me.

Embarrassed and somewhat afraid, I relented. I softly told the group about being rolled and beaten in the paint and tied up with the duct tape and beaten. With the feelings raw, cutting deep into my mind I shared the experience of seeing my daughters and trying to worm away, naked, from the man I believed meant to kill me. Suddenly Heather screamed, "You're a liar. I can't listen to anymore. How could you say this about him. He suffers so much over you and you would say these things?"

She was now crying, and another group member jumped up and wrapped his arms around her. He walked her out of the room and into Aaron's kitchen. Someone else took over the group, and I don't remember a thing about what went on after that. I sat quietly, tears occasionally streaming down my face, deeply buried within myself. I was embarrassed, devastated and betrayed. It took many years for me to see clearly how orchestrated that night had been. Again, this batterer was validated, giving him more fuel to continue.

On another occasion I had been seeing a counselor named Irene who worked through a local hospital. I was seeing her alone and felt good about our relationship and where it was going. She taught me a little about inner child work and a little about imagery. It seemed to me like I had someone who was truly interested in my well-being and in teaching me the things I needed to know to recover from the violence that had plagued my life.

Aaron was pressuring me to turn this into joint counseling. His reasoning was that I no longer trusted anyone he recommended, and he was right. My trust was continuing to atrophy and, as impotent as I was at it, I was trying to protect myself. Of course, I relented again. He had control over everything in my life, including how I could recover and what, if any, future I might have.

Not only did we begin seeing Irene in joint counseling, but she also started individual with each of us. Explaining that he was working hard on himself, Aaron began seeing her twice a week at her home. One Saturday afternoon I accompanied Aaron to her home. We sat on her patio, in front of the pool for this session.

During the session I complained about Aaron's manipulation and continued efforts to control me. He hadn't out-and-out beaten me since he rolled me in the paint, but that was only because he was afraid that I now knew enough to send him to jail. Feeling safe enough to talk to Irene, I shared the different instances of manipulation and control and gave Aaron his due credit, which he demanded, for not beating my brains out.
Irene interrupted, "Jasper, I don't believe he is abusing you and after working with him, I don't believe he ever has."

Defeated I simply stood up, walked around the pool to the gate, down the walkway to the car and climbed in. Again, he was validated and with shame, embarrassment, and betrayal, I was invalidated. He had taken another support from me. He did not do it by being more honest and put-together, but by being more manipulative, fake and charming. I couldn't compete.

Twenty years later, as I waited to do a joint session with Virginia (my mother), Irene walked through the waiting room and into an office, taking a client with her. I hoped the woman was not battered, and if she was, I hoped that in the last two decades Irene might have learned some things. Initially I felt a need to tell Irene how she had effected me so many years ago but as I sat down to write her a letter, I found I had no interest. It just wasn't there.

While counselors may mean well, some may be no more equipped to deal with batterers than battered women are. If they are persuaded by the charm, manipulation, and coercion in only a few sessions lasting an hour or less, how can we possibly blame women who buy into it after weeks, months, years or even decades of exposure? If one who is supposed to be trained and experienced can't counter the charm how can we expect untrained, unsuspecting women to recognize and foresee the quagmire they are about to step into?

I never allowed Aaron to participate in counseling with me again. That's when he began sending long, flowery letters to every counselor I saw in an effort to influence them. These are included in

Letters From A Batterer along with the letter from an attorney telling him that if he didn't stop, she would take action for defamation and libel. Many counselors and coworkers that received these letters never told me about them, at Aaron's request. Those counselors who knew what was going on and understood the intent behind the letter, immediately handed it to me. I didn't understand at the time that Aaron had no right to contact my counselors or that they had an obligation to tell me about his efforts to influence them.

I sat alone in the waiting room of the psychiatrist's office. Aaron made this appointment for me believing that counselors were not equipped to deal with a personality as disturbed as mine. He was supposed to meet me there and, I presume, give the psychiatrist a summary of the problems he had with me.
"It's just getting harder and harder to control her. Once she found out I could be arrested for beating her she has become more difficult," I imagined he would say.
Aaron dragging me from shrink to shrink to be abused was typical, and I had yet to work with anyone who had not been influenced and charmed by his concern for me.
My heart flipped as the receptionist called my name and Aaron had not yet arrived. As I sat across the desk from the man, answering his barrage of questions, his phone rang. Disgusted at the interruption, he picked it up.
"No he can not come back here," he said, "I don't know anyone named Aaron Roberson or Jasper Jameson."
I motioned that I was Jasper, thinking he must not remember my name.
"I don't care how upset he is," he said to the receptionist dismissing my gestures, "I don't know what you're talking about. But I am with a client. Do not send anyone back here," and he hung up the phone. The psychiatrist sat quiet for a moment obviously sorting his thoughts. I was confused and waited for an explanation.
"You said the other counselors you've seen don't seem to think there is a problem?" he asked.
I nodded.

"Have you ever seen anyone without him having contact with them?" he asked.

I told him about Marsha, from the local battered women's shelter. She was supposed to be mine. I was attending the sessions, but it just didn't feel right. She seemed really focused on what I did to cause his anger. This was a center that served only victims of violent crimes and they were supposed to be the experts. I told the psychiatrist about how I found out that she was also having contact with Aaron, without my knowledge. As I listened to myself it was as if another window had been opened and fresh air flooded in replacing the rotting truths that I had been force fed.

Suddenly I understood. This charming, manipulative woman beater was influencing these "counselors". The psychiatrist strongly advised me to find my own counselor and not to even let Aaron know who it was. He explained that my counselor had no business talking with Aaron at all. He explained revictimization and why I felt so hurt by the people Aaron took me to see. He assured me that I didn't need a psychiatrist, that a counselor experienced with battered women would work fine. He shook his head as I explained that Marsha was a counselor from the local shelter, and told me to keep looking.

He gave me the number to the Salvation Army and recommended that I seek shelter for my daughters and myself - especially given that he had probably made Aaron extremely angry. He slid his telephone toward me. I made the phone call and an appointment knowing that I would not move out of my home into a shelter. I was, however, excited by the concept of having a counselor all my own.

Turned out that was the golden number. They assigned me a counselor who gave me the letter from Aaron when she received it and refused to see him when he tried to charm and then bully her. She was the one that helped me change my life, and I am still in touch, twenty years later. There were a couple of service providers who had contact with Aaron and immediately knew what they were looking at. It was no coincidence that they had all been trained by the Domestic Abuse Intervention Project (DAIP) out of Duluth, Minnesota.

And today, fifteen years later, I fearfully faced another counselor with a batterer. As the first court ordered appointment approached with Larry, I could only hope that the field had made some progress. The first session with Larry was horrible but not for the reasons I had come to expect.

I had not been with a battering male for more than a decade yet, because of a court order, I only had to look two feet in front of me to see the man who had brutally battered me for years. He had beaten me during pregnancy, abused my pets to hurt me and tormented me with any weapon he could find for 15 years after I had left him.

Now, he sat only feet from me arguing with a counselor we were court ordered to see. As he argued on and on with this tiny counselor I remembered the pain of those knots on my head and the debilitating pain I felt when he literally put his boot up my ass. The impact was so hard that it chipped the bone and my daughters laughed as he proudly told the story many years later. The impact of their laughter was crushing and was the first time I realized how they had become him.

I felt myself coming unraveled. I found myself remembering that tone of voice. With dread and fear, I worried that he would hit this woman. I realized I needed to protect myself. I pulled deeper and deeper into myself. I projected myself outside of myself, I worked hard to stay present and aware. Nothing worked to provide me the safety I needed. I sat stiff and disjointed through the conflict until the session ended and to this day could not tell you what they were arguing about.

I maintained my composure until I walked across the threshold of that counselor's door and I burst into tears. I drove the hour and a half home crying and spent the next four days in bed, crying, reliving the trauma of those years of violence and the last 15 years of him using my children as weapons.

I did three or four of those court order sessions with my perpetrator and couldn't take anymore. I am careful to differentiate between can't and won't. This was a matter of couldn't. I refused to continue and was threatened with jail. While I was guilty of contempt, there was no doubt I felt that, I did not deserve to go to jail for finally stepping up to protect myself.

I had thought that having the information about how I could be affected would help me prevent being retraumatized. I was wrong. I had thought I would be different than the women I advocated for, and I was wrong. Because of the counseling with the man who had beaten me so long ago, I was rapidly falling apart. With two teenage daughters in crisis, falling apart was not an option.

And I am not alone. Women all over the U.S. are being forced to negotiate, counsel and "reconcile" with men who have brutally beaten them. And women all over the U.S. are being retraumatized. Many women are being forced into "mediation" with men who are (or were) physically and emotionally abusive. While I am a proponent of Restorative Justice programs, mediation in domestic violence cases, or any case where there has been long term contact and a traumatic bond may have occurred, is inappropriate. Can you imagine a judge ordering the victim of a rape to "mediate" with the rapist? Can you imagine a judge ordering the victim of a violent home invasion into counseling with the invader? It would never happen. The fear and harm endured by women in a violent domestic relationship, is often minimized, not seen as a real crime.

Despite my continued explanations and pleas, instead of stepping up and explaining to the judge why it wasn't working and was inappropriate, the counselor told the judge I was in contempt. In an effort to keep me out of jail and to change policy for other women unfortunate enough to come before this judge, we collected position statements from battered women's organizations around the country. There was not one service provider for battered women, who we spoke to, that approved of forced counseling or mediation in domestic violence cases. The following Position Statement is one of those turned over to the court.

Victim's Justice Center Position Statement on Forced or Court Ordered Counseling & Mediations Between Battered or Formerly-Battered Women and Their Perpetrators

The Victims Justice Center Inc. is opposed to forced, court ordered or otherwise coerced counseling and mediations between battered or formerly-battered women and their perpetrators for the following reasons:

- Battered women frequently bond to the perpetrator due to trauma. This is called traumatic bonding. This bond may cause them to behave in a manner that pleases the batterer in an effort to reduce their own injuries. This is not conducive to the honesty necessary for counseling or mediation.
- If the battered or formerly-battered woman has been successful at lessening this bond, counseling or mediation can refresh the bond. For the purpose of mental health, refreshing a traumatic bond is not desirable. See attached on traumatic bonding.
- Counseling or mediation could put the victim/survivor at risk of being abused again because counseling and negotiation by it's nature provokes feelings, which the batterer has historically been inept at managing.
- In a violent relationship the perpetrators use not only verbal but nonverbal cues and threats. It is not possible for a counselor or mediator to recognize all of these, as they can be quite subtle and unique to each relationship.
- Batterers can be very manipulative, charming, and persuasive. Counselors may not always be able to recognize when they are being manipulated or charmed.
- Contact with the batterer may cause intense emotional feelings for the battered or formerly-battered woman. It may also provoke traumatic stress causing the victim/survivor to "relive" the traumatic events or jeopardize the progress she has made.
- Counseling or mediating in domestic violence situations is not something that all counselors are equipped for. The nature of the relationship requires special knowledge and skills.

- The battered woman has been forced, controlled, and coerced enough. It is not the role of the courts to continue this for the batterer.
- Batterers may use the courts, law enforcement, counselors, children or whatever other means they have available to them to continue abusing the woman after she has chosen to end the relationship. The courts must recognize this and refuse to assist the batterer.
- More so than with other crimes, because of traumatic bonding, it is important to minimize contact between victim and perpetrator. Face-to-face contact is one of the most important elements of the relationship in order for the batterer to maintain control. The courts must not encourage face-to-face contact in domestic violence cases.

Forced Counseling & "Mediations" in Domestic Violence

When I asked the judge to order counseling, I was thinking about parenting my daughters. I was not taking into consideration the fact that this man had brutally beaten me. Again, I had separated my own situation from what I knew about the victim's response to forced counseling and mediations and my own position on counseling and mediation in domestic violence cases. I subconsciously felt like I was above the common reaction that I saw in other women who were forced to do counseling with men who beat them. Looking back, I thought that since I had so much information, that I would be able to avoid the trauma that counseling with a batterer could cause. I thought information was all I needed. I was wrong. This time it was the courts that needed the information.

For clarification, and for the record, I use the term amelioration as opposed to mediation. During a mediation there is negotiation in which both parties give, in order to come to a solution. In a victim-offender mediation the victim has already given more than they ever consented to and, by their sheer participation, have shown a gracious spirit. The victim is expected to give no more, including forgiveness.

We (our Victim Services Division) do victim-offender ameliorations. We bring both primary and secondary victims together with the goal of helping them take a terrible experience and find it's highest and best use. There is more on this later. Anyway, back to joint counseling and "mediations" in domestic violence cases -

There are now a number of counselors that will not do joint counseling in a domestic violence situation. I applaud them because often they are fighting an uphill train of thought that believes if people are in a relationship, joint counseling as opposed to individual is required. Many people still believe that if a person is in a relationship then it is better to do the work together. That ignores the individual issues needed to be dealt with prior to dealing with relationship issues.

While victims of domestic violence have many issues, these should not be addressed in joint sessions with the batterers present. There are a number of reasons that joint counseling and "mediations" in domestic violence situations are inappropriate:

Victims Inability to be Honest

A victim who is sitting in counseling with her perpetrator can not be honest about her feelings, thoughts or relationship. Counselors ask for vulnerability and disclosure - two very dangerous requests to make of a victim in the presence of her batterer. Yet counselors arrogantly continue to ignore this fact, believing that their skills are greater than the impact the batterer has had on his victim.

Victims struggle to be honest with themselves about the level of trauma they have survived. They need a safe place even to be able to remember. Expecting her to participate honestly in this vulnerable process is unrealistic, cruel, and potentially dangerous. We often catch women between a rock and a hard spot. If she talks, she exposes herself and gives her batterer more ammo, and if she doesn't, she appears difficult and resistant to therapy. And if she is court ordered to participate, what may be construed as her resistance can weigh heavily against her in court decisions.

Giving Batterer More Ammunition

Having a perpetrator present during counseling with the victim is not only damaging to the victim but also dangerous. As you can see, I can't stress that enough. If she does take the risk of being honest, she is giving the batterer more ammunition with which to abuse her. He already has plenty. For a third party to point out faults in the victim only reinforces what the batterer has filled her head with and supports his position, "She is defective and if we could just fix her I could stop having to beat her." *Letters From A Batterer*, demonstrates this. With every new psychological term Aaron learned came a new barrage of allegations and supposed defects that justified his abuse.

Message That She is Equally to Blame for Her Victimization

Joint counseling, as with a mediation, in a violent domestic relationship sends the message that both parties are to blame and that this is a problem with the relationship that both parties equally have the power to fix. It is not. This is his problem, and it is about power and control - not a dysfunctional marriage. She does not have the power to fix this. If she did, she would have.

Until the violent partner has been held accountable for his actions and has made changes, other communication issues within the marriage can not be explored with any degree of safety. Violence is not a relationship issue - even if both partners use it in a relationship. It is a learned pattern of individual behavior. He has already spent years persuading her that this is her fault, and the batterer often believes this. It is damaging, and again, dangerous for a third party to reinforce this thinking error.

Covert Intimidation

A relationship between two people is private and truly known only to them. This is especially true when violence is involved because of the secrecy induced by her shame and his success at isolating her. It is arrogant of counselors, mediators, and other interveners to think that they can foresee every issue that may arise and every form of threat the batterer uses. The threats that a batterer uses can be so covert and subtle that there is no way for an outsider to recognize them, and this fact makes mediations and counseling in domestic violence situations unrealistic and potentially lethal.

We can try to predict these threats, but remember she has spent years in a hypervigilant state and is reading every move he makes. The slightest change in facial expression (even micro expressions) can send her signals that she is in danger and must submit. We can not effectively recognize all of the threats and coercion. It is arrogant of us to think we can monitor this complicated pattern of hidden messages and behaviors in weekly sessions. Between the two of them, there are words and nonverbal cues that have meaning only to the two of them. He can be threatening her right in front of us, and we won't know it. He can be degrading her with a motion that means nothing to us but is very clear to the victim and sends a very clear message to her.

I was teaching a class for the victim-offender mediation Association (VOMA) on why battered women stay and why mediations should not be done in domestic violence cases. This can be a hot topic, and certainly was this day, especially given that this area has so much money making potential for attorneys. I was struggling to make one of my points when a victim advocate from Ohio, I believe, interrupted me to make my point.

She told of doing a mediation, early in her career, in a domestic case. As the mediation progressed, the woman became more and more unglued as the batterer continued to insist she was unreasonable and crazy. Seemingly, out of the blue, the woman burst into tears and ran from the room.
As she ran out the batterer calmly looked at the mediator and said, "I told you. She's not stable."

Now, under most circumstances like that, a counselor or mediator would not follow the client out, but simply respect their decision to discontinue participation. This woman relied on her instincts and followed the battered woman out, even though the batterer, in her mind, was clearly right about this and, she reasoned probably right about everything else he was saying. She found him to be quite rational, charming, and sincerely interested in the well-being of this woman.

In the hallway, the woman sat crumpled, crying, and shaking. She told the mediator that the problem started when he walked in. The pants he was wearing were the pants he wore when he beat her. They were the "consequence pants". Through her tears she told of several other cues the batterer was sending her, including the endearing pet name "baby" which he only used during a beating.

As this victim advocate continued, I was grateful to her. She had taken my point, in this room full of attorneys and otherwise educated mediators, and made it in a way I couldn't have. The group got it. The cues between any husband and wife are not always apparent to others. In a battering relationship the woman cannot participate in mediation or counseling on even footing because the history and threat of violence is always there.

Using Intervener to Abuse Victim and Support Batterer

Batterers are by nature charming and manipulative. As demonstrated in Aaron's letters, *Letters From A Batterer*, they will go to great lengths to seduce the victim's counselor. Why? Because they need to be in control. Having the counselor look to the controller for the reality of the situation is just what he wants, because the victim's reality becomes invisible, just like at home. If the batterer can make the counselor see how screwed up the victim is, then the counselor will fix her, and he won't have to beat her anymore. Or at least that's how the story goes.

Like children of the relationship, the counselor is an excellent tool for the batterer to use to advance his agenda. In fact, who better? This is an "expert". This is a person who the victim is turning to for help and may be someone she can trust. And when the counselor has been seduced and bought into the batterer's way of thinking, the victim feels betrayed and may end the relationship with the counselor. The batterer's argument is then, "See, it is your fault. Your own counselor told you so, and you just don't want to hear it."

I would not use a counselor that did not openly identify herself as a formerly-battered woman when asked, and I recommend that battered women require that of their counselors. This experience requirement is not unreasonable, given the potential for damage, and counselors who are formerly-battered women are not in short supply. The difficulty is in getting a counselor to admit that up front because of the stigma attached to being a battered or formerly-battered woman and the counselor's aversion to self-revelation with clients. If she buys into the stigma attached to being formerly-battered then she is not for you. Move on.

Conflict of Interest

There is an inherent conflict of interest when doing joint counseling with a batterer and his victim. This conflict of interest extends to counseling itself. Much to my families dismay, I was always a proponent of counseling as a tool for mental health maintenance. As I see more and more from counselors, this becomes less and less so. Instead, I find myself steering the people I work with to people educated and experienced in less traditional manners, yet specific to the trauma or issue.

The conflict of interest inherent in counseling is that the goal should be to help the client get to the point of not needing counseling. If the counselor succeeds at this, then they have an open Tuesday evening slot that they need to fill, in order to make their car payment. It is not in the counselor's best interest to "cure" their clients.

Battered women and other victims of violent crimes do not need therapy; they need radical education regarding oppression; why she stays; offenders; why she is responding to trauma the way that she is; and tools to help her survive and eventually thrive. Treating battered women as if they have a mental health problem supports the position that it's her problem, which he has gone to radical lengths to instill in her. Battered women need information and support. Teaching battered women to think critically about what has happened is constructive - as opposed to questioning their mental health which supports everything the batterer has already done.

She needs encouragement to question the batterer's behavior as opposed to her own.

While I can warn against joint counseling and mediations in violent relationships until my face falls off, it is still going to occur. It will continue to occur because the counselor thinks she can handle it, the victim is hiding the abuse, or the courts order it. The counselor who refuses to accept the advice not to do it is unlikely to accept tips on how to do it. This information is available here, if for no other reason, than to warn the victim who may participate.

Batterer's Groups

Women who are being beaten by their intimate partners cling to the hope they are given by batterer's groups. The honeymoon phase of this dysfunctional relationship keeps the women bonded to and hanging onto the kind side of this man, and there is one. The promise of change keeps hope alive.

The whole relationship is based on control and extremes. As violent and abusive as his behavior may be is how passionate he may be and how sweet he can be during the honeymoon phase of the relationship. The DAIP charted the phases of an abusive relationship. They coined the term honeymoon phase, which is the phase right after an incident of violence in which the man is bringing gifts, apologizing and trying to make sure she stays. Albert Biderman called this Occasional Indulgences (Biderman's Chart of Coercion for Amnesty International) and included it as a necessary component of the coercive behaviors that cause hostages to bond.

When the man enters the batterer's group, the woman frequently believes that it is finally happening – that the batterer is going to change and become the loving partner she yearns for. She hangs onto the relationship with the hope that her lover will stop beating her; these groups reinforce that hope and goal. This seldom happens, and in fact, the groups <u>don't</u> work more often than they do.

A batterer's group that is based on the work of the DAIP has the components necessary for a man to change his behavior, but the question is - does he want it enough to do the hard work necessary to incorporate the information and tools the group offers? Again, he has the power to change or not to change. This is one of the few areas where he may refuse to use the power he has. If the man is ready and willing, there is nothing on earth that will keep him from doing so. If he is not ready and willing to change, there is nothing on earth that can make him.

I have to caution that just because a group is using the model designed by the DAIP does not mean that the facilitator is doing as they were trained. They may have added so much "stuff" in an effort to enhance or add to the DAIP's program, that their program has become useless or even worse, dangerous. When batterers programs fail to do skilled partner contact; when they don't have formerly-battered women monitoring the groups and facilitator skills, and when women's experience and feedback is secondary or nonexistent, a program with the best of intentions may actually be more dangerous for the partners of the male participants.

Some groups do what needs to be done to help the batterer face his behaviors. Whether or not their efforts make a difference is based on the batterer's willingness to look at himself from the inside out, the skill of the facilitator, the facilitator's willingness to be held accountable, and the programs willingness to hold the batterer accountable. There are other groups that give women false hope, reinforce the behavior of the batterers, and collude with them in their justification of woman beating.

While compiling Aaron's letters, for the book *Letters From A Batterer*, I was looking for someone experienced with batterer's groups to help me explain what Aaron was doing and why. As I interviewed facilitators, I insisted they be trained in (and using) the DAIP's program. I found a facilitator and sent him the letters. The analysis that he sent back was shocking. While I will not quote him because he did not agree to be used as a bad example, his analysis sounded just like Aaron himself. Batterer's groups can be very dangerous for the battered women.

After beating me in the yellow paint, Aaron agreed to attend a batterer's group. The first group he entered was one which used the program designed by the Domestic Abuse Intervention Project (DAIP). He was kicked out of the group, after which they called me and told me they believed he was very dangerous and I was at great risk. After being kicked out of that group, he attended another well-known group that was not using the DAIP model. As with every other area of his life, Aaron graduated that program as exemplary.

Had I not had warning from the first program, which I later trained in, I would have thought I was safe, based on his completion of the second program. Facilitators of batterer's groups who are not properly trained put battered women at greater risk in a number of ways.

Some Things To Look For In Batterer's Groups

While these groups offer opportunity, they should be undertaken with safety policies in place for the women and should not be seen as the "fix" for the relationship. They should be undertaken, not as marriage counseling or individual counseling, rather as an opportunity to change a dangerous citizen into one who can be a positive member of his community.

The groups should focus their attention on the belief system of the batterer that reduces the cognitive dissonance allowing them to beat women. In other words, to abuse women, children, animals; to maintain racist or sexist ideas; there has to be a belief system that tells the abuser that the target group or his victims are less important than he is and that somehow they deserve it. Batterer's groups are not an opportunity to talk about how mommy did this or that, rather they should challenge the thinking errors that the offender uses to justify in his own mind his abusive behaviors.

Monitors

Early in my career, some twenty five years ago, the thinking was that batterer's groups needed to be "staffed" with a monitor. These were formerly-battered women who would watch the staff of the batterer's group for collusion (supporting the thinking errors), staff bonding with the batterers, and things that might put the victims at further risk. This is an important safety measure.

Another reason monitors are a good idea is that a survivor can catch subtleties that even a highly trained facilitator would miss. The victims/survivors truly are the experts, and every group should have one present at every session. This would increase the safety and effectiveness of batterer's groups. I do not know whether the idea of monitors caught on, but it should be a requirement for running a batterer's group. **There is no amount of training that can raise the facilitator's awareness to the level of a survivor**.

During one of the groups I monitored, I listened as a batterer described his attack on his partner.
When confronted by the facilitator his response was, "She should have known not to do that. She knows me well enough to know that would make me mad. She knew I would lose it."
I interrupted the facilitator and addressed the batterer, "Do you have any idea how much energy it takes to watch you and try to predict when, where, how, and what will cause the next beating? Do you have any idea how bone-deep exhausting it is to try to make sure you are happy, to watch your every move and mood in an effort to avoid a beating?"
The entire room fell silent along with the batterer who held the figurative talking stick. I watched my words sink into his brain, and I watched him take them to heart.

That was a subtle reality that, during that group, was not seen by the facilitator - someone who had not been in a violent domestic relationship. A male facilitator who had never lived through the exhaustion and anxiety brought on by the hypervigilance it takes to minimize the number of beatings could not have responded in that way, to that justification. Batterer's groups need to be staffed with monitors who have actually survived the self-esteem gutter of a brutal relationship.

For clarification, when I talk about monitors and monitoring I am not talking about taping the sessions to later play back and assess the facilitator's skill. When I use the term monitoring I am talking about using a formerly-battered woman in each and every group to ensure that the facilitator is not further endangering the men's families.

Giving Victims A False Sense Of Security

Often a victim feels a false sense of security when her violent partner begins participation in a batterer's group. Her thinking is that he will be cured and she is now safe. This is not the case, and his participation in the group may raise issues in him that put her in even greater danger because, as I said before, self improvement by it's nature brings up issues. During group, the violence and his beliefs and triggers that lead up to it must be poked and examined. This can cause the batterer's anger to surface again and even escalate. Victims need to be made aware of this. They need to be made aware of the limitations and safety issues brought about by his participation in a batterers group.

Keeping Victims Informed

The victim is seldom privy to what occurs in group, and if she does hear about the group, it is from the abuser and is strictly what he chooses to share from what is a seriously skewed perspective. When issues or feelings that endanger the victim have been raised and or expressed in group, she must be informed. I am insulted by the number of groups that assert they owe their members confidentiality when we know that is not the case when someone is a danger to themselves or others. Many accountable batterer's program will attempt to notify her before he leaves the group. They make it their priority to inform her as soon as possible. The victim should be kept informed of the batterer's progress, or lack of, in group. Even if the group has a policy of confidentiality, it should never mean that she is not fully informed of anything that is a threat to her safety. They have an obligation to alert the woman when she is in danger.

When I was a monitoring, we had a group member who was HIV positive. The offender refused to tell the woman he was beating and, despite my pleas, the facilitators, citing confidentiality, refused to inform the victim that she was being regularly exposed to the AIDS virus.

I was dismissed from group within a few days of my protests, and I have no idea who his victim was and whether she survived her repeated exposure to HIV. If she did in fact contract AIDS, this group and the facilitators have her blood on their hands. They had an obligation to see that she was told about her partner's HIV status, and they refused.

Empathy Considered Guilt

When I began researching and designing Restorative Justice programs, I realized the impact that victims could have on offenders. I began teaching offenders about the reality of women and, in particular, victims of violent crimes. I often take the victims to groups of offenders to share their experiences. This is commonly referred to as victim impact. Often groups welcome us. Occasionally we are told that the victims are not welcome. The reason given is that the facilitator is afraid that the men will feel guilty.

I do understand the foundation for this decision. And while the foundation may be sound, the reality is that as long as the offenders are protected from the true consequences of their actions toward the victims, we can't elicit the empathy the batterers need to make long term changes.

In my offender groups, I do not berate or diminish my participants in any way, and in fact, would stop anyone that disrespected them. Even my adolescents are referred to as "sir," and I model a high level of respect. Like the animals I work with, using violence and abuse actually works against us. At the same time that I am modeling compassion, empathy, and respect, my boys are immersed in the reality of victims, and that information is put back to back with their own traumas. This helps the offenders not only to intellectualize the impact they have on others, but to feel it through their own traumatic experiences.

I have done victim impact with batterers and battered women, survivors of sex crimes and sex offenders, racists and black men, batterers and young men who saw their mothers beaten, and with the American Medical Association and survivors of white coat/white collar crime. Our participants, both victim and offender, are treated with the utmost respect, and if they feel guilt as they listen to how their victims are affected, then we have done our job.

Guilt is an indicator feeling from which we should not shelter our students. Guilt is a red flag telling us that something is wrong with our behavior, that we are doing something we shouldn't. New age thinking and psychobabble would have us believe that no one should feel guilt. That is dangerous. We must not let our psychobabble get crossed up with, and eclipse, our logic. Guilt is being confused with shame. Guilt tells us our behavior is bad. Shame is the feeling that screams at us that we are bad.

Without that red flag feeling of guilt, we are dangerous, as proven by the offenders I work with. The need for victim impact in an effort to elicit empathy should not be denied offenders in order to protect them from the face-to-face and highly emotional consequences of their actions. At the same time we cannot disrespectfully demand respect. We can not cruelly demand empathy and compassion. We can not violently demand peace.

Collusion of Facilitators

Protecting offenders from the victim's reality of being traumatized by the offender, is one way that facilitators collude with offenders. This is collusion because it supports the offender's notion that the victim doesn't need to be heard, that he doesn't have to hear her if it makes him uncomfortable. It supports that his comfort is primary. Self examination and looking at the harm we have caused others is extremely uncomfortable. Listening to the harm I caused my children during the years I was sedating my pain with alcohol was humiliating, embarrassing, and very uncomfortable. Yet I knew that for my daughters to recover they needed to be heard. They needed to know I was willing to go through the discomfort - for them. They needed to know that I "got" it.

But collusion happens in so many more ways than denying the victims a voice. In my groups I insist that the offender refer to his victim by her first name instead of just saying "her" or "my victim" and keeping her depersonalized. Collusion is when we not only laugh at, but allow blond or other degrading jokes.

We are also seeing facilitators of batterer's groups, among others, who are actually asserting that the men themselves are the victims of a society that has taught them not to show their feelings and forces them to be tough. And men are the victims of an unfair society, like the rest of us. There is a relatively new assertion, by a psychologist, being advanced by a talk show host, that batterers are the victims of manipulative, masochistic women who need to be beaten in order to have their needs met. So, not only do we hear the batterers themselves take a victim stance, but the victims, and a surprising array of people, are now taking the victim stance for them.

I am even seeing it in groups who use the DAIP Model. While these facilitators proudly boast that they are using this model, they then spew victim blaming rhetoric that reverses the roles, painting women and society as the perpetrators and the men as victims. This is absurd.

While brought up in an unfair society, men who batter are not generally an oppressed group of people. Living in an unfair world is an experience we all share. With all of the privileges available to the middle-class white man, it is fair that we expect them to embark on a journey of self-discovery as opposed to painting themselves as victims because they did not seek out answers to their behavior. Because they made no efforts to understand their behavior does not make them victims.

These men are not victims. They have made a choice to live in an unexamined world. Because they don't absorb wisdom through their ass from a Hazy-Boy recliner does not a victim make. This whole argument, in and of itself, is a victim stance served up by service providers on behalf of men who would abuse anything they could catch.

Counselor & Facilitator Bonding

I know from working with hundreds of adolescent offenders how easy it is to care about them, and not only them but any other soul we spend time with. Add to that the fact that perpetrators are particularly manipulative and charming and have learned through trial and error what works and how to be endearing. The manipulation and charm is how they prime their victims, get along, and generally get what they want. As with a batterer, they don't just turn that off when they aren't "hunting".

There are many criminals walking around who have never been arrested. After my brain injury, I spent a long time totally isolated on a farm. When I started having contact with people again I looked at my husband, dead serious, and said, "These are all offenders who haven't been caught." And while this isn't completely true, and came from the innocence of a brain injury, the statement was true enough to show my confusion.

Even people who have experience working with incarcerated offenders have to constantly be on guard for manipulation and being groomed and charmed. Not having the experience or training in offenders leaves counselors blind and subject to the skills of those they work with.

This is what sometimes happens in joint counseling, mediation, batterer's groups, treatment programs in correctional facilities, and when law enforcement arrive on the scene. The service provider sees what the offender wants them to see and they don't have the skills to counter it anymore than the victim had the skills to counter it.

6

Common Offender Arguments, Case Problems & Intervener Mistakes

Battered Woman/Victim Looks Crazy

The offender's defense that she's crazy needs to be totally thrown out. As I said earlier, even if she is crazy, that does not mean she deserves to be assaulted, raped, or harmed in any other way. We do not permit people to traumatize others because they have a disability, and the likelihood that she is actually "crazy" is slight. If she meets some type of criteria for "crazy," then we need to look at persistent trauma as a contributing factor and delay any diagnosis.

There are several categories of crimes for which we blame the victim. There are many tools that we use to do that, and calling her crazy is one of them. If a person can't deny the crime, then minimizing and blaming the victim is the next step. Putting the attention on the victim as opposed to the crime or the offender helps the offender stay in his comfort zone, like not hearing the victim's response to trauma.

Discrediting the victim with allegations of "crazy" is so universal that I see it as a predictable justification made by rapists, batterers, and even negligent and criminal doctors, the latter having more serious weight and consequences for the victim. Yet, as common as this defense is, it still works. Just ask any of the victims that have been handed back to their offender with a 72-hour hold. This happens when a doctor who is accused of medical malpractice (negligence or abuse) goes before a judge and has his victim held for a 72-hour psychiatric evaluation. Not only does this serve the purpose of terror and intimidation but discredits her and puts the victim back under the control of the offender. Prior to working with these victims, I would have never believed this was happening. After working with this group of "unpopular" victims I am horrified at how often it does happen.

Whether it is the rich corporation claiming that an entire class action of participants is crazy, the doctor that gets a 72-hour hold on a victim that has filed suit, the celebrity rapist, or the now grown, crack baby that has just raped his sister, this is one of the first, and most expected defenses out of a perpetrator's mouth.

Victims may look "crazy" because they have just been traumatized, and trauma plugs into so many emotions, so fast, that many victims appear to be "overreacting" or "dramatic". The victim struggles to sort through these emotions quickly enough to please onlookers. People in extreme circumstances behave in extreme ways.

Like the prey animal, a person that has just been through a traumatic event may be functioning from the part of the brain that is screaming, "Fight, freeze or flee." Like the spooked horse, they may run, rear, or kick, just in case there's a threat around. Like the rabbit that suspects danger they may freeze. The survivor of a violent crime may behave anywhere along the entire spectrum of behavior, and people often think they can predict what that will be. If it's not what they think it should be, they often draw "crazy" conclusions.

I heard a judge say to a woman, "I have worked in family court for 20 years and seen many battered women, and you are not one of them. I know how they behave, and this isn't it." I can't remember how exactly that woman was behaving, but the judge's judgment was probably incorporated into her self blame despite the fact that she had found the courage to enter a court. How arrogant to think that we can recognize and even predict every response, especially after a trauma has occurred. How unfortunate that people would have any expectation and standard of "normal" for beings that have just fought for their life.

The offender is great at knowing what will turn the victim inside out and then pushing those buttons.
He then calmly points at her and says, "See, I told you. She's crazy."
When this is occurring, it is unlikely that a third party could recognize it, because a victim and offender that have spent a long time together speak in shorthand, in their own language.
Remember, abusers grow calmer as they batter and take control. It is the opposite for victims. It is not hard to see an hysterical, crying woman and a calm man, and see the woman as the problem.

If Someone Wants To Kill You, They Can't Be Stopped

When the system miserably fails a woman and her children, they often respond with, "If someone wants to kill you, they're going to kill you. Nothing can stop them." On the contrary. If a judge, diplomat, former hostage, important witness, government official is at risk, knows the source of the threat and complains, somehow law enforcement and the system find a way to stop them.

Victims Behavior Isn't What It Should Be

The behaviors of traumatized humans and animals can be perplexing. And while they are predictable within a range, that range is quite broad. For example, the victim that is judged harshly for behaving "normally" after an assault has probably not had the experience set in, or she may be dissociated in an effort to protect her mind. She may be called a liar for "under reacting" and called crazy for "over reacting".

We have no business judging the behaviors of a victim/survivor after the trauma. We can expect, and possibly try to head off, some behaviors, but we need to keep in mind that they are responding in whatever way they are behaving for a reason, and that reason may not be apparent to the onlooker, intervener or loved one.

He Says, She Says –
When He Is Certain It Wasn't Rape and She Knows It Was

I consulted on a rape mediation and the lead mediator was truly stumped.

"Jasper, he swears he didn't rape her and, I am certain he really believes this, and I don't believe the victim is lying. I mean this woman was black and blue from head to toe," she said.

Some background – This was a high profile, nationally reported gang rape. One of the fourth or fifth men in line wanted to participate in a victim-offender amelioration. I was a consultant on victimology.

"If she had already been raped repeatedly, and he was the fifth, fourth or even the first man to rape her, at that point she was trying to reduce her injuries. She may have felt the threat was so great that she did become consenting to keep her attacker happy and reduce her injuries. She still was not consenting," I said, "Oh, and by the way, check into rohipnol, the date rape drug. That would explain why she can't remember a thing."

It turned out that the first man to rape her had drugged her, and the offender that participated in the mediation understood how she was raped and apologized for his participation. This rapist participated in the amelioration because he truly didn't understand what had happened and wanted to. The mediation clarified, at least, a part of this for both of them.

But back to the point of a victim's compliance looking like consent. If the victim believes that she will reduce her injuries by making the attacker like her, then we have to respect that tactic. She was there. We were not. We encourage diplomat hostages to follow their gut, comply if necessary and to encourage a bond, yet we harshly judge women who respond this way and choose not to fight back.

This is also not to say that the attacker truly isn't confused. Just when I think I've heard every horrible thing that one human can do to another, humans invent another. Listening to the victim issues of adolescent sex offenders, it is easy to understand how their thinking got so screwed up. While it is not typical that the offender actually believes the victim really wanted it, it does happen.

One way I counter that argument is to ask them to tell me what the victim's face looked like while they committed their crime and what the victim was saying. Describing the victim's face as she was raped usually ends the offender's denial on her consent.

Accusing the victim of consent is also a standard argument, just like the crazy defense. I don't know how many sex offenders I've listened to swear that the four-year-old he assaulted consented, like the rape victim that "wanted it". This is so standard that it should be thrown out when uttered.

I Lost Control

Batterers often use the excuse that they "lost control". My response to them is that they did not lose control. They used as much control as was necessary to achieve their goal. They did not lose it, murder the victim, and then sit down and eat her body. That is losing control.

They exerted enough domination and violence to accomplish the compliance. I often ask them how often they "lose control" in the workplace, with their friends or with law enforcement. That's often the point where it sinks in. They always admit that they never "lose control" in those situations. There was no loss of control with their partner either. They didn't use violence on someone who would fight back. They chose to use violence where there would be little risk of consequence or accountability for them.

Victim Stance

As demonstrated in the book *Letters From A Batterer*, batterers, other offenders, and people who are generally uncomfortable with the fact that they've been "caught" often take what is referred to as a victim stance. This works well with the crazy defense (he is the victim of a crazy woman). This works well with the "she wanted it" argument, and now she's victimizing me by reporting a crime, because she wants revenge. The concept that I lost control and was provoked is a very common theme. And this works well with "I was provoked" and then "lost control."

Just like the conditions necessary for bonding to occur, (outlined in Chapter 3) these arguments work well together when the offender has figured out just how to put them together so he looks as good as he can and to make her look as bad as he can. And again, if counselors, law enforcement, and other trained service providers can't recognize these manipulations and lies, why would we expect women to recognize them and not be taken in by these justifications or violence? These are often young women with little experience, and they have been taught little about these issues, and we expect them to recognize and avoid these relationships.

Negligent (or criminal) doctors and corporations claim they are the victims of "money grubbing", "gold digging" consumers. Child molesters claim they were seduced by the three-year-old who wanted it. Rapists claim they were victims of their hormones, the victim's sex appeal, or a vendetta against them. Batterers claim that they are victims of crazy, promiscuous, provocative, or violent women. Like most of the rationalizations and justifications used by offenders, this argument is as predictable as the sunrise and set.

The victim stance is easy to counter. There is no one responsible for the offender's actions but the offender. Regardless of the behavior of another, they do not deserve to be beaten, raped or otherwise assaulted. They do not deserve to be assaulted and then blamed for the behavior of the offender.

Provocation

While others can provoke a feeling in us, they cannot provoke an action. If actions could be provoked there would be NO law-abiding citizens. We would all be assaulting and killing each other - as opposed to some of us working real hard to control feelings like rage and vengeance. Every battered woman would also be a murderer, and every man would be a rapist. We have to be responsible not only for our own behavior but for the maturity that it takes to respond appropriately to a world absolutely filled with aggravating and provocative people. Provocation of feelings exists. Provocation of an action does not.

Labeling The Batterer
Low Self Esteem (Depression, Codependency)

This is demonstrated well in *Letters From A Batterer*, and is a technique employed by the offender to focus the attention back on him, excuse his behavior, support his victim stance, and seek sympathy. This is an effort to decriminalize his behavior and turn it into a medical issue, which relieves his responsibility. Like the argument of losing control or being provoked, if his crime is due to a medical condition then he may not be responsible in the same way.

The number of service providers, including those that conduct batterer's groups, who buy into this is surprising and dangerous. While they medicalize wife beating, the victim is trying to find some semblance of safety and is believing that because he is now involved in group or receiving "treatment," she is safer.

I have yet to meet a batterer who did not use low self-esteem, depression, or codependency as his reason for violence. It is not in the batterer's best interest, or his victim's, for his behavior to be labeled as a sickness. That only provides another excuse that the batterer can use to cling to these behaviors. Regardless of how you frame it, this is a behavior that is almost always a choice. I say almost because certain brain disorders and injuries can make emotions impossible for some to control. But this is not what we are talking about.

To use a Dr. Philism, this is a "life choice," and when you turn it into an illness you take the control and the fix out of the batterer's power. He batters for power and control and, by medicalizing it, you are telling him that the reason he batters for power and control is out of his power and control.

Labeling Battered Women/Victims

I was teaching a counselor how to work with battered women -for which she was receiving four credit hours of 400 level criminology. I would teach a group of battered and formerly-battered women why they stay and then worked to teach them how to present their stories to an audience of service providers. The counselor's (psychiatric social worker) role was to help the women deal with the issues that this class and preparation brought up.

I became terribly frustrated because the counselor labeled all of the women I taught, and prepared to present their stories, as having borderline personality disorder. Had this been accurate, it would have been very difficult to work with these women. She was so rigid that, again, I found myself unable to shake the counselor out of her training. As I struggled with what to do with her, because she was useless to me, I remembered a warning from the doctor who had spent years teaching me to work with sex offenders.
"Jasper, you have to be careful when referring battered women to counselors. They inevitably label them as borderlines, and you can imagine the implications that has," he said.

He had nailed it. As my student labeled every woman we taught, I thought through the consequence of carrying that label around. These women would be seen as hopeless by everyone who saw that diagnosis. Borderlines are considered resistant and hard to work with, and the prognosis is poor. Trauma survivors may look like borderlines, but need to be dealt with as trauma survivors, not hopeless psychiatric cases. And anyone who believes our health records are private only has to read the forms we are asked to sign when we seek out treatment. Medical records are passed around without inhibition. This is another injustice and barrier to positive intervention that counselors and other mental health providers saddle battered women with. My student had to be moved to another project to finish up her credits because her previous training had been so rigid and inflexible that she couldn't shake it off enough to take in new information.

Labeling survivors of recent trauma is not productive. Trauma causes us to behave in ways that we might not otherwise behave. Often the resulting self-hatred that comes from trauma expresses itself in self-destructive ways. Yes, the survivor is living in chaos and struggling with personal relationships. As transient or permanent as these behaviors may be, they are the result of a trauma and can be modified. And this is a crisis period. Rather than exploring why she feels something, direct approaches like teaching about oppression and power and control are empowering and move a battered woman toward thinking critically about her own situation and what she needs.

As I explained in the section on revictimization, after a trauma the victim/survivor is susceptible to being targeted by another perpetrator. This is not the time for a counselor to be unshakable in their traditional training, filling a time slot, or insisting the client find the answer on her own. Her head is on fire, she doesn't know it, and if you don't tell her she could be seriously injured or killed. Yet an incredible number of counselors will squander this opportunity and watch and wait as the victim is hurt over and over while they take no directive role, simply sitting back and repeatedly asking, "And how do you feel about that?"

Women need a solid advocate, one who gives honest and accurate information and supports her critical thinking and making her own decisions. To give honest and accurate information, we must have honest and accurate information. To have this we must be humble and flexible enough to receive it. The victim also needs an ally who believes she has the skills she needs. These skills must be brought back into her awareness, and she must be respected and encouraged as she practices bringing them back into her toolbox.

"There Is No Reality Only Perception"

While psychology offers us so much information and so many tools it also offers so many opportunities to do harm. From Freud's penis envy to recent phrases like, "There are no victims, only volunteers," psychology has the ability to do incredible damage to the victim and the credibility to make it stick. Just as the diagnosis of borderline sticks with the victim through a lifetime, so does the other damage caused by mental health providers.

One of the most damaging phrases to come along is, "There is no reality, only perception." Somebody said it, it sounded good but apparently, no one actually thought about the meaning of the phrase when all those words are strung together. As I said earlier, I highly recommend offenders try telling that one to the judge, "Your honor, there is no reality only perception. It is simply her perception that I raped her at gunpoint. It is simply her perception that the hospital found tears and evidence. I didn't rape her. That's not real, just her perception."

While this cute little statement may sound good, it fosters bad mental health. From alcoholics, who don't want to acknowledge the damage their addiction is doing to the family - to dysfunctional parents who don't want to own the harm they have caused - to batterers denying the covert manipulation they use to terrorize their victims, the credibility that this statement has been given by counselors and other "authorities" has provided a great big opening for wrong doers to skirt their responsibility. They haven't wasted a second jumping through that opening.

There is reality. There is perception and there is a great deal of gray area. We know that babies come from sex. That is real. We know that the chemicals used in meth labs can explode. That is real. We know what causes a bruise. We know that raping children not only causes them physical pain but emotional pain, and we know that watching your mother beaten hurts a child emotionally.

There Are No Victims Only Volunteers

The first time I heard this pat little, simplistic statement come out of the mouth of a powerful, highly respected psychologist, my mouth hit the floor. Again, tell that one to the judge. I can't imagine how a statement like that hurts the mothers who have lost children to drunk drivers, the victims/survivors of violent home invasions and child abuse and on and on and on. While many of us bear the responsibility of terrible choices that put a target on us, we are not, and can never, be responsible for the choices of another. And when we make bad choices that put us at risk we do so for reasons, either our own thinking errors, lack of information etc… That does not mean we volunteered to satisfy the greed or violent choice of another.

It is so important that we actually think about the words we are saying. My formal education is in communication for reasons like this and my training and experience in victimology offers a bounty of fallacy and opportunity to work with.

Not Being Direct: The "How Do You Feel About That?" Game

The aggravation had become overwhelming. I had explained to the counselor over and over that life was intolerable and I needed more significant changes from my partner, faster, if we were to save the relationship. She had moseyed along for a year as if we had all the time in the world, not concerning herself with how the abuse, or her "cure" was affecting me. And I was responsible for allowing it and trusting her "method".

I had explained to her that every session I had to attend was like - I was going in, she was picking a scab off of a wound to open it up, sticking her finger in the sore, rolling it around and exploring it. She then sent me home with nothing to relieve the pain and she did this weekly, for a year.

By our next session it would start scabbing over again, and my return to "reexamine" the wound only repeated the whole painful process. I pointed out the intense irritation I felt at her technique and mocked the "how do you feel about that?" mantra of the counseling profession.

She explained that instead of walking her client up to the mountain and telling them what it was, she preferred to walk them to the mountain and ask them what they saw. I explained to her that she was standing at the base of a mountain with a blind man who had no idea what to call the view. Without response to that bit of logic, she addressed my comments with, "And how do you feel about that?"

Without hesitation I offered her another metaphor, "I am standing in the kitchen with my head on fire, and if I run to put it out I'm going to do a lot of damage. Running will fan the flames and I am going to do damage to our assets by running through the house."

This was the best metaphor I could think of for the damage that divorce would do to our assets and those who depended on us.
"He can put the fire out with minimal damage," I said, referring to the fact that he could stop the abuse, "Or I can put it out at a higher cost."
The counselor nodded as if she not only understood the metaphor but had thought of it just like that.
"But instead of looking at him and yelling fire, you casually ask him if he smells smoke. Well, my head's on fire, and you want to know if he smells smoke? Obviously he either can't smell, doesn't care or hasn't a clue how to respond. Teach him," I demanded in desperation.

She couldn't be shaken out of her routine and despite the fact that he had seriously injured me, repeatedly, she never got past standing at the foot of the mountain with the blind man, asking him what he saw. The counselor and I were the epitome of a mixed metaphor, and despite the fact that the man had taken actions to end my life, she never told him my head was on fire, or approached the emotional issue with the urgency I felt.

In an emergency like burning heads, it is important that all service providers be able to "shake off" their training. Every situation involving a violent crime is different, and the more tools we have available to intervene, the more successful we will be. We must be creative and flexible to respond to the broad array of techniques that offenders use to traumatize. Waiting for the victim/survivor to bump into the answer is absurd. They haven't bumped into it yet. I think there are a number of basic reasons that the people I work with generally respond well to me:

I do not play games with them. I tell them what I see. They come to me because they are upside down in a vat of tar, or trauma, and they want to know what is going on with their feet. They know they can not upright themselves until they understand their feet. I don't spend six months to a year asking them what they think is going on with their feet. I give them my best assessment and then offer a number of tools that I have seen work with others. Hopefully they find a tool that works and right themselves so that they can see their own feet.

When I think it will be useful, I share my experiences rather than approaching the situation as if self-disclosure is negative. This gives me credibility with the victims and offenders and allows me to share more information and recovery tools, because I am not constantly having to edit myself. This makes me real to my clients and usually alleviates the shame and embarrassment they may have when sharing the trauma.

Mutual Combat

While the term mutual combat is thrown around by the courts, law enforcement, counselors, and virtually every other group called to intervene in domestic violence situations, no one loves it as much as the batterers themselves. While violence against men does exist, it is an extremely small part of the problem. According to Report To The Nation On Crime & Justice, 90% of domestic violence is men against women.

We also have to look at the potential for damage. If I were to hit my husband, it is unlikely that I would even knock him off balance. My husband could end my life with a single blow, and even if he was to attempt to measure the force he uses, the potential for error is great. A miscalculation could kill me.

I was working with a young man and one morning he slipped and accidentally told me the truth. I flipped around to face him, teacup halfway to my mouth and repeated his words as a question, "You beat her. Went to jail, and in the pictures they brought you she looked like she had been in a hockey fight?"
He was grinning, a nervous grin and said in his best prison attitude, "I ain't frontin'. Ain't no woman gonna hit me."
Ignoring the 'tude he had used to survive I ask him, "During your argument with her, when she started swinging on you, did you have any opportunity to get away?"
He nodded, "She hit me first," he said like a little kid.
That argument may work when you are seven, but as you saw, while you sat in jail, it doesn't work for adults and you may be immature, but when you have the strength to beat a woman like that you need to start thinking like an adult. Your mind needs to catch up with your body.

I stood in front of him, legs spaced to give me stability. The teacup had gone by the wayside several sentences ago.

"I'm going to swing at you. You know it's coming so block it," I said.

He stood a good twelve inches taller and started to protest. I drew my fist back and swung with all I had. He blocked it. I took a moment and rubbed the forearm that was going to bruise like a banana. He looked perplexed.

"Now, you hit me with everything you've got and I'll block it. Hit me like you mean it," I ordered.

He shook his head no and firmly said, "I can't do that."

"Why is that?" I ask.

"Because I'll hurt you," he said.

"Exactly," I said, pointing my finger in his face, "It's called a one blow homicide. No one should be hitting any other soul, but the potential for damage is so great that you must NEVER hit a woman, child or animal. Your job is to love and respect them. Not to control them, beat them or cause them any other type of trauma."

Minimizing Damages

It is common for battered women to minimize the damage done to her by the batterer. It is a given that the batterer will minimize the damage he does to his victim. And, unfortunately, minimizing the damage to the victim is also done by the courts, attorneys, counselors, and families.

The battered woman does this to reduce the cognitive dissonance (or the discomfort she feels in her mind) so that it is easier for her to stay and not take the difficult and possibly life-threatening step of leaving. This is not a completely conscious process on her part, but more of a lack of awareness. She may also do this to help to relieve or reduce the guilt that the batterer may feel for having beat her.

The batterer minimizes the damage that he does to his victim for some of the same reason she does. As she hides her pain from him to keep the peace, she often begins to believe the lie that allows for a few moments of peace in the household. Minimizing, denial, and blame are his three main tools. These responses of his regarding the violence toward a battered woman, who is already isolated and fearful, can cause her to internalize those oppressive messages (minimization, blame, and denial) and lead her to even more blame and shame. This blame and shame can keep a victim quiet, hiding pain and bruises, denying the problem for a long time. He also minimizes the damages because he lacks empathy and is probably unaware of just how bad he hurts her. And this is exactly why victim impact is so powerful and effective.

Victim Impact

It is also effective to use surrogates (other formerly-battered women) to teach batterers about the impact they have on their own victims. This is the program (mentioned earlier) that the facilitator of the batterers group refused - stating that she didn't want to make her batterers feel guilty. While these programs are often rejected, that is the first time I had ever heard that excuse.

Our criminal justice system and other service providers are in the habit of keeping victims and offenders as far apart as possible. This has been done forever, and even though we now know differently and have a multitude of options, the majority of service providers prefer to keep it that way.

This policy and habit of keeping victim and offender as far apart as possible is applied backward, totally upside down in the case of batterer and victim. We do little to keep batterers and their victims apart and this is a group of victims and offenders who desperately need to be kept apart in order to reduce and, hopefully, end the bond between them.

Victims/survivors of rape and other violent crimes would often benefit from some types of contact with the offender, (the offender can also benefit) and these are the people that the system works hard to keep from having any type of contact.

Because the offender is kept away from the victim, and often even denied surrogate programs, they usually have no clue as to how they truly affected the victim. For example, the young men I work with often have the idea that women can just cry rape and that's that - there is nothing else involved for her. When I take an hour-and-a-half in group to describe a rape, the rape exam, and the way she is treated by the system (including defense attorneys,) my boys know different. They know a lot more about how the victim is affected by a rape. And when these young men sit across the table from a rape survivor, hear her voice, and see the impact for themselves they learn a lot.

After every single victim impact session or group that I have run, the victim has called me, to say that her life was forever changed - that this was the most positive experience she had and to ask me why this isn't readily available and why it wasn't offered to her sooner.

Victims often have questions that only the offender can answer - like why did you pick me; what did you do with my earrings; and why did you put me in the trunk. With no contact, to the victim, the offender is an all-powerful monster who could grab her up at any moment. By allowing her to get her questions answered, meet the perpetrator and personalize him, we are giving her an opportunity to recover in ways that victims have not had, historically.

At one point, in response to a newspaper article about our program, a facilitator of a batterer's group said that offenders can easily fake empathy. I know that. Regardless of how long lasting our impact is on the offender, based on the long term impact on the victim, these are incredible opportunities for victim recovery that should not be squandered. In other words, if victim impact had no effect on the offender, the victims report being "forever changed." That, alone is a tremendous payoff.

Again, I must stress that victim-offender mediations and ameliorations (and joint counseling) are not appropriate or safe in cases of domestic violence. Victim impact and other restorative justice programs that bring together victim and offender, as opposed to surrogates, are not designed for domestic violence crimes, even though they are intended for and used that way, which is incredibly dangerous. Like forcing women into joint counseling and mediation, these programs will refresh the bond between them, cause her to be further victimized, and possibly cause her to be killed.

And not only are these programs inappropriate for battered women, they are not appropriate for any victim who does not want to do it. I spend months preparing participants to meet. These are not programs that should be implemented by attorneys or anyone else who does not have a high level of sensitivity to victim issues and a high level of training.

Attorneys are lobbying, and have actually been successful, in some states at getting legislation to make it illegal for anyone except attorneys to do these "mediations". This is an incredibly dangerous form of greed that victim advocates are fighting, in some locations more than others.

There are many other pitfalls. Mediators and ameliorators need training. One predictable problem is when the empathy flows the wrong way. At this point I only work with adolescent offenders and, as odd as it sounds, it is easy for the victims to bond to these young men. Once they see the offender as the child he is, rather than the al-powerful monster that hurt them, they tend to want to make everything better for them, as a mother would. This was a particular problem during one of my homicide mediations. The victim saw the young man that killed her son as a connection to her lost loved one.

An inexperienced facilitator can make this wrong-way empathy even worse. Early in my Restorative Justice experience I agreed to do a victim impact panel. The psychologist who normally worked with the group was to prepare the sex offenders, and it was my job to find, assess, and prepare the victims to do panel. When we entered the room and settled in, before anything could even be said, the offenders started talking about the traumas they had suffered in their lives. I allowed it to go on for a moment and noticed tears running down the face of one of the women. I stopped the session, which riled the ire of the psychologist, and he refused to let me work with any of his offenders for years. That was no punishment at all, because there are more than enough to go around.

The victims were prepared to go in and tell the boys their experiences with sexual assault. Instead they listened to the boys tell them about being abused by their mothers, mom's boyfriends, and everyone else. This is valuable, but in it's own session.

The victims/survivors were not prepared for this and the empathy flowed the wrong way.

After a few years, the psychologist got over the fact that I asserted myself on behalf of the victims. This is another example of having to make the tough decisions and forgoing popularity. It is my job to protect the victims/survivors I lure into my programs. I have never had a bad outcome, and that didn't happen because of my concern for my popularity. As I said, popularity is for politicians and cheerleaders. People with a strong need to be popular should not be doing the heavy lifting involved in making changes for oppressed people.

On another occasion, I was about a year into a homicide amelioration. I had been training another Ph.D. level student, who eventually became my partner, who runs the offender side of the program. He had been involved from the beginning of the amelioration. We were scheduled to bring the shooter and the secondary victims together. I called the trainee (who is also a professor) and told him I was running late. I told him to keep the two apart until I got there, and he assured me he understood.

When I arrived, victim and offender were sitting nervously and directly across the table from each other in silence. The victim struggled with that session, and I had to end it early. As we left the facility, it was clear how disturbed the victim was by this. The trainee thought he knew better than I did and that he could handle it. Because he didn't understand the reason for the rule, he was certain there was none.

At the conclusion of this amelioration, my partner went to this victim, behind my back, to get her to sign a statement requesting the killer's release. I had told this man repeatedly and clearly, that he was to have no contact with the victims. He had become attached to the offender and the outcome, running his own agenda. I had suspected this early on and when I did, I tightened my grip on the process. Still, he was certain he knew better despite the fact that he had never worked with a victim, his organization advocated for offenders, and the facility would potentially be looking down the barrel of a lawsuit based on this action and the potential harm to the victim.

Because I could not trust him to make the victim's welfare the priority, I never again allowed my partner to train with me, giving up on training him to work with victims and leaving him to collude with the offenders he was supposed to be teaching. I then turned my attention to training the interns and graduate students he sent. Over the next years my partner did everything he could to prove the nay sayers were right, that victim services should not be cooperating with offender-based organizations. It is sad that some people, with the highest level of education are the least willing to learn. They are the most dangerous to victims because they are certain, whether they know the first thing about trauma and victims or not, that they have learned everything there is to learn.

I could go on and on with stories about the correctional facility, facilitators of offender programs, or offenders trying to manipulate me into manipulating the victims and survivors for them. Victim impact, whether the actual victim or in the case of battered women, with surrogates, is a powerful way to achieve a number of things, including educating the offender on the true impact of his behavior or manipulating the victim for early release or parole. I spend more time on this in the section on Offender Organizations.

As you can see, victim impact also offers a lot of opportunities for the abuse of victims and must be undertaken seriously by people trained to work with victims rather than law, criminology, theology, psychology etc... While these types of education are important the ameliorator/mediator MUST have years of specialized training in victim sensitivity and trauma response.

Why Battered Women Protect The Batterer

Battered women often protect the batterer because it is in their best interest to do so. Maybe it's only in their best interest for the short term, maybe not. One example is with law enforcement. Battered women testifying is good for law enforcement, it makes building their case easier. But it should not be necessary.

Testifying puts a bull's-eye on her chest. They don't need victims to testify in homicide - they make the case. And they could do the same thing in domestic violence cases, if they valued the victims. When they are going to release the man who assaulted her within hours of his arrest, why would she cooperate? That would be stupid on her part and could put her life in great danger. Yet she is often criticized for not cooperating.

Can you imagine expecting the victim of a robbery, rape and assault to cooperate with law enforcement when the offender knows where they live, knows where all their family and friends live and the offender is going to be turned loose within hours? For whatever reason, we are not applying logic to domestic violence. If we did we would not have such unreasonable expectations of the victim.

Victim Blaming

I know I have said this, but it is worthy of repeating for those of you who don't work in the field. There are some offender behaviors that are so predictable that they should be considered a natural extension of the crime. Victim blaming is one and occurs across the spectrum of crimes. Rapists do it when they say she wanted it, and we support them when we question her attire or other choices. Child molesters do it when they accuse the four-year-old of seducing them and, again, we support them when we ask the child why they didn't tell or when we point out every inconsistency in their statement. Corporations and doctors do it when they accuse victims of malingering or somehow causing their own injuries, and we support this in so many ways I couldn't begin to list them here. Batterers do it when they accuse the woman of provoking them or any of the myriad of other excuses they come up with for battering their partner. They have the support of law enforcement and other service providers when they, like my father, ask what she did, which doesn't matter because there was nothing she could do that deserved a beating.

Batterers often have the support of counselors, family, and friends when they ask her why she stays, because inherent in that question is that she could actually leave. There was a counselor here who was "treating" battered women for masochism. This is damaging for her. These are the "experts," and they carry a lot of weight for the victim of a violent crime.

Rapists blame the victim when they say she wanted it, seduced them, or otherwise contributed to her trauma. They are supported by the system, including defense attorneys when they ask what the victim was wearing, go after her psychiatric records, or ask about past lovers.

A young woman could walk down a dark alley totally naked and, while this is a terrible and dangerous choice, she does not deserve to be raped. We need to teach young women what offenders are looking for when they pick their victims and to make better choices. Until we do that, we need to take partial responsibility for the traumas they suffer. As elders, we have an obligation to teach the younger people. If we aren't doing that, we share responsibility for their errors.

Doctors, corporations, and other white coat, white collar offenders blame the victims by accusing them of being gold diggers, crazy, and looking for deep pockets. I have worked with hundreds of victims of white coat, white-collar criminals and only twice have I been used solely for their financial gain.

Victims blame themselves enough, and when service providers jump on board with that blame, it can devastate the victim. Again, these are the "experts," and when they agree with the batterer or other offender, the victim is trashed and her self-esteem plummets. After a barrage of this, climbing out of the hole becomes terribly difficult.

"Emotional abuse is as bad as physical abuse"

Emotional abuse is devastating, and I would not argue otherwise. I object to comparing traumas. What's devastating to one may not be to another. Emotional abuse is not the same as physical abuse. I have always said that the people who say emotional abuse is as bad as physical abuse are the people who haven't been beaten half to death.

Who on earth would actually believe that physical abuse occurs in a vacuum, without emotional abuse. As I said before, physical abuse is emotional abuse with a hefty side of ass kicking. Physical abuse is emotional abuse, with the addition of being potentially lethal. Do we actually think that a man who is beating a woman does so without emotionally abusing her?

There is a hierarchy among offenders in the correctional facilities, which is also a reflection of our society, that puts sex offenders on the bottom. As I point out to my boys, a victim will not die from a sex offense alone, but victims die during assaults all the time. The same is true of emotional abuse. While it is terribly damaging and hurtful, the victim is not at risk of death, as with a beating.

Desperate People Do Desperate Things

Desperate people DO desperate things. Completely sane, rational people can behave "crazy" in crazy situations. As I shared earlier, Aaron did not leave my home until I walked in and told him that he could beat me again, but one day I was going to get fed up, he was going to have to sleep, and I would take the baseball bat he kept behind the door and beat his brains out. It wasn't twenty minutes later that I saw him walking down the hall with a suitcase, but to my surprise and dismay, that didn't end it. As he became more desperate he began stalking me.

While it may have worked to an extent for me, I would never recommend it as a way to get rid of a batterer. It was "a crazy" act of a desperate woman. He could have just killed me then and there. But also, he knew I wasn't that far from "crazy", if not already totally upside down in it. I was "crazy" from being beaten, abused, traumatized, and manipulated. I was desperate, and he knew it.

Our prisons are full of women who hit that point of desperation. They have fought back. They have killed their tormentors. They have burned down their houses, and they have fled with their children -against court orders. When the system can't or won't respond to them and they feel cornered, they may solve their problem in the only way they think they can.

Though being beaten by Larry, I gave birth to my first child. Within a couple of weeks of giving birth I packed up my vehicle, drove 1750 miles, to be exact, crying, with my precious baby and then turned around and drove back home, out of fear. It was "crazy," but I wanted desperately to protect my new baby. And in hindsight, my mistake was coming back.

The number of battered women who have substance abuse issues is through the roof. Battered women find desperate, destructive ways to numb out. They are sedating the traumas of the day and the traumas of yesterday. And yet we judge them. The addictions range from alcohol, to drugs, to shopping, to sex, to cutting, and beyond. And when we treat the addiction, we are only treating the symptom - not the cause. We can get sidetracked in the addiction and miss the underlying issue. Women die all the time as we miss the cause and treat the symptom.

With Aaron I spent years drunk. Initially, he was the drunkest skunk in the hole, but when he found AA, of course I was expected to be just as excited, because he said so. Despite his threats and manipulation, I had no interest in giving up the alcohol. Even though he was no longer beating me because I had learned enough to know beating me was a crime and I could have him arrested, I still spent my nights in terror and my days sidestepping a stalker who I knew could kill me.

Once I was away from him and safe, I had no desire to drink. I had no need for AA or any other treatment program. I just had no more desire for alcohol. The cause went away, and eventually the symptom followed. After more than ten years of sobriety the smell of alcohol only reminds me of the abuse at the hands of my father, Larry, and Aaron.

I did a victim impact panel in one of the correctional facilities that included a combat veteran who was also a formerly-battered woman. She told the men that she would take the combat, death, and chaos she saw in Kuwait over her batterer any day. To my surprise, this was a profound statement for the batterers. They heard her. This statement helped the batterers to understand the impact their actions have on the victim. Unfortunately, the service-providing community often believe they know more than the people who have actually been in the trenches, be it a violent home, Kuwait, or Iraq.

The traumatic stress of dealing with a life of violence can leave us desperate for relief. The symptoms of PTS (Post Traumatic

Stress,) alone can leave an individual, isolated, misdiagnosed, addicted, angry, fearful, and constantly in a state of confusion and desperation. This can be maddening and he demands, from the victim, relief. We see vets filling the homeless shelters and standing on street corners with signs, because they couldn't cope with what they have seen. Victims of violent crimes are also seeking relief from the nerve-wracking startle reflex, the horrifying nightmares, the hopeless depression, and desperation.

    My sister, Rena Jon Jameson, desperately needed acceptance and an end to the abuse. And like her older sister she ended up with one batterer after another. She also desperately sought the approval of our family. She never succeeded, and seeking that approval came with a heavy price - her life. Her husband beat her and according to our children, our father was hitting her even into her 40's.

    Her efforts to win his approval had to be coupled with any drug she could find in order to numb the pain. She was as desperate to win her family's approval as she was to sedate her pain. Sedating the pain finally took more drugs than her body could handle, and it gave out. My sister was desperate to win the love of a family deeply invested in its dysfunction and desperate to sedate the pain that the desperation caused. She was never able to connect the two destructive forces and break the cycle.

    The difference between my sister and me was, until her death, I had a no-contact policy and hadn't seen the family in about ten years. I, too, wanted their love and acceptance, but had realized the price for that was too heavy. I was no longer desperate for that approval, but was willing to accept I had no control over it, that the way they treated me had not one single thing to do with me. The frame of mind that allowed the desperation to dissolve probably saved my life. While we can not control events, as desperate as we may be, we must make choices mindful of the consequences. As desperate as we may be, we must behave as if we are not.

Depersonalizing The Victim

Depersonalization is when we take another being or group of beings and attempt to take away the reality that they are like us and have feelings, in order to make abusing them easier. For example, batterers do it with terms like bitch, ho, broad, chick, etc… We do it in war with terms like gook, pie face, slant eyes, etc… Depersonalization is a necessary part of the degradation and abuse of other beings. Language reflects our attitudes and beliefs more than most people realize. The language Aaron and his friends used in reference to women was telling.

At my sister's funeral, as the priest did his hocus pocus, waving the incense, and talking about God, he never called my sister by the right name. I can't remember what he was calling her, but it wasn't her name. Had it not been for an absolutely packed church of people that I knew, I would have thought I was in the wrong place. No one offered to correct him. Every one in that church was willing to allow my sister (their wife, daughter, and mother) to be eulogized, or whatever they call it, as someone else. I was not.

From the third row, every time he called my sister by the wrong name I corrected him, first quietly, and each time thereafter, my voice got louder. Each time I corrected the priest, Jim, my father, turned around and gave me his "I will stomp you into the ground" look. I knew what that look meant because we grew up with him telling us, in those exact words, and sometimes even with a demonstration. On that day I refused to stop. On that day, I would take a beating to make sure she was called by her name. I would not allow my sister to be depersonalized today. She was depersonalized all her life and in death, I was going to make sure they at least got her name right.

I finally got loud enough that the priest stopped his performance and walked off the stage, where someone behind the curtains must have filled him in. In that entire church, there was no one else that demanded my sister be properly identified into her grave. We had been made such non-persons, and it had spread like a communicable disease. People truly are sheep, and following is so much easier than being disliked.

Law Enforcement

After a night of partying, one of my clients, shared a cab home with one of the men she had partied with. She had consumed too much alcohol, but insisted on a cab as opposed to accepting a ride. She had not known these people long and felt by insisting on a cab she was doing what she needed to protect herself.

The alcohol was a bad choice and the cab a good one. She had no idea where she was when the cab pulled over and the cab driver got out. She watched, perplexed as the cab driver walked behind the vehicle and lit a cigarette. Her questions were quickly answered as the man she had partied with attacked her.

She fought with everything she had as he groped at and slobbered on her body. She didn't know how much time had passed when, during his assault, he ejaculated on her. He was apparently excited by the fight. That night she had chosen a skirt with a one piece teddy that had snaps on the crotch. That was what he hadn't expected and had he not been confused and slowed down by the unexpected lock on her attire, he would have raped her with the cabbie standing right behind the vehicle.

The cab driver dropped her off, hysterical, in front of her home. She went inside to the man who would soon become her husband and told him, as best she could, what had happened. He decided, without consulting her, that she needed to file a police report. Through her shaking and tears, she didn't recall that she ever objected or consented to law enforcement's involvement, they just appeared at the door.

She tried to talk through the tears and shaking. She worked hard to answer the officer's questions, but felt assaulted again with every judgment he made, and he was not hiding his opinions well. "What do you mean you don't even know his name? You partied with strangers? You're engaged to this man and shared a cab with another?" The judgments went on and on. Her boyfriend looked on as she, humiliated, tried to explain why she didn't know where this man lived, what his last name was, or where the party had been.

With the ejaculate still wet on her skirt, she wrapped her arms around herself, stood up, and walked up the stairs to her

bedroom. She was still crying and trying to catch her breath, through the shock as her boyfriend came up and told her that the officer said if she didn't come back down and answer his questions he would arrest her.
At that point she didn't care and just said, "Tell him to have at it. Every one else has tonight."
About twenty to thirty minutes later she heard her lover's voice through her sobbing, "There is a female officer here now. I think it will be easier to talk to her," he offered.

She went downstairs and tried to answer the new officer's questions. Within a few days, she called the office to find out what they had done. She was told that they traced him down through the cab dispatch. After interviewing his friends, who said she wanted it, and the cab driver, who said he never pulled over, to the "suspect" who said it didn't even happen – they determined that there wasn't enough evidence. She later burned the best evidence they had - the skirt - because they had no interest in it.
What happened :

Victim emotions

Productive or not, more often than not someone who has just fended off a rape, been raped, beaten by her lover, or otherwise traumatized is likely to be overcome with emotions. While it is unfair to expect the victim to behave any differently, it is important that the victim be able to communicate what has happened and that law enforcement understand that she may not be able to. Law enforcement needs to be particularly sensitive to the feelings of the victim so as not to make the situation worse.

Lack of Training On Part of Law Enforcement

As aggravated as you may be with the victim, it is extremely important that you be sensitive to language, demeanor, and other nonverbal communication, because someone who has been repeatedly victimized is extremely hypervigiliant and aware. They are likely reading everything in their environment. They are watching for judgments, self-definition, and more danger.

Unwillingness To Invest In Case

While I am sure that police departments are overtaxed, I do believe that investing time in this sexual assault and attempted rape would have been a good investment. The man that ejaculated on her knew what he was doing (despite the fact that the body suit was foreign to him) and certainly had done it before. While that particular case may have seemed trivial to them, it was more about the offender than that one case, because the offender has more than likely done this before. There was no consequence to him that would discourage him from doing it again.

Victim Discredited by Offender and His Buddies

The only time I have met an offender who didn't discredit and blame the victim is when the offender had already gone through a number of rehabilitative programs. When I meet these sophisticated offenders, I am aware of the fact that they may not be sincere. They have had every opportunity to learn what is expected of them and what attitude regarding the victim provides them the best response.

There is a saying, "build a better batterer," which was used early in the battered women's movement as a downside to batterer's groups. Advocates were concerned that teaching batterers would help them learn how to better skirt or comply with the system. Actually, they already know all of the techniques - we are just giving them names for it when we teach them, and we do teach them the proper response and attitude toward their victim. The challenge then becomes ours, as service providers, to see through their charm and manipulation.

Of course the offender and his buddies are going to discredit and blame the victim; yet victims who point out this fact are accused of conspiracy thinking and being paranoid. This is another technique of discrediting the victim that law enforcement actually use themselves against the victim.

This is especially true when it comes to powerful offenders like doctors, politicians, or celebrities. Law enforcement predictably act surprised that doctors would cover for each other in order to dismiss the victim. I use the word "act" because, of course, they know that their colleagues will cover for them. Protecting and covering for each other is as prevalent among law enforcement as any place else.

Victims have an uphill battle anyway, but when you have a poor black female, for example, challenging a powerful doctor and every one covering for him, it's usually hopeless. She will be discredited and will be lucky if one of them doesn't succeed at getting a 72-hour hold (psychiatric detention). And she may never be able to get a doctor again. The thinking error that you are "crazy" to be realistic and honest about offenders and those covering for them as they "conspire" by having a conversation to get their stories straight is absurd. This is not paranoia, but rather a form of human behavior that we see all the time.

Law Enforcement As Abusers

We now know that the rates of domestic violence are higher among families where the men are involved in a paramilitary or military organization. It is a chicken-or-egg argument. Does the regimentation and absolute compliance demanded in the military and law enforcement contribute to the expectation of total compliance in the home? Or does this type of employment and service attract men who have the attitudes and belief systems of men who batter? While I have no supporting research, I believe the latter.

As the child of a cop, I grew up watching them party, drink, and gamble on the week-ends, and any other opportunity. The violence I saw them direct toward their wives, children, animals, and even each other contributed to my belief that all men beat women. The abused wives and children of law enforcement have few, if any, place to turn. And what do you do when you're being beaten by a man who is a friend of the responding officer? Talk about intimidation. Those that have abusive natures do not limit the expression of that nature to their families.

On many occasions, I listened as battered women shared experiences of law enforcement taking advantage of their vulnerability, and I have had my own experiences. There was a point when I was offered a "deal" for protection from Aaron. Looking at my baby girls, I took it. Ten years later this officer, who had risen

through the ranks, was pictured all over the media, being prosecuted, and dismissed, for some misconduct or another.

    I grew up not knowing that there were men in the world who didn't beat women. As a child, because our parents partied together, my friends were also little "piglets", and they lived with the same violence. To this day, one of my friends is certain that his father killed his mother, and he will have no contact with him. Another female was so brutally beaten by her father that she is unable to leave her home.

    When I was a child, the women's movement was in full swing, and I used to say that we needed a kid's movement. Hitting kids wasn't considered abuse, and there really wasn't much of a child protective services. Even if there had been someplace for us to turn, it would have been too risky. Their battered wives face the same dilemma. Who do they turn to? As much as law enforcement, doctors, attorneys etc… deny that they protect each other, they do, and I can line up those who have lived to bear witness from here to God knows where. I've offered to do so, but no one takes me up on that offer.

    Within about ten days of Katrina making landfall, our community raised the money to send me to New Orleans to work with the human and animal trauma survivors. I was expected to work with volunteers suffering from vicarious trauma and the animals that had been abandoned. The staging areas for the firefighters, from all over the country, offered me a retreat when the reality of the situation was overwhelming or dangerous. More often than not that danger was coming from law enforcement in New Orleans, who were a constant threat.

    As I explained to the Office of Emergency Management, Admiral Thad Allen (I believe) and the Attorney General's Office, among others, these service providers were going to hurt someone.

Those who enforce our laws are no different than the rest of us and are deeply effected by the trauma they see.

As I explained to the above mentioned decision makers, "These people have all been traumatized, just like your citizens. As impractical as it is, not one of them should be on duty. Their homes and families, like your citizens, have been damaged by this hurricane. Too much is being expected of them and when one of them snaps it is because they were expected to be super human.. These are trauma survivors with power, anger and guns."

While the decision makers treated me with respect and listened, they made it clear there was nothing they could do, which was probably true. I later walked into a scene where members of the Sheriffs Department had taken a 12 gauge shotgun to peoples' tied up, healthy pets, just because they could. The owners had desperately begged for the lives of their pets, to no avail. This was a terrible scene and with a maximum amount of dissociation, and every other tool in my toolbox, I photographed it.

When they realized I had photographed this horror I then became their target. They were going to hurt me. With the pictures, negatives and CD's stashed I ran home as fast as my short little legs and old truck could carry me. There was nothing that couldn't be accomplished with a good 900 miles between us.

After the national media aired the New Orleans officers beating the man in the streets, a representative from the AG's office called me and told me that when she saw this, my words rang in her head. I have been extremely brief in recounting this story. A detailed version of this event, along with the pictures of the slaughtered pets, appears on our web site and in the book, *Offenders Revealed: How To Avoid Being Picked.* To date, two of the shooters have been indicted and more are expected.

While some men may go into law enforcement for the power they can't achieve in their personal lives, many more go into this dangerous profession because they truly care and want to make a difference. Because of my childhood I have, unfortunately, met more ill-intended cops than not. But, I do not believe that is how it shakes out, overall. While I write about the misdeeds of doctors, cops and others, I do not believe that these offenders are representative of their professions. For every doctor or cop that put me in jeopardy, as you will see in the other books, the actions of at least two more, saved or enhanced my life. So far, the ethical ones have been there to fix the damage done by their peers.

Service Providers & Organizations For Victims of Violent Crimes

Working for social change, if we are doing our jobs, we are not always going to be liked. We can leave the popularity contest to politicians and not judge our success by how many people like us. A better measure is how many lives we can help to turn around, how many unjust laws we can assist in changing, and how much suffering we can reduce.

When our funding is based on how many people like us, then we need to seek alternative sources of funding. During the eight years I spent working with the Department of Corrections, I was able to turn down the cases where I believed the motive was less than honorable. Had I been receiving funding from the state or the DOC, they would have had another tool to manipulate me into taking cases that were not in the best interest of the victims. When we accept outside funding, (and I know why this is advantageous) our programs may be limited by what our funding sources want, as opposed to what our experience tells us is in the victim's best interest.

During a class I was teaching, I expressed my confusion as to why the information on bonding was so unpopular with everyone except the victims themselves. A victim advocate from Maine pointed out that I needed to follow the money. While that is a phrase I have heard over and over, it was really difficult to do. Following the money can be so hard because of the incestuous nature of so many of our social institutions.

For several years I worked only with victims of white coat, white collar crimes. These included victims of Dow Chemical, hospitals, doctors, and pharmaceutical companies. These were the most devastated people I had ever worked with. That was a reality I hadn't expected. I should have known because lack of "justice" is directly proportionate to power imbalance.

While working with these victims, our web site was mentioned in Forbes Magazine. This prompted a barrage of attention. We began getting an average of 250 e-mails a day from victims all over the world asking us for help. This was a nightmare, because every one of them had to be answered so that these victims did not think they were being ignored and dismissed again.

Much to our surprise, we found that the local television stations would no longer work with us. Perplexed, I met with a former political-science professor. What type of dog could the local media have in this fight that would cause them to suddenly shun us? I heard the same response, "Follow the money."
She saw that I still wasn't getting it, "Where do the TV stations get their money?" she asked.
I thought for a minute, "Advertisers?" I said, more as a question.
"And who are their biggest advertisers?" she asked.
I just shook my head, and she gave me what would be my final assignment, "Go home and watch TV," she said, leaving the room.

I did and found the hospital's ads were all over every station - we had just been involved in helping a victim get the license of a doctor who had an incredible number of complaints for children's deaths. We had also named names on our web site and posted the number of formal complaints each one of the hospitals had against them. No wonder we were no longer popular with the media.

That was a decade ago and they still haven't forgotten. Even though we run two businesses that funnel 100% of their net profits back into the community through victim recovery programs, adolescent rehabilitation programs and animal rescue, local media will not tell the community we exist. But they will do story after story on the vandalism of luxury vehicles and other stories that would interest an influential few.

You see, there are popular and unpopular victims. Had we been posting the names of sex offenders, the media would have been all over that, because it's popular to hate sex offenders. They are powerless, and there is little chance they are going to have the resources to advertise with or sue the TV stations. But we weren't posting those names. We were posting the names of powerful doctors and hospitals who had the blood of many victims on their hands, and the offenders had often gone to great criminal lengths to cover up, destroy evidence, and out-and-out squash the victims. Interesting thing about these popular and unpopular offenders is that few people die from a sex offense alone. Yet, the death toll from negligent and criminal doctors is through the roof, equal to three jumbo jet crashes every day.

People are often as afraid of talking about violent crimes as they are afraid of talking about race. They are afraid of saying the wrong thing or showing their bias - to name a couple of issues. As victim advocates, victims, and survivors, we can make it just about impossible to talk about the issues by scaring people to death that they might say the wrong thing - just as in talking about race.

We are hindering the advancement of our own causes by not finding effective ways to keep the dialog open or continually seeking effective ways to share necessary information. One day I used the term "African American" while having lunch with a black woman. She made it clear, rather harshly, that she had never been to Africa, and that she was black. While I still talk about race, and even do victim impact on race issues, you can't make me use the term "African American." The point here is that as we try to initiate dialog on all victim issues, including race, we need to be tolerant and forgiving when people use the wrong terms. We need to teach people to talk about victim issues, not make them more afraid of saying the wrong thing.

Political Action Groups

With the numbers of formerly-battered women available to us, we are a small army. While every movement is advanced by the survivors who work to change the system, many organizations working for political change end up exploiting the victims/survivors who need to make their experience count. We must be respectful of every survivor's process and not push her forward to say things she's not ready for or hold her back by asking her to go back to the victim position (or memories) repeatedly. And when she is ready and we do use her services she should be compensated. Victims/survivors are the experts.

While getting out of ourselves and into our community is a great recovery tool, we have to wait until these victims are ready for political action and then give them the training that they need. If we don't, we are setting them up to fail and then to be possibly revictimized.

When my training and career began, an organization took me in and put me in a position for which I was unqualified. This was my first introduction to the battered women's movement, I was still being beaten and sedated that pain with sex and alcohol. I repeatedly expressed that I was in over my head and sought the help of other, more experienced women within this large, high profile network of service providers. Despite that, I was repeatedly thrown back in, with no more training or counseling. I experienced one failure after another. My drinking escalated and I had to quit.

I was used, and then disposed of, by this organization for the politically unpopular tasks. Yes, I experienced one failure after another but I also facilitated some great changes, with the insight only a victim can offer, and my experience and resume were beautifully enhanced. I have 20 more years of experience, eight of education and hundreds of cases under my belt and still, I hear terrible quotes from this organization despite the fact that we share the same goals.

It is quite damaging to the victim to be thrown into service before they are ready. The experience reinforced what the batterer had told me all along. It was my fault I and deserved whatever I got. While our organizations may be short handed, we must not sacrifice our women at any time, much less while they are trying to build a sustainable sense of self.

Victim Advocates

Controlling The Victim

While I believe that a directive, teaching approach is more productive when supporting people in crisis, there is a difference between teaching a victim/survivor and telling them to do this or that. Whether it be victim-offender mediations, prosecution, or whatever, there can be a fine line between teaching and pressuring.

Advocates and others often tell survivors of rape that they have an obligation to report the crime and participate in prosecution. That is not what I tell them. Until we have a justice system that is consistently sensitive to the victims' needs, the victims only have an obligation to survive and heal. They have no obligation to put themselves in a situation of being retraumatized. Whether or not to report and prosecute is a personal decision for the victim, based on her needs and whether she feels strong enough to withstand the worst possible outcome. Being able to set a boundary and have it be respected may be the first empowering act the battered woman participates in, the first time she's acted in her own best interest.

Inform Victim of Options

I have been shocked at how often service providers even refuse to tell victims they have the option to ameliorate or other types of Restorative Justice options. Relatively few victims/survivors are informed of the fact that they have the option of meeting with the offender. They are seldom told that they can ask that the offender enter a Restorative Justice process that includes restitution not only to them, but to the community. They are not offered the guilt-free option of not cooperating with prosecution or not reporting.

Mediation, amelioration, and Restorative Justice programs are opportunities that are beneficial to victims/survivors in different and personal ways. Whether or not to participate in the programs or processes made available to them should be their choice. In order to make that choice, the choice has to be made available to them. Offering and respecting her choices is honoring and affirming victims - instead of seeing them as tools to be used by the system to build a case, to make a point, to advance a movement etc....

Survivors of rape who need to meet their offenders, encounter a tremendous amount of resistance because tradition has held that the system should keep them apart. Victims may feel a need to meet their offenders for a number of reasons, including questions they may have, putting a face on the offender and telling the offender how they were affected.

Follow Victim's Lead

<u>Whether it's blatant or not, the victim always gives us clues as to what they want and need</u>. Pay attention. It is extremely important that while we teach them as much as we can about victimization, we follow their lead regarding what they need for

recovery. Some victims need for the offender to answer questions. Some victims feel compelled to tell the offender how their life was affected, and others never want to see the offender again. They know what they need for recovery – after they know their options.

Information, Information

As opposed to standing at the edge of the ditch and pulling women out, time and again, which is imperative, it is also imperative that we teach them about the ditch and how to avoid it. We criticize women for getting into relationships with the goal of changing their partner. Yet as a society, that is exactly what we are doing. Instead of teaching young women the red flags and how to avoid becoming prey, we are waiting for the offenders to change.

Much of this is done out of the fear of victim blaming. If we tell women how to change are we then saying that their victimization was their fault? No. We can tell them how to avoid victimization and when it does happen how to get out quickly and the most likely way to survive.

Briefly, On
Offender Organizations & Programs

For more detailed information and particulars on offenders and the organizations that house, teach and support them, see our web site and the books *Letters From A Batterer & Offenders Revealed: How To Avoid Being Picked.*

Correctional Facilities

Adolescents confined to correctional facilities have seldom had resources or positive role models. This is what makes them dangerous. They have been taught that your kindness, generosity or naiveté is an opportunity for them, and a "weakness" on your part. They believe this "weakness" makes you deserving of their exploitation and justifies their behavior. More often than not, their parents, or some other important role model, think like this. I often found myself working with the crack babies, of fetal alcohol syndrome babies, of fetal alcohol syndrome babies. In eight years of working in the facility I never met a young man from a "well-to-do" family. The well-off offender has parents that can, and do, buy their "Justice".

Responsibility & Justice

Not only are families able to buy "Justice" and clearly there is a double standard in society. Every Christmas, one of my sisters-in-laws sends out, what we call, her "brag" letter. They demonstrate their social status at every opportunity and believe that people who struggle brought it on themselves. One of their sons wanted to study medicine and, as she proudly reported in her annual update, was trapping the neighborhood squirrels and cutting them up. Her tone was that of amusement and "isn't that cute".

It is true that violent offenders start with animals and had one of my boys done that, they would have, rightfully, been prosecuted for animal cruelty. The next year she included a similar story only this time it was dogs. That was when we respectfully requested that she remove us from their mailing list. Her son is now a doctor so he can legally trap and cut things up.

The children I work with desperately need role models that hold them accountable and teach them. While we can argue that resources should not be wasted on these violent offenders, the reality is that they will be released. We have them captive and this provides us the opportunity to teach them in the ways that they have been denied.

We can try to teach them empathy, manners, citizenship and the other tools that they need, not only to get along in society, but to reduce their danger to society. This is an opportunity squandered. Even if we put aside the higher goal of protecting society, these are children that have been terribly abused. Out of the hundreds of young men I have worked with, I have never met one that was not a victim. This statement is not meant to excuse their behavior, rather to explain it.

Timmy was a 12-year-old (I believe) who was locked down in maximum security. He was there for repeatedly raping his younger sister. She was also locked down, except in a psychiatric ward. As I do all of my young men, when Timmy first started group I asked him to tell me about his family. He was one of my first cases and, as I listened, I realized I had just ask a fish to describe water. Timmy insisted that he came from a good family. Another word he repeatedly used was "normal".

As groups went on, he reminded me of the period when I thought all women and children were abused. He talked about watching his mother falling down drunk, sitting on the couch using inhalants and bringing home a series of boyfriends. He talked about being beaten by his mother and her boyfriends. And eventually he talked about being raped by more than one of them.

He talked about being the primary caregiver of his little sister, responsible for feeding, bathing and her general well-being. He also reported hitting her, taking his daily frustrations out on her and raping her, like the adults did to him. Timmy behaved in the way it had been modeled for him. I met him at about 12 and he had already been there for a couple of years.

This was a child who knew nothing more than what his elders had modeled. While I held him responsible for his crimes with every word out of my mouth, he couldn't possibly have been responsible for those crimes at the age of six, seven and eight, although I would never tell him that.

His family had repeatedly been investigated by child protective services and a parade of other organizations funded to protect him and those he came in contact with. They failed not only him, but his victims. No one would argue that this child should know how to split an atom or fly an airplane and there was no way that he could have known it was not okay to be violent or sexual. He had no positive example.

Setting Examples

Many of the officers in the facility are there because they truly want to help the kids and make a positive contribution to the communities. Many are there to realize the power and control they cannot, in their personal lives. This is modeled for the children.

One afternoon a bird got into one of the "cottages" at the facility. The boys watched and cheered as one of the officers used a broom to beat the bird to death. Officers at the facility stuck explosives into groundhog holes and disposed of feral cats in terrible ways. For those who would argue that these animals had to be removed from the grounds, I would point out that even if that was the case, these violent offenders are watching with pleasure as they see their role models (because the boys do bond with the officers) cause pain and suffering.

One of the officers set it up to have the cats moved to a local Humane Society so they could be "humanely" exterminated as opposed to the methods being used. With a wink of the eye and tongue-in-cheek, he asked me, knowing the scope of our program, to transport these cats and kittens to the local humane society. These cats are no longer wild and will continue to enjoy the lives they treasured. While we could not let anyone know of the disposition of the cats, this was the example the boys needed to see.

Before I was moved out of maximum security, I worked with a young man who participated in a violent home invasion and the gang rape of one of the young women in the house. He was about 14-years-old and never dropped the hard façade he hid behind. He had been in the facility for about a year and was a constant behavior problem for all of the staff. I worked through the psychology department and our concern with him was that he had never taken one iota of responsibility for what he had done to that young girl.

Despite the facts of this case, his position was an exaggerated version of the predictable position: she wanted it, she was asking for it etc… Like sheer curtains on a window, underneath his tough act, you could make out the outline of issues with racism. Occasionally these issues with whites appeared, but they were usually a mere shadow of his pain.

After months of frustrating games and avoidance on his part, I had an idea.

"Tyree, you know that I grew up with a racist cop and I know how bad they can be," I said.

He didn't respond but his head was hung and his usual icy stare, into my eyes, was gone.

"Tyree, I have taken a beating or two from my father, fighting over racist comments and I have never ignored them much less participated in, or politely laughed at, comments and jokes like that, but I still owe you an apology," I continued, "I am so sorry for the way you have been treated and how white people have hurt you. Please understand that, had I witnessed any abuse, or even disrespect, for you, I would have fought for you."

Tyree knew this was true because the abuse inflicted on the boys was why I had to be removed from maximum security. I believe the head of the psychology department, who was training me, knew I was eventually going to end up fighting physically for the boys and he wisely moved me to areas where I was less likely to see the violence that was consistently directed toward the offenders.

My apology that day continued with no response from Tyree. This apology was not for his benefit alone. At that moment he represented the entire race and provided me an opportunity to express my disgust with our society's abuse and degradation of an entire group of people. I left the young man with no response from him, which was incredibly different from the bravado-saturated show he used to cover his pain.

The next day the department head pulled me aside, "I don't know what you did, but this morning Tyree took total responsibility for not only the home invasion but the rape," he said.

Tyree saw me acknowledge his reality and pain and mimicked that behavior. If we want certain behaviors from our children then we must model that.

Refusal of Training

I watched as one child after another was assaulted by groups of officers and forced to submit. These boys were often misbehaving, but parenting classes and nonviolent techniques would have been beneficial. These were among the many trainings I tried to set up that were rejected.

On one occasion I lined up a neuro-rehabilitation specialist to do a training on the misunderstood behaviors of the young men who had suffered brain injury, and there were many of them. For example, I could see young men freak out because they couldn't stand being touched or because their clothes were touching them.

The estimates of young men, in correctional facilities, suffering from some type of brain injury is astounding. The lead psychologist estimated our numbers in the 90 percentile. As I sat doing the psychiatric notes in the evening, after groups, I could see that many of the disruptions were caused or escalated due to this. The training I had set up was flat-out refused. I was told they refused it because the training would open "a big can of worms". Without that "can of worms" these children will be more dangerous when released than they were upon arrival.

It was the same with training staff on Restorative Justice programs and victim issues. While for years, no one interfered with my groups, staff seemed to see themselves as too smart to be taught anything. And I obliged them, not pushing the issue. After the last election our new Governor decided that we would use all volunteers (which I had always been,) and they wanted to expand my programs. They brought in all new people, from other facilities, and they set about designing this new "system".

For the previous eight years I had done the victim impact and other victim programs in the facility with not a single incident or bad outcome. The amount of respect the victim programs got always depended on the superintendent at the time, but was always positive. My best years were with an extremely progressive female superintendent and we now had a new one.

For the previous years we had operated with a great deal of respect, freedom and sensitivity for our program and the victims. Now our input and advice were ignored, to the point that I resigned, refusing to be involved in such a dangerous program.

I have always refused to work with people who are mandated and don't want to be there. The facility had decided to make my program mandatory for release. Which is a good idea if we are working solely with adolescents who care. This was not the case. My classes went from an average of 10 – 15 offenders to 20-30 young men who were quite unhappy to be there. I was having to send a trainee to get an officer and had to kick out half of the class, every class, because they were so disruptive we couldn't function.

Then the facility decided that I could no longer remove the disruptive, and sometimes violent offenders. All of the boys I work with are violent offenders, but when they begin expressing that in group it becomes unsafe for all. I was told that regardless of how they behaved I had to keep them in group. This was not possible and we continued to remove them anyway.

Among other changes that were not only dangerous to the offender, our staff and the community, the decision was made that victim impact, victim-offender mediations and other Restorative Justice and victim-involved programs would be me and implemented by the staff of the facility, with no further training. Most had not one minute of experience with victims.

We warned the facility that they were putting many people at risk and that if they brought victims into, what was now, total chaos they were setting themselves up for a law suit. We then informed that facility that we could no longer be involved and wished them luck.

Correctional facilities that read an article on victim impact and decide to implement it with no experience and no input from victim rights organizations are setting victims up to be revictimized. Again, we are looking at groups and institutions that refuse to learn. Backward facilities and programs are dangerous in so many ways. Again, I spend more time on this in the books *Letters From A Batterer* & *Offenders Revealed: How To Avoid Being Picked*. You can also find more information on our web site.

Service Providers For Offenders

I founded and ran Nonviolent Alternatives, for about three years. After a time, the women felt the name didn't fit, we were no longer teaching nonviolent skills to batterers, and the victims/survivors changed our name to Victim's Justice Center, to reflect our focus on the victims.

For the next 15 – 20 years, that was the name under which we operated, working with hundreds of victims, teaching them recovery tools, why battered women stay and how to avoid being picked by perpetrators. I was asked to move our program and to work side-by-side and partner with an offender program. The Director reasoned we could do more Restorative Justice programs and we would teach their staff and the students of the University. There are few advocates and victim programs that believe these two types of programs (victim and offender) can work together.

Since I had become friends with Rich, the Executive Director of the offender program, I was certain that the two of us could make it work and agreed, with certain conditions. For example, we would work with them as a sister organization and never under them, for obvious reasons. Rich gladly agreed and was excited to add Victim Services and Restorative Justice programs to his offender program.

Again, as I had done repeatedly, I thought having information about the pitfalls would help me avoid them. I thought the pitfalls we had learned about through the women's movement, battered women's movement, and consumer rights movement wouldn't apply to me because I knew better. I would be watching for the problems, and information would help me avoid them. I thought wrong. There are apparently areas of my skull that are incredibly thick. While I tend to be extremely hard on myself for any mistakes I make, or failures I realize, I often remind myself that to do progressive programs, often stepping into unexplored areas as we do, we will have a high number of "learning opportunities".

I will not go into the details here, you can read short stories about our experiences with our partner (offender) organization on our website and in the books on offenders. Suffice it to say, for now, they behaved like true offenders, not only toward us but toward the adolescents they worked with and with each other. The program's behavior toward us and the victims we brought onto the property, was deplorable and, on occasion, criminal.

While maintaining our relationship, for practical purposes, Victim Services moved out of the office the offender organization had invited us to share. Late one evening I received a call from my partner asking us to house an adolescent offender. This is not unusual - as we house on the properties, victims, the homeless, the disabled, and select offenders.

My partner explained that Ryan had spent his entire life in foster homes, 22 to be exact, that he had never been convicted of a violent crime, and that he was a "nice" young man who loved animals and wanted to be trained at our rescue facility. In hindsight, Rich, again, painted one of his offenders as the victim of circumstances and society. I had heard this defense of violent offenders from Rich for years, and it was the subject of many heated discussions. This time I was terribly weakened by Katrina and didn't "hear it".

To backtrack a little – When the new Governor initiated, what he called, the PLUS Program at the facility I had worked in, I ended my relationship with that facility due to the implementation of policy and procedure that put victims and society at a higher risk. Within a couple of weeks I received a call from the State Victim Advocate. Another facility wanted to release a young man who had stabbed his stepfather multiple times and they wanted me to assess him and to facilitate a victim-offender amelioration. In other words they wanted me to bring together the family of the murdered man and his killer. I knew they were doing this in an effort to keep the victim's family from making waves over the release. I agreed to evaluate the situation.

After weeks of assessing the offender and family members, Katrina hit. After a great deal of consideration and prayer I set up a meeting with the superintendent and other interested parties. I told the facility the young man should not be released, had no remorse, and I shared his frightening quotes from my notes. This was a young man that had not learned what to say and what not to say and he answered my questions with horrifying and appreciated honesty. I told the superintendent that this offender was going to commit another violent crime and I wouldn't be the least bit surprised if it was a homicide. I was assured by the State Victim Advocate that she would continue working with the victim's family and I then walked away.

    I went to work with the human and animal trauma survivors left by Katrina. Within a few weeks of landfall our community had come up with the money to send me into the disaster zone. Had Rich asked me to bring Ryan into our home and shelter prior to that, I would have had access to Ryan's records. At this point I had to take his word and was leaning heavily on my partner's integrity, because I was suffering from vicarious trauma that washed over me in the disaster zone I had just returned from.

    As I said earlier, I had spent close to 30 years working with all types of victims and offenders. I had found bodies, stepped in brains, and survived all types of horrors. Katrina was the experience that took me down and Rich knew it when he lied to me. This was not only my home and refuge but that of other victims and many traumatized animals.

    While Rich had allowed his staff to behave terribly toward Victim Services I never believed he would put me at physical risk. He had dined in my home, we frequently met, just for lunch, and his children had spent a number of afternoons and bon-fire nights enjoying the private park. His family enjoyed the horses along with everything else built by my family for Victim Services.

    It turned out that Ryan had been accused multiple times of violent crimes and convicted more than once. He had also assaulted members of Rich's staff, on more than one occasion, and had no problem letting people (including me) know how he detested women and animals. Rich knew this history because he had the DOC records and knew of the assaults on his staff. But the story here is only partially about an offender program and it's director behaving like offenders. For years that has been predicted by victim service providers in regard to cooperating with offender based organizations and my actions earned me a well deserved, "Told you so."

The response to domestic violence victims has actually gotten worse. I can speak to this from experience because my friend, my partner and the Executive Director of our brother program, embedded a batterer into my home, and our program without warning, and the batterer did what batterers do. He assaulted me.

This catapulted me into a system that I hadn't been exposed to, personally, in decades and a system that was far too hostile for a woman weakened by the human behavior she witnessed in a disaster zone. While the media kept portraying the situation in New Orleans as "bringing out the best in most and the worst in a few" that is not an accurate portrayal.

After working with violent offenders in the state's most serious maximum-security facility for male adolescents, I expected that I would be assaulted in the facility. I spent years pushing violent offenders to the point of tears and self revelations, without incident. I did this with no security, arguing they would never be honest as long as the guards were present. I knew that pushing them into self awareness, my only security had to be mutual respect. But I still believed a violent response was inevitable and knew that eventually I would be assaulted and I accepted it as a hazard of the job. But it was not in the facility that I was assaulted. Instead, due to the actions of my partner and friend, I was assaulted and would have the "opportunity" to compare my current research with my current reality, again.

The System…Again…

Law enforcement's behavior was worse than it was more than 20 years ago. I knew the potential for local law enforcement's abuse was there because a lot of media attention had recently been focused on Sheriff's deputies that tazed a tiny woman whose only bad behavior was that she refused to be quiet when the two large deputies told her to, as displayed on the video.

After being assaulted by the offender, there were many threatening and disrespectful incidents by the prosecutors office and law enforcement. Ryan continued to come back and threaten us. On one occasion, a victim living at another property tried to make a police report because Ryan continued entering the property. When she tried to make a police report they refused to come to the property or take a report. When I then called them, the officer hung up on me telling me never to call back. When I complained to his superior, I was told Officer Mc Minnis was there on loan from the State Police and there was nothing they could do about his behavior.

There was one incident after another, including an officer charging up the drive as if he was going to assault me and then explaining it as, "I didn't know whether you were the victim or offender." Which is absurd given that I am obviously female and the offender is obviously male. Neither one of us are androgynous. I finally decided I was more likely to be harmed by law enforcement than the offender and let Ryan do as he pleased until he derived no more pleasure from it. The details of these experiences (law enforcement and our 10 year partnership with the offender program) can be found on the website and *Offenders Revealed*. The point is, that nothing much has changed.

A service provider that I tried to talk to about the trauma of New Orleans and being assaulted again, continued to insist that we needed to start with my childhood. Ignoring my need for help regarding the horrifying experiences of New Orleans which included photographing law enforcement using a 12 gauge shotgun on peoples' healthy, tied-up pets when the owners had begged them not to. Once officers in St. Bernard Parish found out I had photographed the criminal behavior; the pictures and I then became the target. This counselor insisted my trauma response was due to childhood, until I finally gave up and found my own way.

After returning from the Gulf, I found out the offender I had assessed had committed a serious assault and was never released. The victims reported that they had not been contacted by anyone from the State, including the State Victim Advocate and, almost two years since, they still have not heard from anyone other than me for a follow-up, explanation or anything else.

One of the most important issues here is to be able to shake ourselves out of our training, stereotypes and labels so that victims can get the help they need. Law enforcement can't get past the labels and stereotypes. Treating victims as crazy, dramatic etc… doesn't work for the victims or their children and supports the offenders' presentation of fact.

Talk shows are presenting "experts" that claim battered women need to do joint counseling with a focus on their childhood and another spews victim-blaming statements that become gospel to the women watching. This is not just about the "system" but all of us. And teaching accurate information to all would seriously reduce the numbers of battered and revictimized women. This needs to be done by the true experts and needs to answer the questions, "Why do you stay?" and "how do perpetrators pick us?"

Quick Reference

After Being Traumatized:

-Use your hindsight and examine what choices may have put you at risk
-Ask yourself what gut feelings you had that you ignored
-Are there any patterns? Has this happened before?
-What choice could you have made to keep you safer
-Thoroughly examine how the attack or event has effected you
- What symptoms are you left with? How is the trauma showing?
-Examine yourself for any actions that make you stand out as a weaker member of the herd, more vulnerable.
-Seek out counseling or a third party for information you may not see
-Take extra precautions during your vulnerable time
- Don't use mind altering substances that leave you impaired. An obviously drunk or high woman is an easy target, like a zebra walking on her knees.
- Examine the dynamics of, and reason for, the failure of your previous relationships. If you have just left a batterer you may not see the next one coming.
- Surround yourself with supportive, emotionally healthy people who will be honest with you. If you have to "fire" everyone in your life, do it.
- Seek out a good counselor. If you are not comfortable, then change. Some people just don't fit. Don't stay with a counselor that isn't working for you.
- Expect any counselor to be more of a teacher than a listener. If you are not learning from them, then you need to move on. The jokes about, "And how do you feel about that?" are true. Your sister can ask you how you feel about things. You want a counselor that helps you to see into yourself.
- Listen to your gut instincts and follow them. If you have survived a trauma you have a lot of important information filed away in your brain.

Some Things Perpetrators Look For:
Again, this is a brief list. For more information on offenders and staying safe, please see our book, *Offenders Revealed: How To Avoid Being Picked*

- Anything that makes you stand out (sexy clothes, etc...)
- Impaired senses (drunk, drugged etc...)
- Neediness
- Low self esteem, need for approval
- Opportunity (victim walking in alley, unlocked doors etc...)
- Absence of male figure
- Kindness
- Lack of assertiveness, fear of being rude
- lack of healthy boundaries (not assertive, afraid to say no)
- The newly widowed may be lonely
- The incest survivor may keep her secret but sexualize her relationships
- The stoic POW may drink himself into a stupor daily but refuse to talk
- The formerly-battered woman may unconsciously display low self esteem

Victim's Justice Center Position Statement on Forced or Court Ordered Counseling & Mediations Between Battered or Formerly-Battered Women and Their Perpetrators

The Victims Justice Center Inc. is opposed to forced, court ordered or otherwise coerced counseling and mediations between battered or formerly-battered women and their perpetrators for the following reasons:

- Battered women frequently bond to the perpetrator due to trauma. This is called traumatic bonding. This bond may cause them to behave in a manner that pleases the batterer in an effort to reduce their own injuries. This is not conducive to the honesty necessary for counseling or mediation.
- If the battered or formerly-battered woman has been successful at lessening this bond, counseling or mediation can refresh the bond. For the purpose of mental health, refreshing a traumatic bond is not desirable.
- Counseling or mediation could put the victim/survivor at risk of being abused again because counseling and negotiation by it's nature provokes feelings, which the batterer has historically been inept at managing.
- In a violent relationship the perpetrators uses not only verbal but nonverbal cues and threats. It is not possible for a counselor or mediator to recognize all of these, as they can be quite subtle and unique to each relationship.
- Batterers can be very manipulative, charming, and persuasive. Counselors may not always be able to recognize when they are being manipulated or charmed.
- Contact with the batterer may cause intense emotional feelings for the battered or formerly-battered woman. It may also provoke traumatic stress causing the victim/survivor to "relive" the traumatic events or jeopardize the progress she has made.
- Counseling or mediating in domestic violence situations is not something that all counselors are equipped for. The nature of the relationship requires special knowledge and skills.

- The battered woman has been forced, controlled, and coerced enough. It is not the role of the courts to continue this for the batterer.
- Batterers may use the courts, law enforcement, counselors, children or whatever other means they have available to them to continue abusing the woman after she has chosen to end the relationship. The courts must recognize this and refuse to assist the batterer.
- More so than with other crimes, because of traumatic bonding, it is important to minimize contact between victim and perpetrator. Face-to-face contact is one of the most important elements of the relationship in order for the batterer to maintain control. The courts must not encourage face-to-face contact in domestic violence cases.

Fact Sheet

"Almost 90% of violent attacks occurring within the home were males attacking females ... Over 50% of all murder victims were women with longstanding relationships with the murderer." Dobash & Dobash 1987

"1 of 4 female children will be incested" <u>Betrayal of Innocence</u> Susan Forward, M.S.W. 1978

"70% of all young prostitutes and 80% of all female drug addicts have been incested as children." <u>National Abortion Rights Action League Fact Sheet On Child Sexual Assault</u>

"9 out of 10 assaults are committed by men against women." <u>Report to the Nation on Crime & Justice, Dept. of Justice 1982, FBI Uniform Crime Report</u>

"Over 80% of children in juvenile halls have been sexually abused prior to placement, regardless of the reasons they are being held." "The Ultimate Violence" <u>KPFA Radio Station Folio, San Francisco</u>

"...women's violence not only causes less injury but is largely in self-defense or retaliation." The State of the Debate: <u>A Review Essay on Woman Battering</u> Ed Gondolf

"Men commit violence against women in over half of all relationships." <u>Wife Beating: How Common & Why?</u> Strauss 1978

"1 out of every 2.8 women in Los Angeles County over the age of 14 will be raped at least once in her lifetime." <u>Los Angeles County Protocol For the Treatment of Rape and Other Sexual Assault, 1981. Fact Sheet on Child Sexual Assault</u>

"90-95% of all sexual assault cases go unreported. Fabricated sexual abuse cases constitute 1-4% of reported cases" <u>National Victim Center Handbook, 1991</u>

Definitions

These definitions are meant to clarify how the author is using the terms. While they may disagree with others and in many cases there may be better definitions available, this section is meant to clarify the authors use.

Abuse – mistreatment of another soul. Can be physical, emotional, sexual or mental. A few examples below:
>**Emotional abuse–** Passive aggressive behavior, name calling, threats, manipulation etc…
>**Physical abuse–** Any type of unwanted touching that doesn't end when asked and that causes discomfort.
>**Sexual abuse–** Any type of unwanted touching, with or without sexual intent in an area considered sexual that does not stop when requested, was not consented to, or where the recipient resists.

Advocate – a person that supports, argues for, protects etc… those who are unable to do so for themselves.

Amelioration – to make better, to find the highest and best use for an experience or situation.

Anger – an outwardly expressed feeling that is apparently directed toward someone outside of the person experiencing the feeling. It is a feeling that is often used to cover feelings that may leave us feeling more vulnerable (like hurt or sadness) or feelings that may be perceived as weaknesses.

Anxiety – a stress reaction from current, past, or perceived future events that causes the person to have symptoms like sweating, fast heart rate, fear, etc… The reactions resemble what a prey animal feels while determining the right response to a perceived threat (fight, flight, or freeze).

Appropriate victim – a person who is considered by perpetrators, and even society, to be acceptable/justifiable to harm or hurt due to some characteristic of that person. For example, a woman with an active sex life may be seen as a justifiable target for rape, or a child who has been repeatedly sexually assaulted may be seen by offenders as an excusable target for their own sexual outlet.

Assault, physical – an action intended by the actor to cause harm to the target. The action can be physical, as in hitting, or it can be verbal.

Assault, verbal - is an insult or words intended to hurt or humiliate the person it is directed toward. Verbal abuse can be overt as in screaming, cussing and name calling or it can be harder to detect and more subtle as in passive-aggressive comments. Verbal assaults are not generally illegal and cannot provoke an action or assault. See provocation.

Batter – to abuse another physically.

Batterer – one who physically abuses another.

Batterer's group – groups that try to teach men who batter not to batter.

Blame – to focus responsibility elsewhere.

Closure – a term used to describe a person's acceptance and incorporation of a traumatic experience. It is often meant to say they are "over" the experience. While the goal is to ameliorate the experience and to gracefully and smoothly incorporate it into our identity and knowledge base, there is no "closure". The door is always open, to some degree. We live with the experience, to some degree for the rest of our lives.

Collusion – to support covertly or overtly the behavior(s) of another. For example, when we turn our head to, or laugh at a racist joke, we are colluding with the racist.

Common sense syndrome – Often used as a synonym for the Stockholm Syndrome or Hostage Identification Syndrome. The term is telling in that it reflects the logic of a victim (hostage) trying to satisfy, or not antagonize, someone who has complete control of their welfare and has threatened to kill her if she tries to leave. The constant nagging, by people who don't fully understand the dynamics of the situation, that she should leave despite her best judgment, gut instincts etc... does not, to the battered woman, constitute common sense.

Conflict – to disagree

> **Conflict of interest** – When someone is advising or counseling someone whose best interest is contrary to their own.

Conflict resolution – an effort to work out a disagreement
Control – to have significant, if not total, input into the behaviors of another.
Corporation – Used here as an umbrella term for a business, organization, or other entity that is structured in a manner to avoid accountability.
Compliance – to get someone to do what we want.
Counseling – ideally to advise and teach another.
Counselor – Typically meant to describe a person who listens to us talk about our current and past issues, often around childhood, and helps us to find insight into those issues. Ideally this role would be a person who actively guides and teaches us as opposed to having us talk - in hopes that we will eventually "bump into" the skills, tools, and answers that we need to find perspective and insight into our own and the behaviors of others. The more dangerous the predicament of the counseled the more necessary it is that the advisor take an active teaching role.
Crazy – generally used to describe someone who struggles with mental and emotional health issues. Term is historically and still commonly used to discredit victims (usually female).
Debilitation – a weakened state either through exhaustion or illness.
Degradation – to insult, humiliate and otherwise put another being down to the point where they believe they are less significant than they actually are and less significant than others. A vital element of the process of traumatic bonding.
Denial – to argue to yourself/others that a single or series of events did not happen or is not true, contrary to the obvious.
Depersonalization – to persuade yourself/others that another being does not have the components necessary for them to have feelings and to be deserving of compassion. This is used to deny that "enemies" or targets have feelings - making it easier to hurt them.
Detachment – to emotionally pull yourself out of a situation in an effort to get a better perspective on the events and to reduce the chances of being emotionally injured.
Dissociation – to emotionally project yourself outside (or to pull yourself deep inside) of your body in order to protect your mind

when you are unable (or believe that you are unable) to protect your body.
Domestic Abuse Intervention Project (DAIP) – the DAIP is the grandmother of a productive program for batterers and the training of facilitators.
Empathy – being able to understand, imagine and relate to the feelings of another being.
Euthanasia – to take the life of a being in order to stop its' suffering.
Extermination – to take the life of another being because they are an inconvenience. Often referred to as euthanasia by animal shelters.
Exhaustion – to be physically, emotionally, and mentally worn out.
Facilitator - a person who moves a group of people along, helps to keep them focused and orderly in order to accomplish a predetermined goal.
Formerly-battered women – a woman who was abused in the past.
Generational – being passed down from grandparents to parents to their children to their children.
Guilt – a mental warning of ill feelings, sometimes manifested physically, that you have done something wrong.
Honeymoon phase – the phase in an abusive relationship where the batterer often begs, pleads, makes promises, and brings gifts to the victim in an attempt to keep her from taking an action in her best interest, like leaving or calling the police. This phase is vital to traumatic bonding.
Hostage identification syndrome – often used interchangeably for traumatic bonding or the Stockholm syndrome.
Hurt – an emotion that is usually covered by anger, especially with males as it is often seen as weakness. It is a painful emotion because it is internal as opposed to the outward expression of anger.
Hypervigilance – to watch and otherwise study the behaviors, moods and triggers of another - usually in an effort to predict their next or future behaviors.
Inner child – represents one (out of many) aspects of our personality that reflects a point in our development (or childhood) that was a problem, traumatic, unresolved or even successful and

positive. It has been incorporated into who we are, "as is". For example a woman raped at ten may have an inner ten-year-old Add to that parents divorcing at six and a change of school at 12 and she is working with an inner six, ten and 12-year-old, among others.

Intimidation – behaviors employed to threaten, scare or otherwise control the behaviors of another. These behaviors can be obvious (overt) or hidden and subtle (covert).

Isolation – to be physically or emotionally secluded from others. A vital part of domestic violence that maintains compliance and the development of a Traumatic bond. Isolation prevents others from having input into the victim's thinking.

Justice – an abstract term used in reference to a righteous payback or "evening" things out for a wrongdoing.

Justification – to give a good reason for doing something. To try to make an action appear to be the right thing to do.

Mandatory Arrest Policy – a policy put in place by many law enforcement agencies that takes the responsibility for arresting a batterer out of the hands of the victim. The policy calls for law enforcement to arrest if they see, believe, etc… that one person has committed an assault against another. This policy is intended to keep the victim from being put in greater danger by taking the responsibility for arrest out of her hands.

Mediation – a process where a third, neutral party attempts to help people work out their differences. A dangerous venture for battered women in domestic violence cases.

Medical malpractice – bad or below standard medical treatment. Different than medical/corporate crimes.

Minimization - an effort to make a statement or behavior less significant than it was.

Molest – to touch in an unwanted or inappropriate manner.

Monitor – in this context, to observe educational or treatment programs in an effort to prevent/point out the manipulation, collusion, dangerous, behaviors, statements, and beliefs that may be supported by the facilitator(s). The monitor is someone with extensive experience in that particular type of trauma. For example, the monitor for a sex offender group is the survivor of rape or incest,

a formerly-battered woman is the monitor in a batterer's group, etc...
Mutual combat – a term used by law enforcement, courts etc... when they believe that both parties in a domestic violence case were "fighting". The term does not take into consideration self-defense, defense of children and potential for damage.
No-drop policy – a rule that prevents the courts and law enforcement from dropping a case. Initially intended to reduce the pressure that batterers put on their victims to prevent them from cooperating with law enforcement.
Occasional indulgence – part of the honeymoon phase where a captor, batterer etc... offers the victim gifts or other benefits they wouldn't normally offer.
Offender – a person who intentionally harms another and has been convicted of doing so.
Oppression – to hold down (figuratively) another being. To keep them from realizing their full abilities.
Omnipotence – all powerful.
Perpetrator – a person who intentionally harms another.
Popular victim/unpopular victim – a person who has been harmed by another who falls within a group of people that are seen by society as worthy of compassion. This is usually determined by who has the best, most powerful and well-funded advocates and movements. For example, generally and as a group (even though as individuals they cross all socioeconomic lines) sex offenders are poor and powerless as opposed to doctors, hospitals, and other corporations who have been successful at labeling their victims as "gold diggers" etc... This is one example of unpopular victims.
Post traumatic stress disorder – a group of responses to past trauma which include nightmares, night sweats, anxiety, hypervigilance, and an overactive startle reflex.
Predator – a being that watches for and seeks out other beings to "exploit" for their own perceived benefit.
Prey – a being exploited, or apt to be exploited by a predator.
Provocation – an act that contributes to the onset of feelings another may have in response to the action or comment. While, despite the vehement testimony of many a batterer, it is not possible to provoke

an action (assault) from another. While our words can cause someone to have thoughts or feelings, they are responsible for how they respond to that. There is no provocation of action, only thoughts and feelings. Our response to someone else is our choice.

Reality – truth, what is actual or real as opposed to how we see it once it goes through our filters. Contrary to popular definitions, reality does not change with the perceiver. For example someone who is colorblind may see your dress as green. That does not change the fact that it is actually the color we call red.

As the author writes, "Your honor, I did not rape her. That is her perception."

Tell that one to the judge, which she hears all the time (she wanted it, she provoked me etc…). Please see Reality in the index.

Restitution – a monetary or behavioral payment by an offender intended to restore or offset damages, as much as possible, for the wrong doing of the offender. Commonly described as an intention to make the victim "whole" again, which is not possible.

Restorative Justice –where crime is a violation of people, relationships, and communities. Rather than being defined by law-breaking and guilt, the obligation is to make things right, and justice involves the victim, the offender, and the community in a search for solutions which promotes repair, reconciliation, and reassurance. (Howard Zehr)

Retraumatize – to be traumatized a second, or more, time after the initial trauma - due to being singled out by a predator, or by having an old wound reopened by an unskilled therapist, or any number of other triggers.

Revictimization – for a person to be injured more than once, often due to the fact that they are presenting a weakened state to those that would prey on them.

Satellite – in this context, to carry on the agenda and goals of another.

Secondary victim – Where the primary victim would be the murdered child, the secondary victims of that crime would be the friends and family.

Sedation (sedating) – to make yourself feel better/stimulate desired brain chemicals/cause yourself to forget certain events and feelings.

Self-mutilation – to cut, burn or otherwise injure yourself.
Service provider – someone who provides services to the community.
Sexualize – to express or try to fulfill your needs and wants through sex.
Shame – to believe that an event in your life has degraded and devalued who you are.
Startle reflex – an uncontrollable jump or fear reaction that can become overactive after a traumatic experience. It is manifested when someone or something suddenly and unexpectedly appears or otherwise surprises someone. The person surprised may jump, scream and even cry.
Stockholm syndrome – a bonding that sometimes occurs when the welfare of one person depends on the goodwill of another.
Survivor – a person who has been able to physically and emotionally overcome and integrate a trauma.
System – in this context, those that come in contact with victims/survivors.
Threat – to try to achieve the compliance of another by telling them you will do something that is detrimental to them if they don't comply.
Tolerance – to withstand another. In the case of race, sexuality etc… the term is inappropriate insinuating there is something regarding race or sexuality that must be suffered by someone else.
Trauma – a negative, cumulative, life-changing event.
> **Vicarious trauma** – to suffer negative effects by viewing or hearing the trauma of another.

Traumatic bonding – a bond that occurs between two people, usually the victim and offender, due to trauma.
Trivial demand – requirements made of victims by offenders to degrade the victim and maintain the habit of compliance.
Vengeance – a desire to get "even".
Victim – a being that has been injured by another and has not been able to integrate the experience into their way of being in a positive, or even a neutral manner.
> **Victim blaming** – arguing that the person injured is actually to blame for their injuries. One of the first efforts made by

an offender to deflect and avoid responsibility for their actions. This is used by most all offenders regardless of socioeconomic status. Like the victim stance this is a universal defense.

Victim empathy – to understand and relate to the pain and suffering of a being that has been targeted for abuse.

Victim impact – when the survivors of a violent crime share their experience with offenders, service providers or the community in an effort to teach them about how they are effected by the actions of another.

Victim impact statement – when the subject of a crime makes a statement to the court in an attempt to effect sentencing and often to finally be heard.

Victim-offender mediation – The commonly used term "mediation" is in appropriate in that inherent in the term is that both parties "give" and the victim has already given more than she ever consented to. The author uses the term amelioration, which is when, at the victims wish, both victim and offender are brought together in an effort to find the highest and best use for the experience. With a facilitator highly experienced in trauma response, both victim and offender can benefit immensely from the experience.

Victim stance – is when an offender takes the position that they were actually the victim. This is another predictable move made by offenders to deflect and avoid responsibility for their actions. This is not only used by a repeat offender rapist but white coat, white-collar offenders.

Violence – an act that causes physical injury or harm.

Intermittent – violence that occurs off and on causing the recipient to stay off balance, unsure of what will happen next.

White Coat, white collar – used to describe corporate and medical entities.

Sources Cited/Consulted

While these references and sources may seem old, as pointed out in the introduction, when updating research there was NO change in statistics.

Factors Influencing the Development of the Hostage Identification Syndrome   James T. Turner   Political Psychology, Vol. 6, No. 4, 1985 Pgs. 705-710

The Stockholm Syndrome: Toward an Understanding   Irka Kuleshnyk   The New School for Social Research 1984   Social Action and the Law, Vol. 10, No. 2 pgs 37-42

Survivors of Terror: Battered Women, Hostages, and the Stockholm Syndrome   Dee L. R. Graham, Edna Rawlings, Nelly Rimini   Rethinking Clinical Approaches pgs. 216-231

Conflict Interaction in Domestic Violence   Courtney, Jameson, Thompson, Wallace

Backlash: The Undeclared War Against Women   Susan Faludi

Battered Women's Litigation Against Police   Response To the Victimization of Women and Children Journal of the Center for Women Policy Studies Vol. 9, No. 3, 1986 pg. 29

Crime Victim Model Legislation   Response To the Victimization of Women and Children Journal of the Center for Women Policy Studies Vol. 9, No. 3, 1986 pg. 29

The State of the Debate: A Review Essay on Woman Battering   Edward W. Gondolf   Response To the Victimization of Women and Children Journal of the Center for Women Policy Studies Vol. 11, No. 5 1988 pgs. 3-8

Battered Into Submission   James & Phyllis Alsdurf   Christianity Today June 16, 1989 pgs. 24-27

Battered Women: The Transformation of a Social Problem   Liane V. Davis Social Work July – August 1987 pgs. 306-311

The Case Against Anger Control Treatment Programs for Batterers   Edward W. Gondolf and David Russell   Response To the Victimization of Women and Children Journal of the Center for Women Policy Studies Vol. 9, No. 3, 1986 pgs. 2-5

On the Relationship Between Wife Beating & Child Abuse   Lee H. Bowker, Michelle Arbitell, J. Richard McFerron   Rethinking Clinical Approaches pgs. 158-173
Battered Women: Mourning the Death of a Relationship   Susan F. Turner, Constance Hoenk Shapiro   Social Work Sept.-Oct. 1986
A Tale of Abuse   Barbara Kantrowitz with Pat Wingert, Patricia King, Kate Robbins & Tessa Namuth   Newsweek Dec. 12, 1988 pgs. 56-65
Prisoners of Pain   David Gelman with Regina Elam Newsweek Dec. 12, 1988
Factors Used to Increase the Susceptibility of Individuals to Forceful Indoctrination: Observations & Experiments   Group for the Advancement of Psychiatry Symposium no. 3 December 1956
Domestic Violence & Victim-Offender Mediation: From Theory to Application   Alan Edwards & Judith Lake The Mediation & Restorative Justice Center
The Battered Woman   Lenore Walker
The Domestic Abuse Project   Research Update No. 2, June 1989
Hostage Hallucinations: Visual Imagery Induced By Isolation and Life-Threatening Stress   Ronald K. Siegel, Ph.D. The Journal of Nervous and Mental Disease Vol. 172, No. 5, 1984
Battered Women As Survivors: An Alternative To Treating Learned Helplessness   Edward W. Gondolf with Ellen R. Fisher   Lexington Books
Not So Benign Neglect: The Medical Response To Battering   Demie Kurz, Evan Stark   Rethinking Clinical Approaches
Battered Or Schizophrenic? Psychological Tests Can't Tell   Lynne Bravo Rosewater   Rethinking Clinical Approaches
The Secret Trauma   Diana Russell, et al., 1986
Beyond the "Duty to Warn" A Therapists "Duty to Protect" Battered Women & Children   Barbara Hart   Rethinking Clinical Approaches
Protecting Abused Children, Supporting Battered Women: A Model Policy for CPS Intervention   The Exchange A Forum On Domestic Violence Vol. 2, No. 3 August 1988 National Woman Abuse Prevention Project
Getting Free   Ginny NiCarty

A Multisystems Intervention in Woman Battering Mary Pat Brygger, Jeffrey L. Edleson The Domestic Abuse Project
Legal Remedies and the Role of Law Enforcement Concerning Spouse Abuse Ellen Pence Abuse & Religion 1988
Violence Against Wives Dobash & Dobash 1979
Wife Beating: How Common & Why? Strauss 1978
Confronting Domestic Violence: A Guide For Criminal Justice Agencies Goolkasian U.S. Dept. of Justice 1986
Guidelines For Mental Health Practitioners in Domestic Violence Cases S. Schecter National Coalition Against Domestic Violence 1987
Betrayal of Innocence Susan Forward, M.S.W. 1978
The Justice System's Response to Domestic Assault Cases: A Guide For Policy Development Pence & Galaway 1985
The Gift of Fear Gavin DeBecker
Hostage Survival B. McClure 1978
Negotiating Tactics Edward Levin
Reviving Ophelia Mary Pipher
Political Psychology James T. Turner Vol. 6, No. 4, 1985
Sociometry Albert Biderman Social-Psychological Needs and Involuntary Behavior as Illustrated by Compliance in Interrogation 1960

Index

AA 175, 248,
Abuse 17, 21-22, 29-31, 49, 58, 61, 64, 69, 73-74, 82-83, 85-86, 88, 109, 111, 115-116, 118, 122, 132-134, 136, 140, 145-146, 148, 150-153, 168, 179, 185, 187, 189, 191, 194, 196, 199, 208-209, 216, 221-222, 226-227, 239, 245
    Animal 180
    Child 21, 30, 88, 92, 120, 129, 134-135, 145, 207
    Emotional 12, 86, 218-219
    Mental 118, 173
    Physical 12, 21, 89, 173, 218
    Sexual 35, 58, 67, 135
    Substance 26, 128, 137, 167, 220
Addiction 31-32, 49, 101, 107, 114, 120-121, 134, 155, 176, 207, 220
Advocate 60, 85, 93, 129, 145, 157, 167, 181, 186-187, 206, 214-215, 225, 230, 232-233, 242, 242
Alcohol 2, 9, 25, 30-31, 67, 83, 88, 102, 108, 135, 159, 161-162, 172, 195, 207, 220, 223, 227, 233, 236
Amelioration 50, 94-95, 100, 183-184, 201, 213, 215, 234, 243,
Animal 7, 23, 28-30, 33, 50, 52, 62-67, 88, 94, 102, 104-105, 115, 123, 137, 166-167, 171, 191, 194, 199-200, 211, 226-227, 231, 236, 238, 243-244, 252
Anger 10-11, 20, 26, 107, 111-112, 119-121, 126-128, 130, 141, 152, 157, 168, 179, 193, 228
Anxiety 28, 88, 122, 192
Assault 19, 25, 29, 33, 43-44, 46, 48-49, 52-55, 81, 88, 98, 104, 106, 109, 129, 132-133, 135, 137, 140, 160, 162, 165, 170, 198, 200, 202-203, 214, 216-217, 219, 223, 225, 240, 243-245
Batter 4-5, 11, 16-19, 21, 23-27, 30-32, 38-39, 49-50, 56-58, 68-78, 80-97, 101, 109-110, 116, 118, 120-121, 124, 132, 136, 138-141, 143-158, 166, 169-170, 172, 174-200, 202-207, 211-214, 216-221, 225-227, 232-234, 242-244, 246
Blame 2, 24, 30, 44, 47, 49-50, 77-78, 80-81, 83, 92, 102, 120, 132-133, 136-137, 143-144, 147, 153, 157, 167, 170, 177, 185, 198-199, 203, 211-212, 218, 225

Bonding 69, 71, 73-75, 77, 83, 91, 93-94, 96, 140, 182-183, 197, 203, 230
Child 6-7, 12, 16-27, 30-32, 35-38, 40-44, 46, 48, 50-51, 55-59, 61, 67, 70, 72, 74, 76, 79, 81-84, 88, 91-92, 94-95, 100-102, 106, 111, 113-118120, 129-137, 140-142, 144-145, 148-150, 152-154, 156-161, 164, 166-167, 169-170, 172-174, 176, 180, 183, 191, 195, 200, 203, 207, 211, 214, 217, 219, 221, 226-227, 229, 231, 236-238, 240, 244, 246
Closure 111, 184, 210
Collusion 191, 195-196
Combat 66, 76
    Veterans 30, 33-34, 88, 99-100, 122, 220
    Mutual 157, 210
Common sense syndrome 83-84, 104
Conflict 43, 180
    Of interest 188
    Resolution 87
Control 4, 16, 18-19, 21, 34, 41-42, 51, 59, 69-71, 73, 75-76, 80, 84-85, 88-92, 96, 108, 110, 113, 116, 118, 121, 124-125, 128, 140, 142-143, 147, 149, 152, 154, 156, 159, 175-178, 183, 185, 187, 189, 199-204, 206, 211, 215, 221, 233, 238
Corporation 199, 203, 217-218
Compliance 74, 87-88, 201-202, 226
Counseling 8, 20, 92, 94, 109, 141, 147-148, 157, 160, 162-166, 175-177, 181-189, 191, 197, 208, 213, 233, 246
Counselor 8-9, 18, 32, 34, 57, 71, 92, 109, 129, 141, 146-147, 150-151, 153, 155, 157, 168-169, 175-189, 197, 203, 205-211, 217
Crazy 35-36, 124, 129, 152, 156, 186, 198-200, 202-203, 218-219, 226, 246
Custody 20, 92, 149, 157, 159-162, 164-165, 168, 175
Debilitation 85
Degradation 33, 45, 49, 78-79, 85-87, 91, 222, 239
Denial 35, 37, 52, 56, 109, 115, 127-128, 202, 211-212
Depersonalization 222
Depression 173, 204, 221
Detachment 116-120, 124
Dissociation 2-3, 17, 29, 34-35, 120, 129-130, 228

Divorce 20, 26, 70, 145, 158-159, 169, 209
Dysfunction 49-50, 58, 107, 152, 170, 185, 189, 207, 221
Emotion 11, 26-27, 35, 38, 44, 61, 70, 88-89, 100, 106-107, 118, 123-126, 132, 138-139, 149, 182, 195, 199, 204, 207, 209, 224
Empathy 112, 125, 194-195, 212-215, 237
Enmity 94
Exhaustion 24, 82, 85, 89-90, 192
Facilitator 92, 146, 175, 190-197, 212-214, 216
Family 3, 7, 19, 26-27, 31-32, 36-37, 42-43, 46, 50, 52, 55, 56-58, 60, 70, 74, 76-83, 86, 98-99, 101, 106, 111, 115-116, 119-120, 135-136, 138, 143-145, 148-150, 153-154, 162, 166, 170-171, 174, 199, 207, 217, 221, 236-238, 244
Forgiveness 62, 130-132, 136, 184
Friends 1, 8-9, 11, 27, 32, 44, 46, 52, 54, 57, 73-74, 77-82, 86, 98, 137, 142-143, 153-154, 160, 172, 202, 214, 217, 222, 224, 226-227, 237, 242
Generational 58, 74, 76, 135, 154
Girls 3-6, 8-10, 20, 23-25, 38-46, 48-50, 53, 59, 61, 76-77, 104, 138, 142, 153, 159-164, 171, 227
God 18, 21, 32, 61-62, 89, 102-103, 109-110, 117, 130, 135, 149, 222
Guilt 68, 31, 43, 83, 92-95, 128, 132-133, 137, 171, 181, 194-195, 211-212, 234
Honeymoon phase 80, 89, 147, 150, 189
Hypervigilance 30, 66, 88, 90, 93, 192
Incest 18, 75, 134, 138, 230, 231,
Inner child 111, 113-115, 127, 130, 132, 140, 166, 176
Intimidation 185, 199, 226
Isolation 73, 82, 85-86, 90-91, 140
Justice 18, 41, 49, 84, 126, 150, 153, 181-182, 194, 205, 210, 212-214, 230, 233-234, 236, 240, 241-242
Justification 60, 82, 120, 190, 192, 198, 203
Kill 3, 9, 16-18, 20, 27, 40, 54, 59, 62-64, 74, 80-82, 88, 90-91, 93, 99, 103, 110, 113-114, 120, 123-124, 127, 129, 133-135, 146, 148, 156, 159, 176, 182, 184, 190, 192, 197, 200, 203, 206, 210, 213-215, 219-220, 227, 242, 244
Labeling 204, 205

Mandatory Arrest Policy 26,
Mediation 87, 94, 99, 157, 175, 181, 182-187, 189, 197, 201, 213-214, 233-234, 241
Medical 122, 155, 195, 199, 204-205
Minimization 212
Molest 48, 50, 55, 170, 203, 217
Monitor 25, 174, 186, 190-193
Mutual combat 157, 210
Objectify 94
Occasional indulgence 73, 79-80, 85, 88-89, 127, 150, 189
Offender 17, 25, 30, 33, 49-50, 54, 58-63, 66-67, 70-71, 73, 76-77, 91-92, 94-95, 99-100, 102, 104, 108-109, 112, 117-118, 120, 128, 130, 135-138, 144, 147, 154-155, 157, 167, 183-184, 186, 188, 191, 193-205, 207, 209-210, 212-220, 225-226, 228-229, 231, 233-239, 241-246
Oppression 188, 206
Omnipotence 81, 85, 87, 89
Panic 105, 122-124
Perception 79, 85, 90-91, 106, 109, 138, 143, 152, 206-207
Perpetrator 18, 32, 34, 36, 49-51, 60, 66, 72, 76, 83-84, 88, 91, 93-94, 117, 129-130, 135, 137-139, 175, 180, 182-185, 196-197, 199, 206, 213, 242, 246
Post traumatic stress disorder 65, 119, 122, 124, 144, 220
POW 74-75, 82-85, 92, 138
Power 7, 18, 33, 54, 56, 80, 85, 89, 91, 94, 110-111, 127, 129-130, 135, 140, 152-154, 166, 185, 190, 204, 206, 228, 230, 238
Predator 33, 52, 0, 62-65, 67, 70, 104, 158
Prey 30-31, 42, 52, 62, 64-65, 67, 88, 104, 137, 199, 235
Provocation 50, 80, 95, 203
Racism 7, 87, 95, 203
Rape 19, 30, 32-33, 35, 43-44, 46-47, 49-50, 66, 75-76, 84, 94, 97-98, 101-102, 109-112, 121-124, 129, 132, 136-137, 147, 155-156, 181, 198-199, 201-203, 207, 212-213, 217-218, 223-225, 233-234, 237-239
Rationalization 203
Reality 1, 25, 31, 33, 86, 100, 109, 138, 143, 151, 155-156, 187, 192, 194-195, 206-207, 222, 227, 230, 237, 240, 245

Religion 21, 42, 69-70, 72, 79, 102, 147, 170
Restitution 234
Restorative justice 181, 194, 213-214, 234, 242
Retraumatize 35, 181, 234
Revictimization 30, 41 49-51, 56, 65, 82, 85, 91, 116, 118, 125, 127, 131, 133, 176
Satellite 96, 153, 166
Scapegoat 120, 132, 135
Secondary victim 99, 215
Sedation 31-32, 100, 108, 149, 221, 233
Self-mutilation 28, 30, 49
Service provider (system) 9, 21, 24, 30-31, 60, 71, 73, 96-97, 109, 116, 141, 146-147, 149, 154-155, 158, 175, 179, 181, 196-197, 203-205, 209, 212, 217-218, 225, 228, 230, 233-234, 242, 245, 261
Sex 21,41-47, 61, 139, 159, 163, 172, 207
    Abuse 35, 58, 67, 135
    Assault 19, 33, 43-44, 49, 52, 54, 106, 132-133, 135, 140
    Gratification 41, 43
    Life 8, 194
    Offender 17, 49, 54, 58, 67, 94, 100-101, 112, 144, 167, 170
    Sexist 191
    Sexualize 30-33, 49, 51, 107, 128-129, 138
Shame 4-5, 6, 11 23, 25-26, 29-30, 43, 51, 81,83, 86, 93, 110, 128, 133, 138, 144, 147, 150-151, 177, 185, 195, 210, 212
Stalking 23, 147, 219
Startle reflex 28, 64-666, 122, 221
Stockholm syndrome 73-75, 77, 84-85, 92
Survivor 23, 28, 30, 32-34, 36, 58, 63, 65-66, 75, 94, 98-101, 106, 109-110, 123, 125, 129, 134, 138, 144, 146-147, 153-156, 182, 192, 195, 199-200, 205-207, 209, 212-213, 215-216, 227-228, 232-234
System 36, 84, 92, 95, 97, 101, 128, 146-150, 152-154, 156-157, 168, 191, 200, 212-213, 218-219, 225-226, 232-234, 240, 244-246
Threat 2-3, 8, 10-12, 27, 35, 52, 54-55, 64, 80-82, 85-86, 88-91, 94-95, 105, 114, 117, 143, 145, 148, 153, 160, 162-165, 167-168, 172, 181-182, 186-187, 193, 199-201, 211, 220, 228, 245
Tolerance 31, 33

Trauma 3, 23, 26, 28, 30-36, 49, 57-59, 61-67, 73, 76, 78, 82, 94, 97-103, 105-110, 112, 120, 122-125, 127-129, 133-134, 136, 138-139, 144, 149, 154-156, 158, 180-184, 188, 194-195, 198-200, 205-206, 209-211, 214, 216, 218-220, 224, 227-228, 244, 246
Traumatic bonding 69, 71, 73-75, 77, 83, 91, 93-94, 96, 182-183
Trivial demand 79, 80, 83, 85, 87
Vengeance (revenge) 203
Victim 16-18, 24-28, 30-36, 49-51, 55, 58-60, 65-67, 69, 73-77, 82, 84, 86, 88-92, 94-102, 109-110, 117, 122, 127-129, 135-136, 143-144, 146-156, 170, 179, 183, 185, 188-189, 192-194, 196, 199-201, 204, 207, 209-211, 213-214, 216, 219, 221-222, 224, 226, 230-231, 233-234, 237-238, 240-246
    Advocate 19, 60, 186-187, 214, 230, 232-233
    Animals 243
    Appropriate 49, 61-63, 67, 70, 76, 85, 137, 152
    Blaming 30, 50, 67, 119-120, 137-139, 148, 152, 156, 185-187, 196-203, 205-207, 212, 217-218, 224-225, 235, 246
    Empathy 94, 194, 215
    Grooming 51, 104, 137, 197, 222
    Impact 86-87, 95, 122, 145, 194-196, 212-213, 216, 220, 232, 240-241
    Victim-offender mediation/amelioration 94, 99-100, 181-184, 201, 212, 214-217, 233-235, 241
    Popular 219
    Revictimization 36, 49, 59-61, 66-67, 77, 97, 101, 109, 136, 138, 140, 147, 150, 154, 158, 179, 206, 224, 232, 241
    Secondary 99, 215
    Stance 152, 187, 196, 201-203
    Unpopular 199, 218, 230, 231
    Victimology 54, 61, 66, 155, 201, 208
Violence 1, 4, 7-8, 17-23, 25, 29, 31, 41, 49-50, 53, 58-59, 61, 69-70, 73, 76, 80, 82, 85-86, 88-90, 93-96, 101, 116-117, 120, 134, 140-141, 143, 145, 147, 149, 154-155, 157, 167, 171, 176, 180-187, 189, 193-194, 202-204, 210, 212-213, 216-217, 220, 226-227, 232-233, 239, 244
White Coat, white collar 134, 218, 230

www.ingramcontent.com/pod-product-compliance
Lightning Source LLC
Chambersburg PA
CBHW032035150426
43194CB00006B/284